Coming Alive from Nine to Five

Coming Alive from Nine to Five
THE CAREER SEARCH HANDBOOK

Fifth Edition

Betty Neville Michelozzi
Corralitos, California

MAYFIELD PUBLISHING COMPANY
Mountain View, California
London • Toronto

Library of Congress Cataloging-in-Publication Data

Michelozzi, Betty Neville
  Coming alive from nine to five: the career search handbook/
Betty Neville Michelozzi. — 5th ed.
    p.   cm.
  Includes bibliographical references and index.
  ISBN 1-55934-534-9
  1. Vocational guidance.   2. Job hunting.   I. Title.
HF5381.M46   1995
650.14—dc20   95-35004
                                                         CIP

Manufactured in the United States of America
10 9 8 7 6 5 4 3 2 1

Mayfield Publishing Company
1280 Villa Street
Mountain View, California 94041

Sponsoring editor, Franklin C. Graham; *production editor,* Merlyn Holmes; *copyeditor,* Patterson Lamb; *text/cover designer,* Susan Breitbard; *cover art,* Randy Lyhus; *manufacturing manager,* Amy Folden. The text was set in 10.5/12.5 Sabon by Fog Press and printed on 50# Ecolocote by Malloy Lithographing Inc.

 This book was printed on recycled, acid-free paper.

Contents

Chapter 7

THE JOB HUNT: Tools for Breaking and Entering   209

Chapter 8

DECISIONS, DECISIONS: What's Your Next Move?   248

Chapter 9

WORK AFFECTS THE SOUL: The Final Analysis   282

Preface

Coming Alive from Nine to Five is a unique handbook that develops, demystifies, and integrates the various facets of career/lifestyle search and choice. A handy reference book, it draws together into one comprehensive, practical, easily usable and reusable source the essentials of career/life decision making. Flexible enough to be adopted in whole or in part by individuals or groups, previous editions have been used in semester-long courses, workshops, individual counseling sessions, in colleges and high schools, and industry and business. In short, *Coming Alive from Nine to Five* is intended for anyone searching for meaningful life activities—from students to retirees, from managers of households to managers of corporations, from job trainees to career-changing professionals.

This updated version of *Coming Alive from Nine to Five* focuses on career preparation not only for the last shred of the twentieth century, but for the twenty-first century as well. Using the same personal approach as earlier texts, the fifth edition expands awareness of the career search process as it relates to a person's whole life.

Writing yet another edition has provided an opportunity to develop new material, integrate overlapping exercises, eliminate what seemed less helpful, and update innumerable bits of data. Feedback from those who have used the first four editions has been especially useful in the revision process.

The book begins with an upbeat discussion of success and moves quickly into self-assessment activities. It then considers a variety of societal factors that influence work, beginning with the interrelationship between people's roles and their career choices. Because vast social changes are happening very rapidly and the twenty-first century will no doubt be very different from the present, Chapter 5 enables us to look at the future in terms of challenges, options, and opportunities.

The leader/instructor's manual includes a discussion of study skills especially useful in a career course and other materials to facilitate the task of assisting students with this most important activity: reflection on life goals, including, specifically, career choice.

B. N. M.

Acknowledgments

Acknowledgments are a very personal thing. They point out the impossibility of accomplishing anything of importance alone. I am grateful to all these people:

Peter, my husband, for his caring support, "thought-full" suggestions, and assistance with many tasks. He helps me keep perspective on life's deeper meaning when a sea of paper and words threatens to engulf me.

Supportive colleagues at West Valley and Mission Colleges who read, reviewed, and gave helpful feedback and/or materials: Bill Allman, Joanne Anderson, Veronese Anderson, Chloe Atkins, Don Cordero, Ken Gogstad, Tom Heffner, Carolyn Hennings, Michael Herauf, Jo Hernandez, Sharon Laurenza, Joyce McClellan, Susan Monahan, Gladys Penner, Richard Przybylski, Jack Seiquist, Sylvia Sellect, Pat Space, Jill Trefz, Pat Weber, and Jan Winton, Patti Yukawa, Dave Fishbaugh and the Mission library staff.

All the caring, careful typists who contributed way back, especially my neighbor Ruby Garcia, who goes beyond neighborliness to heroism, and Kay Koyano at West Valley College, whose patience with the first manuscript was unmatched. Aptos, Santa Cruz, and Watsonville library staff, who at the drop of a phone call searched out many details and even called back—in minutes!

Academic reviewers who use the text and made valuable suggestions and comments: Lynn Hall of Bakersfield College, Carey E. Harbin of San Jose, California, Dolores McCord of Valencia Community College of Florida, Sydney E. Perry, Jr. of Old Dominion University in Virginia, Sharon L. Speich of Inver Hills Community College in Minnesota, Charles Ward of Pasadena City College, and Susan Wood of Indiana University Southeast.

West Valley and Mission College students who taught me to teach Careers and Lifestyles and shared the beauty of their life journeys. Staff and students in many places who attended workshops and lectures and gave generous feedback. Career people who share their stories and give support and resources to career searchers.

Colleagues and resource people in many places who have been supportive and given assistance and information: Judy Shernock, for her work on the Personality Mosaic, and Cora Alameda, Sally Brew, Dorothy Coffey, John French, Mel Fuller, H. B. Gelatt, Lynn Hall, Phyllis Hullett, Jean Jones, Barbara Lea, Ritchie Lowry, John Maginley, Gene Malone, Lillian Mattimore, Stephen Moody, Art Naftaly, Chuc Nowark, Ruth Olsen, Julie Pitts, Alex Reyes, Kay Ringel, Jo-ann Seiquist, Mary Kay Simpson, Pat Thompson, Judy Barry-Walsh, Ed Watkins.

Instructor who shared class time to test materials—too numerous to mention by name but remembered with gratitude.

People (past and present) at Mayfield who have been so great to work with: Naomi Angoff, Liz Currie, Bob Erhart, Laraine Etchemendy-Bennett, Frank Graham, Pat Herbst, Yaeko Kashima, Carol Norton, Nancy Sears, Laurel R. Sterrett, Pam Trainer, April Wells-Hayes, Merlyn Holmes, and Julie Wildhaber. Manuscript editors Patterson Lamb, Susan Geraghty, Carol King, and Victoria Nelson, who contributed above and beyond the call of duty.

Family and friends, who gave me "living love," you have all enriched me.

Betty

Introduction

A Letter to You

Career search can be a special, very precious time to orient and organize your life. It can be a time when you look deeply at yourself and what you have been doing. It can lead you to question how you intend to spend your life for a time, or your time for the rest of your life: to keep or not to keep certain goals, to change or not to change certain behaviors, to aspire or not to aspire to certain positions—all with a view toward life enrichment.

Career search involves more than simply figuring out what job might suit you best. (That is the short-range view.) Your perspective expands when you ask yourself what you want that job to do for you. Once you ask this question, you may very quickly find yourself face to face with some of your deepest values. Do you want power, prestige, profit? Peace, harmony, love? Are some values incompatible with others? Can you have it all?

Can you work sixty hours a week moving up the corporate ladder, nurture loving relationships with family and friends, grow your own vegetables, recycle your cans on Saturday, jog daily, be a Scout leader, meditate, and play golf at the country club? How fully can all your interests and values be actualized in the real world? What is the purpose of work? What is the purpose of life? These questions lead to that all-important question, What do *you* want out of *your* life?

This text is written for those who are in transition and would like the opportunity to learn a "thought-full" career/life decision process: beginning college students, graduating seniors, parents whose children are grown, the newly divorced or widowed, job changers, the disabled, the unemployed, grandmothers and grandfathers kicking up their heels, corporate tycoons stopping to smell the flowers, people in mid-life crises, veterans, ex-clerics,

PEANUTS reprinted by permission of United Feature Syndicate, Inc.

people becoming parents and providers, people retiring, and all others willing to let go behaviors that are no longer appropriate and risk new ones. A book about career choice is inevitably a book about life and all its stages for people from nineteen to ninety-nine.

Because a career decision is so important, some people approach it with fear and trembling, lest they make a mistake. Others avoid the process altogether, certain it will nail them down to a lifelong commitment they can never change. Still others feel that any job will do just to get them started on something! And then there are those who feel that even if they did a thorough career search, it would turn up absolutely nothing. In reality, a careful career search can help everyone. It can help *you* to see many possibilities, develop flexibility, and gain a great deal of confidence. It can even help people who have already made a career decision better understand themselves and their connection to the work world. The result can be greater career/life satisfaction.

The Process

What process should you use in making a thoughtful career decision? Many people choose their first career using the "muddle-about method." They consider subjects they've liked in school: if it's math, then they'll be mathematicians; if it's history, they'll be historians. They consider the careers of people they know and ask the advice of friends—a good beginning, but not always a broad-enough perspective. If Uncle Jim the firefighter is a family hero, a new crop of firefighters is launched. If the career seekers fry hamburgers for a time, they're tempted to judge the whole world of business through the sizzle of french fries. If models and airline pilots capture their attention, they long for a glamorous life. They may try one job, move from here to there, get married, have a family, and move again, trying different positions, grabbing different opportunities. Then one day, they aren't sure just how it all happened, but there they are: spouse, children, house, job—"The whole catastrophe," as Zorba the Greek said. And they may wonder, "Is this all there is?"

Some folks make very early decisions: "I knew when I was two that I wanted to be a chimney sweep." Although deciding early may work out well and satisfy the need some people have to firm up choices, in other cases it means the person has closed off options that might have been more satisfying. Career choice is sometimes treated as trivial. Adults ask six-year-olds what they want to be when they grow up. Are they going to sell shoes at Penney's or invade the corporate complex of Microsoft? Will plumbing be their outlet or travel tours their bag? Even while quizzing the children, many adults aren't always sure what their next career would be if they had to choose.

At least occasionally, however, the image of life's wholeness will flash before you and you will catch a glimpse of the time and energy that you will invest in work. You see that work will affect your life in many ways. But unless you keep a tight lid on it, the ultimate question will eventually present itself: "What's it all about?" If you deal in depth with career choice, you are bound to slip into philosophic questioning of life's meaning.

Stages and Steps

Because you are reading this book, you're indicating that "muddling around" is not the way you want to approach your career decision. There are stages and steps in the career search process. For many people, the journey begins at ground zero with not an idea in sight. As you gather career information, you may reach a point where you seem to be engulfed by too many ideas; things seem to get worse before they get better. Eventually you must begin to lighten the burden by choosing. You simply can't follow every career in one lifetime. The calmer you stay, the more easily you will arrive at your decision point.

The steps you need to take to reach a career/life decision must be part of a clear, understandable, and reusable *system,* one that

1. helps you articulate who you are and what you do well.
2. describes the work world as simply and completely as possible.
3. helps you see where your personal characteristics fit into the work world.
4. empowers you to secure the job you have chosen by improving your job hunting skills.
5. sharpens your decision-making skills, for you probably will make many decisions, and each choice leads to others.
6. raises your consciousness about work as only one part of your personal journey, one aspect of your total lifestyle.
7. addresses issues of global concern, showing how work is part of the world picture with its many challenges and how the solutions are provided by your work. Career planning breaks barriers and builds bridges.

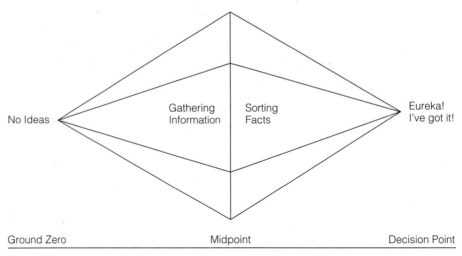

No Ideas

Gathering Information   Sorting Facts

Eureka! I've got it!

Ground Zero   Midpoint   Decision Point

The Career Choice Continuum

In *Coming Alive from Nine to Five*, you will find such a system. It is based on identifying clear values that lead to good decisions. At first glance, this book may look like a conventional careers manual. Read the book, fill in the blanks, and (even if you're already over forty) you'll know what you want to be when you grow up.

You *will* find blanks to fill in as part of the step-by-step process of getting to know yourself and the job world. You *will* find exercises to explore your needs, wants, and values, to discover your personality orientation. You *will* be guided to examine your past and select the activities you've enjoyed as well as skills you've developed over the years. A job group chart will help you to put *you* and *work* together in a meaningful way. A final inventory will collect all this "you" data and help you to see it as a unified whole.

Each of these steps represents small decisions designed to fall into a general career pattern that is compatible with your personality. This in turn leads you to choose an appropriate educational pathway such as a college major; a career that will lead you into a field of your choice; and a lifestyle that both results from and supports your career choice.

No two people will do the process in exactly the same way. Some people find that doing every exercise will lead them to a career. Others may want to use this book for ideas but not follow it exactly. Some may wish to skip around, looking for what is most helpful as long as they are not doing so to avoid the issues involved in making a career/life decision. For example, those who find decision making difficult may want to read Chapter 8 for more structured decision-making exercises.

But this book also touches on some of the heavier issues of life. How can you fulfill your potential? Be happy? Be content? It deals with such

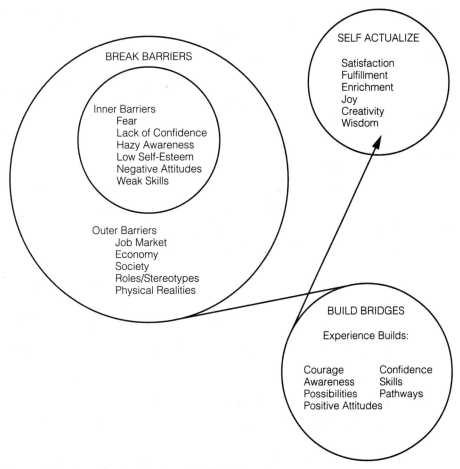

Career Planning: Breaks Barriers, Builds Bridges

issues lightly—sometimes whimsically—because life is meant to be joyful. After a good chuckle, you will get serious and *think* again because your life is also serious and sometimes even sad. Career search, then, is really a time to *stop out* to see who you are and where you're *growing*.

This handbook works best when the searcher approaches it in a relaxed, lighthearted manner. But a serious career search also calls for commitment and motivation. Those who get thoroughly involved will experience new confidence in themselves and greater clarity about their lives. Their goals will be easier to recognize and reach. Besides providing a living, a career can satisfy some of your deepest longings. The career search, then, will become a profound journey of personal growth on the path toward self-actualization.

The Career Search Guide

Most people base career decisions on incomplete information. As you begin your career search, it may help to focus on some important questions.

1. Gather information about yourself.

a. Needs, wants, and shoulds

What do you *need* to survive? What do you *want* to enrich your life? Do your *shoulds* help you or hold you back?

b. Interests and values

The choices you've made over your lifetime have developed into a strong pattern of interests. These reflect what you value most in life. Are your values clear?

c. Skills

Analyze your most enjoyable activities. Through repeated choices in your areas of interest, you have developed many skills. Of all the skills you have, which do you enjoy using the most?

2. Become informed about societal issues that affect your career.

a. Roles

What *roles* do you play now? What expectations do you and others have about these roles? Do you wish to change or adapt these roles?

b. Challenges, options, and opportunities for the twenty-first century

What are the major challenges that face the world today? What are the many positive and viable options already being taken to meet these challenges?

3. Job Market Exploration: Where to Start

a. Explore the job market

Interest and skill inventories lead you to an overview of the entire job market. What jobs fit your self-image?

b. Research workplaces

What are the important characteristics of various workplaces? How do you find out which will work for you?

World Monitor, July 1989

c. Research job market opportunities

Check the job market outlook and relate it to needs and wants in society. Will there be a need for people to do the job you'd like? What workplaces will you choose? Do you have alternatives?

d. Information interview

Have you talked to people in careers that interest you? Have you surveyed and evaluated possible workplaces? Does the survey show that you need to re-evaluate your choices?

e. Tools for the job hunt

Do you know how to network, portray yourself effectively through résumés, applications, interviews, letters? Can you talk fluently about yourself?

4. The Final Analysis: Wrap-Up

a. Decisions

Finalize your decision.

b. Goals

Set realistic goals with time lines.

c. Strategy

Develop a strategy for action.

d. Values/Philosophy

Review the whole picture to make sure it fits your value system, your philosophy of life and work.

 Self-Assessment

Before you begin your career exploration, discuss either in writing or with a group where you are on the Career Search Continuun, p. 4 and how you feel about doing a career search process at this time.

1/

Needs, Wants, and Values

Spotlighting You

FOCUS

- Define success in terms of needs, wants, and goals.

- Examine important values in your personal and work life.

- Identify steps to begin making desired changes in your life.

Success Is Everybody's Dream

Everyone who begins a career search dreams of what he or she would like the process to achieve. Some simply want a job of any sort, the sooner the better. Others may be able to take the time, not only to choose a career, but also to get the education it requires. In any case, when a change is in the air, success is the goal.

Hold up the word success and almost everyone will want to follow it. It's so upbeat, so cheerful, so, well . . . successful! We certainly favor it over failure. Success, though an elusive concept, is compelling in its power. We chase it, we work for it, we long not only to be successful but to be considered successful by everyone we know. But many career searchers forget to define this coveted creature in terms that are uniquely theirs.

What is success? Often an array of vaguely defined dreams crop up in answer to that question: we have arrived, we have climbed the mountain, we have achieved our goals. How do we find our way to success? What does success look like? Media images bombard our consciousness; family and friends confuse but compel us; half-formed dreams lure us up one pathway and down another.

Is it high-speed movement? Go places, hit the floor running, travel in the fast lane. Is it competition? Get ahead, be number one, swim with the sharks. Is it battle? Set your sights, maneuver, get to the top. Is it labels and logos? The right outfit, the right house in the right place with the right car? Society's images of success can make the thoughtful person's head swim. Yet achieving success is a basic human need. From getting a meal to making a deal, both the street person and the billionaire work each day to succeed.

Success Defined

Success has many layers and many definitions. We generally think of it in broad terms: A person *is* successful. We seldom ask what that means, what it consists of, how a person gets there, how that compares with our idea of success, and whether that is the kind of success *we* would enjoy. The fact is, success is "all in your head"; it is what matters most to *you*.

Success also relates closely to failure. We achieve, and then we find ourselves looking at the next step. Some steps work and some don't. What we learn becomes a part of life's experience. The steps that don't work might be considered failure, but they are temporary as well. We need to recognize that no one has the time, energy, and interest to "do it all," to become good at everything.

Failure often causes us to reassess our goals, strive harder, and hence attain greater success. Most successful people admit they have had some "good luck" that helped them along the way. Chances are they have had

"bad luck," too. They have made some mistakes, but they were not defeated. Success comes most often to those who set realistic and reasonable goals and who work hard persistently and with enthusiasm, without giving up when things go wrong. Townes Duncan, Chair and CEO of Comptronix, in Gunersville, Alabama, once said:

> Seymour Cray was a friend of my dad's. I asked him once what
> it was like to know the genius who had built the world's first
> supercomputer company. My dad said, "Well, actually, son, he
> wasn't so much smarter than me. He just made mistakes
> a hundred times faster."[1]

Surprisingly, the setbacks we experience in life are often those that precipitate deeper, more valuable, and often painful insights into ourselves that cause us to make changes. And, when they look back, some people are grateful that a failure led them away from some serious pitfalls. Author Bill Cane asks, "Is it possible to accurately plot out a lifetime without budgeting in the possibility of change, darkness, and personal pain?"[2]

> Failure is a greater teacher than success.
> —*Clarissa Pinkola Estés*[3]

Some people see success as a secure niche they'll occupy when they are finished with the hard work of achieving and changing. But we are all in transition and usually required to meet new challenges and draw on new abilities. No one stands still forever. Growth, marriage, family, divorce, death, degrees, promotions, transfers, new technology, layoffs, cutbacks, mergers, reorganization, management changes, company bankruptcy, illness, disability, and retirement represent some of the changes that affect life and careers and make us face new choices.

Goals that were appropriate for us at an earlier age fall by the wayside as we acquire and uncover new skills, as our values become more certain, as our experience opens up new horizons. What we view as a great and exciting success today may fall into a more modest perspective later in life as we move toward greater maturity and fulfillment. Our definition of success changes as we grow.

As surprising as it may seem, some people are afraid to succeed. Success brings more responsibility, higher visibility, and the expectation that the good performance will continue. Success requires continued effort to get there, to stay there, and to continue growing. The person who accepts failure, however, no longer has to keep trying. Failing can be a way to exert independence against the real or imagined demands and expectations of others.

Sometimes people really are successful right now, but they haven't been giving themselves credit. The powerful image of the dynamic, hard-working business person reaping tons of profits, prestige, and power can make other types of achievement seem trivial. Someone noted that today's maxim is "Nothing succeeds like excess." Artist Thomas Hart Benton lamented that the ideals and practices of the go-getter were ranked "above all other human interest."[4] We often honor the workaholic, who in fact may be quite self-destructive. We revere the ideal of individual success—being number one; but some might ask, at what price? We continually "up the ante" in the amount of material goods that make us look successful. We have to question such prevailing madness and ask, "Must success cost so much?" And further, "Must my success be the success defined by others?" Some people measure success in terms of their ability to simplify their lives, to live with less.

At the very least, success is finding happiness, which may be defined as being reasonably content with the choices you have made in life. Unless you see more broadly, with a more penetrating look, you may simply continue searching for success, and hence happiness, where they are not to be found. Through self-exploration you will begin to see how capable you are, how much more is possible for you, and how wonderful you are and could become on the road to success. If you have grown accustomed to feeling "unsuccessful," find success by setting one small, short-term, realistic goal each day and achieving it: exercise for five or ten minutes; learn five dates in history; straighten out one drawer. And then congratulate yourself on your achievement. Expand your goals little by little each day.

Luck is preparation meeting opportunity![5]

Clarifying Needs, Wants, and Values Determines Success

All our activities are motivated by human needs and wants, based on our value system, and work is one of the chief ways to obtain our needs and wants, express our values, and find success. To start the career process at its roots, ask yourself what you *really* need. A genuine need is something you *must* have to survive, something you literally cannot live without. After these basic needs are identified, begin to look at your *wants*. Wants can enrich life beyond the level of needs. Then look at *shoulds* because sometimes they create confusion about what we really want. What we want reflects our *values* and gives meaning to our lives. Looking at needs, wants, shoulds, and values is the root of a career search and can open a new phase of personal growth as well as clarify goals.

Basic Needs Relate to Our Survival

We can divide all human motivation or needs into four areas: physical, emotional, intellectual, and altruistic or spiritual. Minimal survival needs in each of these areas are the foundation for becoming a fulfilled and self-actualized person. All human beings have basically the same needs.

Air, water, food, clothing, shelter, energy, health maintenance, exercise, and the transportation required for these necessities are the vital elements of our physical need system. We also must feel physically safe and secure, and we must have the time and usually the money to satisfy our physical needs in a dependable and orderly world.

> Even God cannot talk to a hungry man except in terms of bread.
> —*Gandhi*

Yet we've heard stories about orphaned infants whose physical/safety needs were met but nevertheless died mysteriously. We've heard of old people "dying of loneliness" or of a person dying after receiving word of the death of a loved one.[6] Human beings need love, some kind of faith and assurance that they are lovable, someone to give them courage in order to develop a sense of self, self-esteem, and a sense of belonging. Atlanta psychologist, Perry W. Buffington, said, "The love you have for yourself is the nucleus of all motivation . . . If you love yourself, you feel worthy. If you feel worthy, you feel competent. If you feel competent, you're ready to achieve and work and love."[7] We fool ourselves when we say we have no need for others, that we can do it or have done it ourselves. Without the support of others we would not have survived. Without their caring, we would have little or no sense of self-worth. The how-to-get-rich-quick, look out for number one, and win-through-intimidation books override the basic need that people have for caring and cooperative emotional support that "swimming with the sharks," "winning with weapons," and "guerrilla marketing attacks" don't quite fulfill. A certain level of emotional nurturing is important for survival and growth.

We may tend to view intellectual needs as nonessential, but every culture has a system to teach its young how to satisfy needs. Education begins when we are born and does not stop until we die. In this complex, fast-paced, high-tech world, it is ever more important for survival. Ideally, education leads to deeper knowledge and understanding of ourselves, others, and the world around us and to the wisdom needed to make good life choices. School is only one avenue to education because people learn in different ways. Those who relate best to the physical world seem to learn through their hands. Some learn best through their ears, some through their eyes. Some learn best from the emotion-laden words of people they love. Media-lovers learn easily from books, pictures, diagrams, and other symbols. But however we learn, our intellect lights the way.

Altruistic needs—setting aside our desires to meet the needs of others—sound as if they are only the frosting on the need cake and not a real need at all. But actually, a certain degree of altruism—looking out for others, winning by cooperation—is necessary for our individual survival. As we begin life and often as we age, we are dependent on the altruism of others. In a recent magazine article, authors Growald and Luks say that "scientists are now finding that doing good may be good for the immune system as well as the nervous system" and "may dramatically increase life expectancy."[8]

There is no doubt that our individual decisions affect other people and the planet. Human survival depends on the social responsibility of each one of us and is endangered when we totally disregard the needs of others. For example, imagine your daily commute. Without regard for others, the freeway would become a free-for-all! Most societal problems are the visible product of many individual choices made without regard for the health and well-being of all. We all experience the consequences.

> In this age we can no longer afford to be self-aggrandizing.
> —*California Business Owner Joanne McKohn*

When people reflect on their own needs and those of others, they often feel drawn to find answers to the riddle of life, to understand the problems that face them, to live a more meaningful life. They also sense that simply having knowledge does not imply that they will have the wisdom and will to act for their own good and that of others. A desire to develop morally and spiritually often results. As they search for answers to the whys of their existence, they may find motivation to live nobly and to accept with a graceful and adventurous spirit all that life brings them. To live one's life without any sense of meaning is often to live with a vague despair and hollow emptiness that diminish life.

These needs can be thought of as a hierarchy, with physical needs first on the survival agenda, then emotional, then intellectual, and then altruistic/spiritual, according to psychologist Abraham Maslow. If a person's most basic needs are unfulfilled, it is difficult for that individual to be motivated by higher needs. (You've noticed how hard it is to concentrate on a class right before lunch!) If you have survived modern life thus far, a good share of your basic needs have already been fulfilled. Many people have contributed to your well-being on all levels along the way.

> I have the audacity to believe that people everywhere can have three
> meals a day for their bodies, education and culture for their minds,
> and dignity, equality, and freedom for their spirits.
> —*Dr. Martin Luther King*

Needs Relate to Wants

Satisfaction of needs is absolutely necessary for life. A cup of water, a bowl of rice, and a few sprouts a day, one set of clothes, and cardboard box for shelter will do. A large percentage of the world's people live on such meager rations. Because most people choose not to live at a survival level if they can help it, they begin to search for the means to satisfy their wants. It's important to know what is clearly necessary for survival and what can wait—a great difference. Risks such as changing jobs are less frightening if you know that you can survive on very little. Once your needs are satisfied, you can work more calmly toward achieving your wants. If all our needs and wants were completely satisfied, all the action in our lives would stop. Need/want satisfaction is not a straight line where at some point we are "finished."

Think of basic needs and those wants that are truly enriching: clean air and water; nourishing food; simple, attractive clothing and warm, decent shelter; adequate health care, practical transportation, reasonable protection from risk; close relationships with caring people; the opportunity for satisfying work, a job that provides money, time, and leisure to enjoy these things, creativity; and personal, intellectual, and spiritual growth not only for ourselves but others. If we were to focus on these, the world as well as all of us would be transformed in amazingly positive ways.

There is a large gray area between survival needs and wants. To what extent is physical health important? Just surviving may mean barely dragging along day by day. On the other hand, high-level wellness for certain individuals may require extraordinary amounts of expensive health care. It is important to know what is *real,* what is important—to be able to appreciate the difference between a make-believe forest and a real one, or between a fast-food burger and a special meal made with care by someone who loves you.[9]

Needs and Wants Relate to Feelings and Shoulds

How does each person's unique set of wants evolve? Most wants come from the culture in which a person lives. Ideally, people are taught by parents and teachers to find the balance called *common sense* that exists between going for everything that feels good and reasoned judgment telling us that not everything that feels good is good for us. Life experience teaches us over and over that some things work and some do not.

Everyone has a range of emotional responses to life's events. Growing means learning to understand and manage them, not let them manage you. Anger, for example, can be a natural response to adversity. Staying angry, "grinding" about bad luck, and plotting revenge keeps a person from using "anger energy" in a productive and positive way to grow through the problem. It's obvious that impulsive people may act on feelings to such excess that they bring harm to themselves and others.

But it's less obvious that overly cautious people may become so dependent on rules that they are slaves to shoulds. When you say, "I should," you are implying that you neither need nor want to do this thing, but some force or some person outside you is saying you ought to. Shoulds are energy drains because they create a feeling of resistance and apathy. They cause people to shift responsibility for their choices somewhere else. When you make life changes, it's important to know whether your shoulds are value inspired. Shoulds will either evaporate as unimportant or, if value related, will be owned as a want.

Needs and Wants Relate to Values

Needs are absolute survival minimums on the physical, emotional, intellectual, and altruistic levels. *Wants* go beyond survival to a place of enriched choices. When you make such choices based on reasoned judgment, good feelings, and common sense with no pressure from shoulds, you are clearly indicating that this choice is something that *you* value. You will generally feel confident and enthusiastic about your decision. Making an important value decision may also bring some feelings of regret or guilt. Other good choices may have to be left behind; shoulds may still linger. But in time a true value will become a comfortable part of your life pattern. Values are what you *do*, not what you *say*. Becoming aware of what you really value and cherish is a lifelong process.

Surprisingly, struggles, disappointments, worries, hopes, and dreams indicate a value area as well, for if something is not a value it would not be of concern. There are bad values as well as good ones. Sometimes people sense that they are choosing values that are not good for them, that do not nurture them, and they struggle against a "good value" decision. Murky values can result in many conflicts. People who seem turned off, confused, indecisive, complaining, hostile, alienated, or "lazy," and who over-conform or over-rebel probably have conflicts over values.[10]

Values are unique to each person. For King Midas, gold was everything. For some people, it is the love of a pet, as we have seen when a person

astounds the public by leaving a million dollars to a pet cat. Sometimes your choices can lead you far from the kind of success you originally had in mind. Hoping for attention and love, people who acquire all sorts of status symbols may instead alienate those they are trying to impress. Endless acquisition of satisfiers on one level can cause neglect of needs and wants on other levels. A wise person once said that everything you own, owns you. Clarifying your values helps you avoid pitfalls on your journey. You don't want to find yourself halfway down the block before you realize you've turned the wrong corner.

Values Influence Your Lifestyle and Act as Motivators

Your values lead you to make decisions about your whole life, not just your career. All the elements of your lifestyle, including family, love and friendship, home and work environments, religious preference, education, and recreation—in short, all the choices you make—will reflect your personal values.

Your choices will in turn further affect your values and will thus influence your lifestyle in many ways. In your career, for example, you will learn new skills, change some behaviors to fit your new role, make new friends, and learn a new vocabulary. Your work can lead to new involvements and even new ways of seeing yourself.[11] In fact, work roles can be so overpowering that some people find it hard to relate to a new acquaintance without knowing what that person does for a living.

Most important, the work you choose will fulfill many of your needs and wants and will directly reflect your values. Without needs and wants to motivate them, people would not work. Most people work for money to fulfill their basic needs. Some people work because the work is intellectually satisfying. Others go to work to be with people, to be noticed, be approved of, and for a whole host of individual enticements. Those with enough resources to fulfill their basic needs and wants then work for enrichment and for the good of others.

It may seem difficult or impossible at times to align your lifestyle with your values. Life is not always obliging. To write the Great American Novel may be on your dream agenda, yet you find yourself typing engineering specs. Your choice says that you value feeding yourself and your family over feeding your love for writing.

Clarifying your values and their order of importance can eliminate a great deal of conflict as well as help you set goals. When you have realistic goals, both immediate and long term, you have a far greater possibility of actualizing your dreams. With this book, you will be clarifying many values as you learn about yourself and your own characteristics. You will be making decisions based on those values. And achieving your needs and wants in harmony with your values spells success. This process is bound to enhance your personal growth.

> The unexamined life is not worth living.
> —*Socrates*

Personal Growth

Getting acquainted with yourself—your feelings, needs, wants, and most cherished values, changing shoulds to wants or dropping them—is a continuous process of growth. Growing as a person means adjusting but not losing our dreams and desires as we explore the realities of the world. The need for growth on all levels is a powerful force within us. It means expansion into new and exciting areas of life. Never before in the history of humankind have people of all ages had such opportunity for growth. Many people now live longer, are more affluent, have access to vast amounts of technology, and are more aware of possibilities. There are new dimensions to life that were not present even twenty years ago. People are going back to school at ages seventy and eighty, getting degrees, starting businesses, publishing their first books, painting, initiating nationwide political action groups, or teaching swimming! People are discovering that their powers are about as strong as their attitudes: physical (including sexual) ability, the ability to learn, the capacity to develop new ideas.

The alternative to growth is a diminished life that closes out self by put-downs, lack of confidence; many shoulds that close out others by bitter, angry thoughts and blaming/projecting; and many demands that close out life by tension, guilt, and anxiety.

Growth is not always easy. Sometimes exploring these ideas and feelings with a trusted guide can help you learn to channel your energy in positive ways and to accomplish your goals more effectively.

"It seems like only yesterday I was on the verge of getting it all together."

Drawing by Stevenson; © 1974 The New Yorker Magazine, Inc.

Reviewing past experiences can uncover important clues to your skills and interests as well as promote growth. Your "free spirit" years, those beginning at about age five or six when you became independent enough to make some choices, are especially important. You weren't as worried about what people thought as you might have been when you were ten or twelve. What gave you satisfaction then and what proved disappointing? Some people find great motivation striving for success in what was once a so-called area of failure. Timid speech students become noted speakers; inept Little Leaguers become strong athletes.

Times of transition can be fearful periods in which life seems so empty that we'd give anything not to face reality. But when we do face it, we are amazed at how much more there is of all good and joyful things. We begin to like ourselves better and are able to care more for others. We gradually begin to see life differently. In a sense we create our own world, and in the words of Ken Keyes, Jr., a humanist who developed a system for handling strong feelings, "a loving person lives in a loving world."[12] Self-awareness leads to self-acceptance, which leads to self-confidence. Then we are on the way to self-actualization.

When minimal needs are fulfilled on every level, when our wants are becoming reality, when our shoulds have dissolved or turned to wants, when our feelings are helping rather than hindering the process, it seems that endless vistas of growth open up for us. Psychologist Abraham Maslow said, "We may still often (if not always) expect that a new discontent and restlessness will soon develop, unless the individual is doing what he's fitted for. A musician must make music, an artist must paint, a poet must write, if he is to be ultimately at peace. What a person can be, he must be. This need we call self-actualization."[13]

A self-actualizing or growing person might be described as follows:

- is authentic, open, doesn't hide behind roles or masks
- is ruled neither by ego nor emotion
- is simple, natural, with little need for status symbols
- is autonomous, centered, not pulled along by every fad
- can make decisions, take responsibility
- takes life seriously, with a generous touch of whimsy
- can see through the pretenses of others with a benign view and maybe even a chuckle
- is emotionally balanced, enjoying peak experiences, delighting in people, art, nature, yet able to "get the job done"
- is not burdened with the anxiety, guilt, or shame that go with shoulds
- is spontaneous, passionate, creative, an enjoyer of life—yet is moral, ethical, concerned
- sees all useful work as dignified and treats all workers with respect
- takes time for self-renewal and relaxation
- can be alone or in a group with equal ease
- values self as well as others
- is able to find common ground in opposing views and help reconcile people's differences
- values privacy, yet feels one with humankind
- tends to form deep personal relationships, based on love and caring, with other self-actualizing people
- has a basic set of beliefs, a philosophy of life
- acts not out of greed, fear, or anger, but out of love and caring for the whole world

The flowering of our growth
brings aliveness, effortlessness,
individuality, playfulness,
completion, richness.

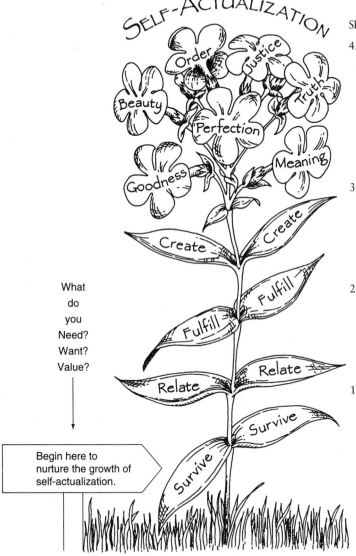

SELF-ACTUALIZATION

4. ALTRUISTIC NEEDS: We
all must interact with others to survive, but to live
life fully is to have that
generous, loving spirit that
promotes truth, goodness,
beauty, justice, perfection,
order, meaning, and all that
is noble and good in the
world.

3. INTELLECTUAL NEEDS:
A degree of knowledge and
understanding are neces-
sary for survival, but a
truly developed mind is one
in which wisdom and cre-
ativity flourish.

2. EMOTIONAL NEEDS:
Basic caring from others is
necesssary for our growth.
Rich relationships bring us
joy and the courage that
comes from emotional sup-
port, love, and respect.

1. PHYSICAL NEEDS: We all
have needs for food, clothing, shelter, safety—the
things that keep us alive.
Our carefully chosen wants
enrich us and enable us to
simplify our lives and feel
self-sufficient.

Four NEED/WANT/VALUE areas leads to Personal Growth and Development.

The Flowering of Personal Growth

As people find balance and sufficiency in their needs and wants, life becomes greatly enriched: fulfillment of physical needs and wants is ample yet not excessive; relationships bring respect, support, love, and joy; wisdom and creativity flourish; and the human spirit becomes noble, compassionate, and good.

When people have it all then, where do they go next? Heroic deeds make up the fabric of some people's lives as they achieve the highest form of self-actualization. At this level, a person is motivated by natural altruism or spirituality. Service to others becomes the primary value, and the person strives for what Jakob von Uexkull, founder of Right Livelihood Awards, called "the ability to empower, uplift, and heal the human spirit."[14] For example, Millard and Linda Fuller wondered why so many people in rural Georgia were living in run-down shacks. Instead of getting angry, they got busy, organizing volunteers and raising money. They began to build low-cost housing in partnership with needy people who pay the cost back so that more homes can be built. The organization they founded, Habitat for Humanity, has built over 40,000 homes worldwide since 1976.

Pat Cane brings school supplies and teaches art and relaxation techniques to war-torn Guatemala and Nicaragua, but above all, she brings love. Gradually others are joining her in her ministry of healing for an afflicted world. She writes, "All of these communities are very poor, some in the countryside are without running water and electricity. Most of the families earn less than $10 a month. Their lives are, for the most part, simple and very humble, but very rich in love and faith and truth and many of the deep human values that matter most of all. What they have to share with us is a very different view of reality not found in the media nor in the rhetoric of the powerful and wealthy of our world. And this can lead to many awakenings within ourselves of the deeper meaning of love and justice in the world."[15]

David Suzuki talked to some destitute homeless children on the streets of Brazil and found amazing altruism. One child said, "I wish I was rich. And if I were I would give all of the street children food, clothes, medicines, shelter, and love, and affection!"[16]

The more talents you develop, and the more you can make a positive contribution to the world you live in, the more self-actualized you are on all levels from physical through emotional, intellectual, and altruistic/spiritual. This world is filled with challenges. It is our work that provides many of the options and solutions.

> Hope . . . is not the same as joy that things are going well, or willingness to invest in enterprises that are obviously heading for . . . success, but rather, an ability to work for something because it is good, not just because it stands a chance to succeed.
>
> —Vaclav Havel
> former president of Czechoslovakia[17]

The Work Ethic: A Personal Philosophic View

An integral part of our value system and a reflection of our personal growth is our attitude toward work, our *work ethic*. Is work really necessary? Is it valuable? Demeaning? Enhancing? Often we are ambivalent. While necessary, work is viewed differently by various cultures. In the modern technical world, people are expected to work hard and achieve much, leaving enjoyment and fun for ever-shrinking leisure hours.

The American work ethic has its roots in early colonial days when the maxim "Idleness is the devil's workshop" was not to be questioned, nor was Ben Franklin's dictum, "Time is money." Americans value those who have "made it" and often look down on people who haven't. People should work hard for their just rewards. Thus, by and large, we are work addicts—striving, struggling, sometimes becoming ruthless and immoral to succeed. (Work itself sometimes becomes the devil's workshop!)

The backlash from our national policies and attitudes has been vividly described in *Work in America,* a special task force report to the secretary of Health, Education, and Welfare that is still relevant today.

> Because work is central to the lives of most Americans, either the absence of work or employment in meaningless work is creating an increasingly intolerable situation. The human costs of this state of affairs are manifested in worker alienation, alcoholism, drug addiction, and other symptoms of poor mental health. Moreover, much of our tax money is expended in an effort to compensate for problems with at least a part of their genesis in the world of work. A great part of the staggering national bill in the areas of crime and delinquency, mental and physical health, manpower and welfare are generated in our national policies and attitudes toward work. . . . Most important, there are the high costs of lost opportunities to encourage citizen participation: the discontent of women, minorities, blue-collar workers, youth, and older adults would be considerably less were these Americans to have had an active voice in the decisions in the workplace that most directly affect their lives.[18]

Not everyone subscribes to the American Work Ethic. Senator Edward Kennedy recounts how, during his first campaign for the U.S. Senate, his opponent said scornfully in a debate, "This man has never worked a day in his life!" Kennedy says that the next morning as he was shaking hands at a factory gate, one worker leaned toward him and confided, "You ain't missed a goddamned thing."[19]

Somewhere between these two extremes of workaholism and alienation you will develop your personal work ethic, your personal perspective on the meaning of work for you.

Just a Job, or a Career?

Your career choice will more completely match your values when you decide on the degree of commitment you are willing to make to your work. Do you want a career or just a job? A job might be defined as something one does to earn money, requiring little involvement beyond one's physical and mental presence. Many people of all levels of intelligence and creativity approach work this way; some, because their job is the only work they want or can get; others, to support hobbies and creative activities for which there seem to be no work opportunities.

In contrast to a job, a career can be seen as a series of work experiences that represents progression in a field. This kind of work usually absorbs much of a person's energy. A career is often planned for and trained for, and it often involves dedication of time and talent beyond the minimum required.

Two people may do identical work, yet one may view the work as "just a job" whereas the other sees it as "my career." Sometimes a person trains and sacrifices to achieve a career only to face disillusionment and ends up just putting in time. Conversely, some people have been known to perform what society calls "menial" work with a level of dedication worthy of a career professional.

A demanding career may cause a loss of family, health, friendship, and leisure. How much are you willing to sacrifice? Some people can pursue a career with great dedication and yet manage to keep a balance. How much involvement is enough for you? Keep the question of commitment in mind, as well as your other values, as you consider your career choice. When you find work that matches your needs, wants, values, interests, and abilities and see that it brings you many rewards, your respect for your workplace and colleagues will grow. You will be eager to put forth your best effort, and you will enjoy the challenges that each day brings. What began as a job may become your career.

We seem to be in a period of rising expectations about ourselves and about work, even in a frequently shaky job market. As T. George Harris, former editor of *Psychology Today*, once said, "We were doing all right until some idiot raised the ante on what it takes to be a person and the rest of us accepted it without noticing."[20] Well, why not? Why not expand our vision? To paraphrase Elizabeth Cady Stanton, the true person is as yet a dream of the future.[21] Why keep that idea forever in the future? Why not begin to make it a present reality? The premise of this manual is that even in a time of tight employment, work and life can be a joy! For the first time in history we can allow ourselves the luxury of thinking of work as both fulfilling and a responsible way to provide good things for ourselves and others. And each person will find that fulfillment in a unique way. A carpenter will put each nail in a little straighter; secretaries will prepare reports with extra-special care. We all can contribute in some way to the well-being of others as well as to ourselves as responsible, productive, and contented workers.

If we can find a place where we feel some measure of success, some value, we will find new energy to put into our work. Dr. Hans Selye, a world-renowned, biological scientist, describes the relationship among aging, work, and stress: "Work wears you out mainly through the frustrations of failure. Most of the eminent among hard workers in almost any field lived a long life. Since work is a basic need of man, the question is not whether to work but what kind of work is play."[22] And Yehudi Menuhin expresses it well when he says, "All my life I have reveled in the sound of the violin."

We have many resources of mind and spirit. Can we move to a place of greater joy in work and in life? Harvard researchers, Bartolomé and Evans tell us, "You will fit your job/life activity, and we can say, be more successful if you feel confident, enjoy the work and if your moral values coincide with your work."[23] Reflecting on what success means to you, what your values are, is essential in deciding what you want to do with your life. The paths that open up can be quite surprising and different from what you may have expected.

As you go about the process of choosing a career, your image of success will sharpen. May your career choice contribute to your dream of the future.

 ## *Self-Assessment Exercises*

The following exercises are designed to help you with your inward search. Use *only the ones that are useful to you. You may not need to do them all.* Chapter 9, "Work Affects the Soul: The Final Analysis," has been set aside for summaries of some of the Self-Assessment Exercises. It may help you to note the results of your surveys there, either as you finish each chapter, when you reach the end of the book, or not at all. It's up to you.

1. Needs and Wants: Dream your goals.

a. Survival needs plus: Your enriched wants reflect your values

What lifestyle is important to you? Dream—let your imagination soar—describe your ideal.

Your home _____

Your clothing _____

Your food _____

Your family_____

Your friends _____

Your associates_____

Your transportation_____

Your pets/plants_____

Your gadgets and playthings _____

Your activities _____

Other_____

b. People needs

What do you expect from each group around you—for example, family, friends, associates? What would you like to change?

_____

_____

_____

_____

c. Fulfillment needs/wants

Dream again! If you could instantly be in your ideal career/lifestyle, already skilled and trained, what would it be?

- To delight yourself and amaze your family and friends?

_____

_____

- To improve the world?

_____

_____

d. Checking the balance

Check the balance in your life. What do you do, over and above absolute need, to contribute to your well-being on each of the following four levels?

Physical_____

Emotional_____

Intellectual _____

Altruistic/Spiritual _____

2. Tapping into Feelings and Shoulds

What seems to block your effectiveness? It's easier to make career/life decisions if problems are not getting in the way.

a. Life problems checklist

Identify the factors that you feel are a problem for you. Rate the items listed by checking the appropriate columns: I am happy with; I am managing with; I am having trouble with. Year + = This problem has been going on for a year or more; Chronic = This problem has been present for a great deal of my life. Then go back and circle the numbers of the items you would like to change.

	Happy	Managing	Trouble	Year+	Chronic
Parents/brothers/sisters					
Spouse/children					
Family closeness					
Friends/relationships/love					
Privacy/freedom					
Dwelling					
Work					
Finances					
Personal achievements/success					
Confidence					
Health					
Diet/drugs/drinking/smoking					
Exercise					
Physical appearance					
Physical well-being					
Time/leisure					
Recreation/hobbies					
Emotional/mental well-being					
Status					
Intellectual ability					
Artistic ability					
Education					
Social concern					
Political concern					
Spiritual/religious well-being					

b. Feelings checkpoint

Check (✓) any of the following feeling responses that often create problems for you. Mark with a plus (+) those areas you'd like to improve.

_____ Anger	_____ Discouragement	_____ Pessimism
_____ Apathy	_____ Fear	_____ Resentment
_____ Boredom	_____ Frenzy	_____ Skepticism
_____ Confusion	_____ Frustration	_____ Violence
_____ Cynicism	_____ Hostility	_____ Worry
_____ Depression	_____ Hurt	

c. Shoulds

List and examine the shoulds that hold you back. Can you drop them or change them to wants? Answer below.

_____

_____

_____

_____

3. Rating Values

Here are five incomplete sentences that encourage you to think about values. In the lists that follow each one, check (✓) *every* word that finishes the statement correctly *for you* as you or your life are *now*. Put a plus sign (+) in front of every word that describes things you would like to *develop more*. Feel free to add, delete, or change words on each list.

a. Career values

In my career, I do (✓); I would like to (+):

_____ Create beauty	_____ Help people
_____ Create ideas	_____ Improve society
_____ Design systems	_____ Make things
_____ Experience variety	_____ Organize things
_____ Explore ideas	_____ Perform physical tasks
_____ Follow directions	_____ Take responsibility

b. Result values

I have (✓); I'd like to have more (+):

_____ Adventure	_____ Money
_____ Beautiful surroundings	_____ Pleasure
_____ Comfort	_____ Power
_____ Fun	_____ Possessions
_____ Happiness	_____ Prestige
_____ Independence	_____ Security
_____ Leisure time	_____ Structure

c. Personal qualities

I am (✓); I'd like to be more (+):

_____ Accepting	_____ Famous
_____ Affectionate	_____ Friendly
_____ Ambitious	_____ Good-looking
_____ Balanced	_____ Healthy
_____ Brave	_____ Honest/fair
_____ Calm	_____ Intelligent
_____ Caring	_____ Joyful
_____ Compassionate	_____ Kind
_____ Competitive	_____ Loving
_____ Confident	_____ Loyal
_____ Conscientious	_____ Mature
_____ Cooperative	_____ Neat
_____ Courteous	_____ Needed
_____ Creative	_____ Optimistic
_____ Decisive	_____ Peaceful
_____ Disciplined	_____ Poised
_____ Efficient	_____ Prompt
_____ Enthusiastic	_____ Self-accepting

_____ Sensitive   _____ Understanding

_____ Strong   _____ Verbal

_____ Successful   _____ Warm

_____ Trusting   _____ Wise

d. People satisfiers

I have good relationships with (✔); I'd like good (or better) relationships with (+):

_____ Spouse/lover   _____ Children

_____ Relatives   _____ Friends

_____ Parents   _____ Neighbors

_____ Siblings   _____ Colleagues

_____ In-laws   _____ Supervisors

e. Personal growth satisfiers

I am satisfied with my development in the following need/want areas (✔); I'd like to develop more in (+):

_____ Physical   _____ Intellectual

_____ Emotional   _____ Altruistic/spiritual

f. Global values

I am working toward (✔); I would like to work more toward (+):

_____ Economic development   _____ Industrial/technical development

_____ Environmental protection   _____ Weapons control

_____ Ethical/spiritual development   _____ World food or housing supply

_____ Human rights   _____ World peace and prosperity

g. Values checkpoint

Star (*) your top three values in each section a–f. Describe yourself to someone or write a brief paper describing yourself using these value words. Explain any contradictions.

4. Goal Setting

Set goals! Go back over the above exercises and pick one area for improvement. Write down a key word and post it someplace where you can see it, perhaps on the bathroom mirror. What specific steps, little or big, can you take to improve your life? Perhaps see a counselor to talk over such issues as problem areas, strong feelings, or values conflicts.

I'd like to improve: _____

Steps to take: _____

_____

_____

5. Your Expectations

At this point, do you feel that you want a career or "just a job"? Explain.

_____

_____

_____

6. Drawing a Self-Portrait

a. Your free-spirit years

Between the ages of five to ten, what activities did you enjoy the most? Remember various seasons, indoors, outdoors; remember friends you played with. List and then check (✓) those you enjoyed most.

_____	_____
_____	_____
_____	_____
_____	_____
_____	_____
_____	_____

b. Your lifeline

Even very young people have had significant experiences that changed them. Beginning with the young childhood period, draw a lifeline representing the ups and downs of your experiences at various times of your life. Draw your first impressions without concern about detail. Begin by skimming over the surface of your life, noting the high and low points, such as times of joy and times of unhappiness. Look for people who had profound and positive effects on you.

	Young Childhood Teddy Bears/Goblins 3–5 years	Elementary School Free-Spirit Years 6–13 Years	High School Teenage Traumas/Triumphs 14–17 Years	New Beginnings College/Work 18–22 Years	Developing an Adult Lifestyle 23–28 Years	Family/Commitment Career Involvement 29–39 Years	Midlife Crises Is There Life After 40? 40–45 Years	Settling In Facing Up 45–55 Years	Putting It All Together Once More/Preretirement 56–70 Years	Reflecting/Integrating A Time for Wisdom 70+
High Points										
Low Points										

■ List your low points/hardest times.

_____

_____

_____

_____

_____

_____

■ List your high points/happiest times.

_____

_____

_____

_____

_____

_____

■ List your most important life decisions.

_____

_____

_____

_____

■ List three to five people who influenced you the most *in your life* (include teachers, authors, etc.). Tell what they did. Rate the importance of their influence now by rating them: 1 = Very important; 2 = Important; 3 = So so; 4 = No longer important.

_____

_____

_____

_____

7. Candid Camera—3-D

Each activity you've chosen to do contains important clues about you, your skills, and your interests. This exercise will be one of the first steps on the road to career decision making. It is also the first step toward preparing a résumé and getting ready for an interview. Your life in 3-D will help you discover who you are, decide your goals, design your strategies. Spend an intense hour doing this exercise as outlined here. Use scratch paper. Then save it and add to it, refine it, and organize it according to the exercises that follow.

■ **Loves:** Make a list of ten to twenty activities you love to do, not *like* or *should* but *love*. Don't *think* too much; just list whatever comes to mind first.

■ **Jobs:** List five to ten or more of the most important jobs you've held for pay, way back to baby-sitting or lawn mowing.

■ **Other:** List five to ten of your most important extracurricular activities, community volunteer jobs, hobbies done at home or on vacation, sports, anything you've done that is important to you.

■ **Activity Components:** Then take a separate sheet of scratch paper for each of two or three items in each category and begin to list what you did to accomplish each activity. For example, if skiing is on your list, you might say buying equipment, doing fitness exercises, deciding where to go, making reservations, budgeting funds, what else?

■ **Date, People, Things:** Become aware of the times when you are dealing with people and things. Notice when you are dealing with ideas and information alone—for example, when reading, analyzing, and organizing material—just what this exercise requires. You will see that in dealing with people and things, you always need ideas and information (data). Then code each activity D, P, or T. We will use this code later on to help you sort out various types of job qualities.

P = activities when you deal directly with people (some use of data always implied).

T = activities when you deal directly with things (some use of data always implied).

D = activities when you deal just with ideas and information, called data (there is little or no interaction with people or things).

8. Data File

Here is an example of file cards done by students. They summarize activities performed in various jobs or important activities. Notice that any activity can be expanded with more detail. Make a file card for each of the jobs and activities that is important to you.

X-Mart, Inc.   Supervisor: Buster Brown

347 Snow Valley Lane   Salary: $5.20/hr

New Castle, DE   Dates: June 1996–present

Title: Cashier

• Process customer merchandise through check stand

• Collect cash and make change

• Verify check or credit card information

• Bag items and present sales slip

• Help unpack merchandise in storeroom and stock shelves

> Happy Lake Summer Camp   Supervisor: Jane Golden
>
> Route 555   Salary: $50/week plus
>
> Happy Lake, Wisconsin 53950   room and board
>
> Title: Camp Counselor   Dates: Summers 1995, 1996
>
> • Supervise group of 8 children ages 8 to 10
>
> • Organize swimming activities
>
> • Teach leather crafts
>
> • Do conflict resolution, listen to problems
>
> • Oversee bunk room

9. Creating an Autobiography

Many people find that creating an autobiography is a valuable way to rediscover themselves by looking over their past lives. Use one of these suggestions.

- Simply write the story of your life.

- Write a summary of Exercise 6b, "Your Lifeline."

- Using Exercise 6b, "Your Lifeline," write about the people who influenced you. What were their messages to you?

- Make a poster or collage out of magazines or old pictures that illustrate you and your life line.

- Use the three circles on the next page as a basis for an autobiography. Discuss each item in the past, present, and future circles as it applies to your life.

- Create a personal "I Wheel" like the one on p. 37.

 ## Group Discussion Questions

In addition to these group discussion questions below, share with others the exercises in this and all the chapters.

1. Discuss with a group what basic needs you could supply for each other and how much money that would save you. What wants are important for you?

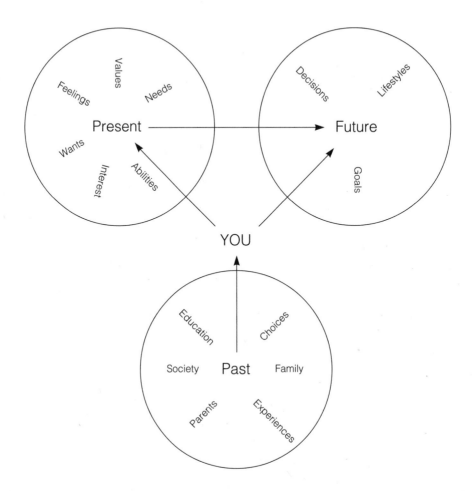

Have you covered all the areas: physical, emotional, intellectual, altruistic/spiritual?

2. What is the connection between our needs and wants and the work we and others do?

3. What limits and demands do your personal wants place on your career choice?

4. Name the last five items you've purchased. What basic needs did they fulfill? What wants? Could you survive without them for a year?

5. List all the devices in your home that use electricity. On a scale of l to l0, rate how necessary each appliance is to you. If you could use only five, which ones would you choose? Is electricity a basic human need?

6. Do the basic human needs change over time?

7. Discuss success and failure.

   a. Define success and failure for yourself.

   b. Try substituting the word *happiness* for *success*. Is there a difference?

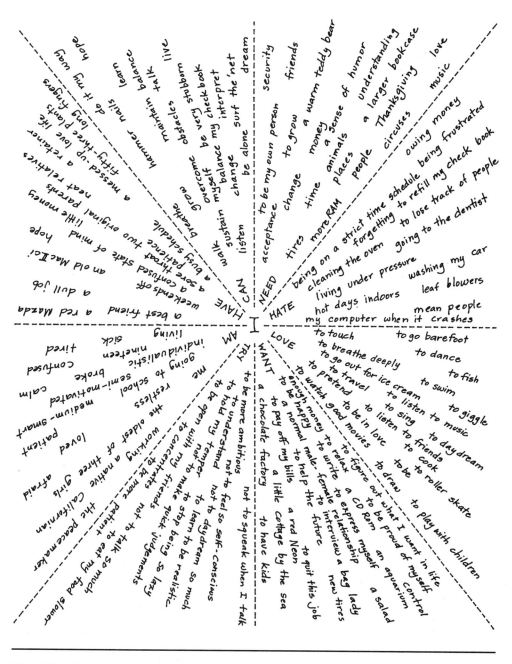

The I Wheel

8. Give as many answers as you can to this question: Why do we work?
9. Has this chapter clarified your image of the kind of person you are now and would like to be in the future; the kind of lifestyle you would like to lead?
10. Has this chapter caused you to begin making some decisions that will bring you closer to your goals? How?

2

Personality and Performance

Pieces of the Puzzle

 FOCUS

- Assess your personality.

- Pinpoint your relationship to Data, People, Things, and Work Qualities.

- Identify your skills.

You are gathering information to match a special person—you, and your needs, wants, and values—with satisfying positions in the world of work. When you finally enter the workplace, you may have had to make some compromises, but the ideal is to minimize the compromises and maximize the match.

A major decision point is interest area. Where do you, with all the unique facets of your personality, feel most comfortable? The human personality is like a stained-glass window—a mosaic of light and color. A stained-glass window is an enduring object of carefully chosen colors, yet it changes with the changing sun. In darkness it seems to disappear, but in the light it comes alive with color.

> It takes
> > its life from light
> > it sleeps at night
> > and comes ablaze at dawn
> > > it holds the day
> > > 'til shadows fade,
> > > its brilliance strangely gone.

Analogously, the human personality can be seen as a mosaic of six major themes.

Areas of Interest: The Personality Mosaic

Psychologist and vocational counselor John Holland says that one of six major personality types—or perhaps a combination of two or more types—plays a highly important role in an individual's career choice. We become more interested in some areas than others early in life. These areas become focal points, largely because of choices that stem from our needs, wants, and values.[1]

Notice what interests draw individuals when family or friends get together. Sports and cars are a magnet to some; the lives and loves of people are a concern to others; mind-bending discussions, plotting a financial move, or sharing creative endeavors can keep some members of a group going until all hours. Because each person notices and experiences things differently, *you* are unique in the combination of things that interest *you*. Those interests make up your predominant personality characteristics and are keys to career satisfaction.

Becoming aware of your "lesser lights" can also provide some illumination and enrichment. We are all born with innumerable possibilities. Some talents may remain undeveloped for half a lifetime only to surface in the middle and senior years. Personal growth leads to the discovery of new dimensions in ourselves.

Then there is that "Renaissance person" who seems able to be and to do all things with apparently equal ease, who is at home in all settings and with all people.

In this chapter, you can identify the predominant orientation of your personality in an inventory called the Personality Mosaic. It's important to take this inventory before reading the interpretation that follows. Then you can analyze the kinds of activities you've been enjoying all your life. Having reminded yourself of your interests, you will be ready to tie this data into the Job Group Chart in Chapter 3.

 ## Personality Mosaic

Circle the numbers of statements that clearly sound like something you might say or do or think—something that feels like *you*. Don't stop to analyze your responses too much. Put question marks (?) in front of doubtful items. Put an X on the numbers of statements that feel very unlike you.

? 1. It's important for me to have a strong, agile body.
2. I need to understand things thoroughly.
3. Music, color, writing, beauty of any kind can really affect my moods.
4. Relationships with people enrich my life and give it meaning.
5. I am confident that I'll be successful.
6. I need clear directions so I know exactly what to do.
? 7. I can usually carry/build/fix things myself.
? 8. I can get absorbed for hours in thinking something out.
9. I appreciate beautiful surroundings: color and design mean a lot to me.
10. I'll spend time finding ways to help people through personal crises.
X11. I enjoy competing.
12. I prefer getting carefully organized before I start a project.
13. I enjoy making things with my hands.
14. It's satisfying to explore new ideas.
? 15. I always seem to be looking for new ways to express my creativity.
16. I value being able to share personal concerns with people.
17. Being a key person in a group is very stimulating to me.
18. I take pride in being very careful about all the details of my work.
? 19. I don't mind getting my hands dirty.
20. I see education as a lifelong process of developing and sharpening my mind.
X21. I like to dress in unusual ways, try new colors and styles.
22. I can often sense when a person needs to talk to someone.
23. I enjoy getting people organized and on the move.
24. I'd rather be safe than adventurous in making decisions.
? 25. I like to buy sensible things I can make or work on myself.
? 26. Sometimes I can sit for long periods of time and work on problems or puzzles or read or just think.
? 27. I have a great imagination.

28. I like to help people develop their talents and abilities.
29. I like to be in charge of getting the job done.
30. I usually prepare carefully ahead of time if I have to handle a new situation.
31. I'd rather be on my own doing practical, hands-on activities.
32. I'm eager to read or think about any subject that arouses my curiosity.
33. I love to try creative new ideas.
34. If I have a problem with someone, I'll keep trying to resolve it peacefully.
35. To be successful, it's important to aim high.
36. I don't like to take responsibility for making big decisions.
37. I say what's on my mind and don't beat around the bush.
38. I need to analyze a problem pretty thoroughly before I act on it.
39. I like to rearrange my surroundings to make them unique and different.
40. I often solve my personal problems by talking them out with someone.
41. I get projects started and let others take care of details.
42. Being on time is very important to me.
43. It's invigorating to do things outdoors.
44. I keep asking, "Why?"
45. I like my work to be an expression of my moods and feelings.
46. I like to help people find ways to care more for each other.
47. It's exciting to take part in important decisions.
48. I am usually neat and orderly.
49. I like my surroundings to be plain and practical.
50. I need to stay with a problem until I figure out an answer.
51. The beauty of nature touches something deep inside me.
52. Close personal relationships are valuable to me.
53. Promotion and advancement are important to me.
54. I feel more secure when my day is well planned.
55. I'm not afraid of heavy physical work and usually know what needs to be done.
56. I enjoy books that make me think and give me new ideas.
57. I look forward to seeing art shows, plays, and good films.
58. I am very sensitive to people who are experiencing emotional upsets.
59. It's exciting for me to influence people.
60. When I say I'll do it, I do my best to follow through on every detail.
61. Good, hard manual labor never hurt anyone.
62. I'd like to learn all there is to know about subjects that interest me.
63. I don't want to be like everyone else; I like to do things differently.
64. I'll go out of my way to be caring of people with problems.
65. I'm willing to take some risks to get ahead.
66. I feel more secure when I follow rules.
67. One of the first things I look for in a car is a well-built engine.
68. I like a conversation to be intellectually stimulating/challenging.
69. When I'm creating, I tend to let everything else go.

70. I feel concerned that so many people in our society need help.
71. It's challenging to persuade people to follow a plan.
72. I'm very good about checking details.
73. I usually know how to take care of things in an emergency.
74. Reading about new discoveries is exciting.
75. I appreciate beautiful and unusual things.
76. I take time to pay attention to people who seem lonely and friendless.
77. I love to bargain.
78. I like to be very careful about spending money.
79. Sports are important to me in building a strong body.
80. I've always been curious about the way nature works.
81. It's fun to be in a mood to try something unusual.
82. I am a good listener when people talk about personal problems.
83. If I don't make it the first time, I usually bounce back with energy and enthusiasm.
84. I need to know exactly what people expect me to do.
85. I like to take things apart to see if I can fix them.
86. I like to study all the facts and decide logically.
87. It would be hard to imagine my life without beauty around me.
88. People often seem to tell me their problems.
89. I can usually connect with people who get me in touch with a network of resources.
90. It's very satisfying to do a task carefully and completely.

Scoring Your Answers

To score, circle the same numbers that you circled on the Personality Mosaic.

R	I	A	S	E	C
1	2	3	4	5	6
7	8	9	10	11	12
13	14	15	16	17	18
19	20	21	22	23	24
25	26	27	28	29	30
31	32	33	34	35	36
37	38	39	40	41	42
43	44	45	46	47	48
49	50	51	52	53	54
55	56	57	58	59	60
61	62	63	64	65	66
67	68	69	70	71	72
73	74	75	76	77	78
79	80	81	82	83	84
85	86	87	88	89	90

Count the number of circles in each column and write the total number of circles in the spaces, 15 being the highest possible score:

R _4_ I _9_ A _6_ S _15_ E _11_ C _11_
   7?   6?   6?   0?   3?   4?

List the letters R, I, A, S, E, and C, according to your scores, from highest to lowest:

1st _S_ 2nd _E_ 3rd _C_ 4th _I_ 5th _A_ 6th _R_

Put question marks (?) on the score chart that match those you marked on the inventory. Does adding in the items you're unsure of (?) change the order? _____

How? _____

Put your Xs from the inventory on the score chart, also. In which areas do you have the most "unlike you" scores (X)? _4-R_   _3-A_   _1-E_

_____

Were you aware at any time of responding according to "shoulds"? _____

When _____

Do you have a tie score in two more or columns? If so, the remainder of this chapter will help you to decide which column represents the "real you."

To get more in touch with yourself, read aloud some of the statements for each orientation from the Personality Mosaic. *Be* that kind of person. Embellish and dramatize the statements to see how that kind of behavior feels. You may want to role-play this activity in a group.

Interpreting the Personality Mosaic

The inventory you have just taken is based on the six personality orientations identified by John Holland. As you can see from your score, you are not just one personality type—that is, you are not a person with fifteen circles in one area and no circles in any of the others. In most people one or two characteristics are dominant, two or three are of medium intensity, and one or two may be of low intensity. A few people score high in each category because they have many interests. Others, who don't have many strong interests, score rather low in all areas.

Here is an overview and discussion of the six personality types and their relationship to each other. Try to find yourself in the following descriptions.

Realistic Personality

Hands-on people who enjoy exploring things, fixing things, making things with their hands

Express themselves and achieve primarily through their bodies rather than through words, thoughts, feelings

Usually independent, practical minded, strong, well coordinated, aggressive, conservative, rugged individualists

Like the challenge of physical risk, being outdoors, using tools and machinery

Prefer concrete problems rather than abstract ones

Solve problems by doing something physical

Realistic individuals are capable and confident when using their bodies to relate to the physical world. They focus on *things,* learn through their hands, and have little need for conversation. Because they are at ease with physical objects, they are often good in emergencies. Their ability to deal with the physical world often makes them very independent. Because these characteristics describe the stereotypical male, many women shrink from displaying any capability in this area, and often women are discouraged from doing so. Realistic people sometimes get so absorbed in putting *things* right that they can forget about everything else.

Investigative Personality

Persons who live very much "in their minds"

Unconventional and independent thinkers, intellectually curious, very insightful, logical, persistent

Express themselves and achieve primarily through their minds rather than through association with people or involvement with things

Like to explore ideas through reading, discussing

Enjoy complex and abstract mental challenges

Solve problems by thinking and analyzing

The investigative type deals with the "real world" of things but at a distance. These individuals prefer to read, study, use books, charts, and other data instead of getting their hands on *things.* When involved with people, they tend to focus on ideas. Wherever they are, they collect information and analyze the situation before making a decision. If they enjoy the outdoors, it's because they are curious, not because they enjoy rugged, heavy, physical work. Their curiosity sometimes leads them to explore their ideas to the exclusion of all else.

Artistic Personality

Persons who are creative, sensitive, aesthetic, introspective, intuitive, visionary

See new possibilities and want to express them in creative ways

Especially attuned to perception of color, form, sound, feeling

Prefer to work alone and independently rather than with others

Enjoy beauty, variety, the unusual in sight, sound, texture, people

Need fairly unstructured environment to provide opportunities for creative expression

Solve problems by creating something new

The artistic types express creativity not only with paint and canvas but with ideas and systems as well. Those sensitive to sight, sound, and touch will be drawn to the fine arts such as art, drama, music, and literature. The weaver designs and makes fabric; the poet creates with words; the choreographer arranges dancers in flowing patterns; the architect creates with space. But the industrialist creates systems for the flow of goods; the program planner creates better delivery of services. Others will be content just to enjoy aesthetic experience.

Artistic types often love the beauty and power of the outdoors to inspire their creativity—but not its ability to make them perspire with heavy work. They would rather create ideas than study them. They like variety and are not afraid to experiment, often disregarding rules. Their ideas don't always please others, but opposition doesn't discourage them for long. Their irrepressible spirits and enthusiasm can often keep them focused on a creative project to the exclusion of all else, though plowing new ground can be lonely and agonizing. Not producing up to standard (their own) can plunge them to the depths of misery.

Social Personality

People persons who "live" primarily in their feelings

Sensitive to others, genuine, humanistic, supportive, responsible, tactful, perceptive

Focus on people and their concerns rather than on things or intellectual activity

Enjoy closeness with others, sharing feelings, being in groups and in unstructured settings that allow for flexibility and caring

Solve problems primarily by feeling and intuition, by helping others

The social personality focuses on people and their concerns. Sensitive to people's moods and feelings, these individuals may often enjoy company and make friends easily but not necessarily. Some, with a concern for people, may be shy individuals and even introverts who need time alone, but they will still focus on people's needs. Their level of caring may range from one person to the entire human race. Their relationships with people depend on their ability to communicate both verbally and nonverbally, listening as well as speaking. Their empathy and ability to intuit emotional cues help them to solve people problems sometimes before others are even aware of them. They can pull people together and generate positive energy for the sake of others, but not for themselves. Because the social orientation seems to describe the "typical female," many men shrink from expressing or dealing with deep feelings. The social personality types sometimes focus on people concerns to the exclusion of all else. They sometimes appear "impractical," especially to the realistic types.

Enterprising Personality

Project persons who are thoroughly absorbed in their strategies

Energetic, enthusiastic, confident, dominant, political, verbal, assertive, quick decision makers

Self-motivated leaders who are talented at organizing, persuading, managing

Achieve primarily by using these skills in dealing with people and projects

Enjoy money, power, status, being in charge

Solve problems by taking risks

The enterprising person is a leader who initiates projects but often gets others to carry them out. Instead of doing research, these people rely on hunches about what will work. They may strike an observer as restless and irresponsible because they often drop these projects after the job is under way, but many activities would never get off the ground without their energizing influence. They need to be a leader of the "in crowd," but because their relationships center around tasks, they may focus so dynamically on the project that the personal concerns of others and even their own, go unnoticed.

Conventional Personality

Persons who "live" primarily in their orderliness

Quiet, careful, accurate, responsible, practical, persevering, well organized, task oriented

Have a strong need to feel secure and certain, get things finished, attend to every detail, follow a routine

Prefer to work for someone of power and status rather than be in such a position themselves

Solve problems by appealing to and following rules

The conventional person also is task oriented but prefers to carry out tasks initiated by others. Because these individuals are careful of detail, they keep the world's records and transmit its messages, on time. They obey rules, and they value order in the world of data. They like to be well prepared ahead of time and prefer minimal changes. Getting tasks finished gives them immense satisfaction. Their sense of responsibility keeps the world going as they focus on the tasks at hand to the exclusion of all else.

FOR THE MOST PART
I do the thing which my
own nature drives
me to do.
—*Albert Einstein*

The Personality Hexagon

The six personality types can be arranged in a hexagon. In the figure, "Personality Types: Similarities and Differences," the types next to one another are most similar. The words linking them indicate their shared traits or interests. For example, realistic and investigative people focus on things. The R person does something to or with the thing; the I person analyzes it. Investigative and artistic types are both "idea" people. The I explores and may develop ideas logically; the A invents them intuitively. Artistic and social people like to be in tune with their feelings—the A person with feelings about surroundings, the S person with feelings about people. Social and enterprising people are people leaders: the S person is concerned about people; the E person wants to get people motivated to undertake a task. The conventional person will carry out the details of the task to the last dot. Thus the E and C are both task oriented in different ways—the E person initiating and leading, and the C type carrying through to completion with the utmost responsibility. Both C and R types value order: the C values data/paper order; the R values physical order.

People seek out work activities that enable them to be with others of like personality. Workplaces, too, tend to gather similar types and reflect the style of these workers.

The types opposite each other on the hexagon are most unlike. For example, the artistic personality is independent, doesn't mind disorder, and likes to try new things. The conventional person depends more on other people, likes order, and would prefer things to stay the same.

Two people who are strongly opposite in personality can improve their relationship by understanding the differences between them. A realistic per-

Personality Types: Similarities and Differences
SOURCE: *Adapted from John Holland,* Making Vocational Choices: A Theory of Careers *(Englewood Cliffs, N.J.: Prentice-Hall, 1973), copyright © 1970, by special permission of John Holland and Prentice-Hall, Inc. See also John Holland,* Self-Directed Search *(Palo Alto, Calif.: Consulting Psychologists Press), copyright © 1970.*

son doesn't deal much with people's feelings, while a social person sees much of life through feelings. The introspective I person is amazed at the outgoing E person's ability to act without doing much research. Because opposites complement each other, it can be advantageous to see a radically different personality as a potential source of support and enrichment. Wise employers will hire those whose personality orientation is appropriate for the work to be done.

Imagine six people sitting around the hexagon. Each person is a strong representative of a personality type. Give the group an issue to discuss (such as lower taxes, in the figure "Personality Types: Typical Talk,"), and each person will look at it in a different way.

Sometimes we have personality conflicts within ourselves. We'd like to be creative and try something different, but our conventional nature tells us that's a "no-no." We'd like to take an enterprising risk, but our investigative side wants to gather all the facts before deciding. Realistic folks who mostly like to be alone dealing with physical objects need some people interaction, too. Each personality type is surprised to learn that the characteristics of an

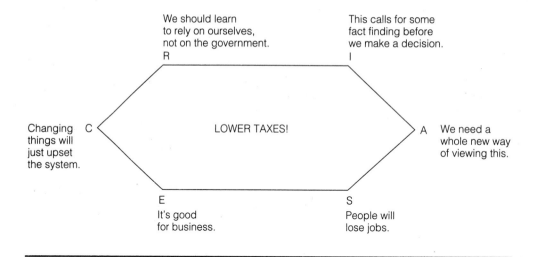

We should learn
to rely on ourselves,
not on the government.
R

This calls for some
fact finding before
we make a decision.
I

Changing C
things will
just upset
the system.

LOWER TAXES!

A   We need a
whole new way
of viewing this.

E
It's good
for business.

S
People will
lose jobs.

Personality Types: Typical Talk

opposite type can help make their own lives work better. The social personality may need to learn a certain amount of independence from people; the enterprising one, to find out facts before acting; the artistic, to be careful of detail; the realistic person, to stay in touch with other people; the investigative person, to take a risk; and the conventional person, to try something new!

It is likely that you will find a job difficult if it lies in an area very different from the interests of your personality type. An engineer with thirteen years' experience in the field admitted that he had thought engineering would involve his hands and now wished to become a technician. An industrial arts teacher wished that his job didn't involve motivating people all the time. His industrial specialty was also "too clerical" because it dealt with safety and time studies. Both these people would have been more content with work that let them use machines and tools in some way.

Rose Marie Dunphy, a realistic/artistic woman, illustrates what it feels like to be doing "what you are fitted for," as Maslow says. She says about her sewing, "Each time I touch a piece of fabric, magic occurs. I don't see corduroy or cotton but a dress, a shirt, curtains with tiebacks. Each time I sit on my chair facing the sewing machine, I disappear. I've gone into my hands . . . fabric, foot, and needle join hands to perform one function. In the process, they become one, and as in a chemical reaction, a totally different thing emerges. Not just a dress or curtain, but a new me."[2] And

---

PERSONALITY TYPES: AN EYE OPENER

An engineering manager is orienting a group of older women exploring careers in his company. The conversation turns to personal matters, and he shares with them his early difficulties in communicating with his wife. He found it hard to understand her continued wish that he would *talk* to her. When a divorce threatened, he sought some communications training and struggled with this strange new activity: sharing feelings he never knew he had. The women related well to this story. After a tour of the plant, they agreed that working with electronic circuits wasn't for them. Then the engineer replied that it would be as hard for them to work in his more realistic/ investigative area as it was for him to learn the social skills of dealing with people and their feelings!

Wynne Busby describes the same sensation he observes happening in a young carpenter who puts in a window for him. "I could sense all the skill, years of experience, of loving handling of tools and wood, which was available to him even for such a simple task as this." And he sees the same absorption, the same intimacy of hand, mind, tool, materials in his calligraphy teacher. "Her hand remembers the shape of the pen. The ink flows and the letters curve, black and clean on the page. All the skill which her hand remembers is available for her work of creation.[3]

On a whimsical note that illustrates the differing approach of the investigative/idea people and the realistic pragmatic ones, an old "Down-easter" said, "One of the things that struck me and . . . other Maine people [was that] the bright young people had all the ideas and could name things and . . . the way things should happen. The Maine people were more used to . . . getting the hay in before it rained.[4]

At first, you may not see yourself clearly in the results of the Personality Mosaic. One woman told her class that she was certain she was not investigative. Then she admitted to the delight of the group that her next thought was, "I wonder *why* it turned out that way?" Take time to study and understand each personality type and only then accept the data that really seem to fit you well.

Understanding your personality can help you make a good career decision. Understanding the personalities of others can improve human relationships and ease your acceptance of the choices that others make. And note that we may act in each of these six modes more than we realize. They represent activities that we need and want to do.

Realistic: Physical Mode	**Social: People Mode**
Running on the beach	Laughing with a friend
Eating a pizza	Hugging the baby
Fixing the sink	Listening to an aging person
Investigative: Mind Mode	**Enterprising: Accomplishment Mode**
Discussing politics	Organizing a party
Reading *War and Peace*	Saying "hello" first
Planning a trip to Europe	Applying for a job
Artistic: Aesthetic Mode	**Conventional: Structure Mode**
Enjoying a sunset	Stopping at a stop sign
Wearing complementary colors	Straightening your closet
Decorating a cake	Finishing a paper on time

Does growth mean allowing all these dimensions to surface and to actualize them to the best of your ability? As you grow, will you feel more comfortable in all these areas? Your career decision may fall within the area of your highest personality type; it may reflect a blend of several types. Stop and take a good look at your personality; then discuss your dominant personality characteristics with someone and explain why they feel right to you.

Dealing with Data, People, and Things

The world around you has only three areas your personality can relate to: data (ideas and information), people, and things. We will organize much of the decision-making material that will follow into these three areas.

Data

The human mind can take in and give out great quantities of information, or data, in the form of words, numbers, and symbols. All day long the mind clicks away, taking in and expressing thoughts and ideas, often creatively and always in a way unique to the individual. When you notice you are out of milk and jot it down on the grocery list, you've just processed some data. Reading, writing, speaking, and listening all deal with data. Every activity deals with data, from simple to complex. The cry of the newborn gives us data about how the baby feels. Lights blinking on your car dashboard can be saying, "Stop and get oil—now!" Some people think of data as complex

Well, what have we here?

The Pick Of Punch © 1980 by Punch Publications Ltd. Reprinted with permission. New York Times Syndication Sales Corp.

numbers and computer printouts. But data include all kinds of ideas and information: the words you speak, read, hear; the music you enjoy; the smiles of your friends; the colors of the sunset. Anything that is not a person or a concrete object is called data and we deal with it on various levels of complexity, from just noticing it to copying it to developing or creating it.

People

Another kind of activity depends on interaction with people. We deal with people at various levels of complexity, from greeting and waiting on them to dealing with their long-term personal growth. A rent-a-car clerk in an airport observed that she liked working with people, but not with the public! Conversely, a person who thought she wanted to be a counselor found the less-involved people contact she experienced as a bank teller to be just right. And managers find that people generally respond better to genuine respect and affection, the basis for good human interaction, rather than to competition and control. *We use a great deal of data when we deal with other humans.* We involve all sorts of body/mind perceptions and linguistic skills.

A FEW ACTION WORDS DEALING WITH DATA, PEOPLE, AND THINGS

DATA	PEOPLE	THINGS
Analyze	Assign	Assemble
Budget	Assist	Clean
Compare	Communicate with	Cut
Compile	Counsel	Decorate
Compute	Direct	Demonstrate
Decide	Encourage	Drive
Design	Entertain	Fit
Evaluate	Evaluate	Guard
Illustrate	Hire	Inspect
Learn	Interview	Install
Organize	Manage	Lift
Plan	Motivate	Measure
Read	Negotiate with	Mix
Record	Organize	Move
Research	Refer	Operate
Schedule	Represent	Process
Process	Serve	Repair
Synthesize	Sell	Set-up
Visualize	Supervise	Tend
Write	Teach/Train	Test

The emotions, which are physical responses to sensory information, permeate our mental processes and influence our behavior and relationships with others.

Things

We relate to physical objects in any number of ways: building, repairing, carrying, making things, running machines; tinkering with gadgets from food processors to power saws. The physical object that we use may be our bodies in such activities as sports and dance. Involvement with things can range from simple activities (putting up a picture) to complex ones (repairing a satellite). The body skills used require various degrees of strength, agility, and coordination in relating to other physical objects. The way the body fixes and builds things often requires creative ability. And, of course, we need the data required to deal with those things.

You learned to deal with data, people, and things at all levels early in life. Look again at your Candid Camera 3-D lists from Chapter 1. How many times have you planned events, organized people, or repaired objects in your lifetime? Using data, people, and/or things, individuals do work from repairing clocks to creating music, art, literature, and scientific and technical wonders. And amazingly, very day—using your body, emotions, mind, and spirit—*you* create your life.

Activity Analysis

In the Candid Camera-3D exercise in Chapter 1, you listed every activity you could think of that you've done in your life: jobs, community and extracurricular activities, education, and other projects, along with all the things you had to do to accomplish each activity. This expanded activity list contains data that will help you choose satisfying life activities.

It's important to analyze activities in detail. A woman says that she is realistic because she likes to garden. Her notebook shows that she obviously loved collecting, organizing, and analyzing data as she had a list of seeds, a planting schedule, a layout of her garden. Asked how her garden was, she said, "Not so good!" She didn't get out there very much. Her personality type and then her activity analysis showed that she was much more investigative than realistic and that data were more interesting than things. So study your lists to be sure that you have broken down each activity into as many specific component activities as possible. And check that you have coded them D, P, and/or T for their involvement with data, people, or things. These lists will be important for the skills identification exercises that follow.

Skills

If you actually listed all the activities you've ever done, your list would be enormous. Now here is one of the most important connections for you to make. When you've *done* any activity, that means you *can* do it! You've shown you have the ability, and that ability is a *skill!* Many people think they have no skills because they can't play the oboe or dance up a storm. But in reality they have been accomplishing things successfully for many years and have the capacity to accomplish much more. One factor is confidence. If you *think* you can, then you are well on the way to accomplishment. At least you can probably do something that has some of the satisfiers of your dream job.

For example, a teacher completed an interest inventory that suggested a career in the performing arts. Acting seemed intriguing, but not likely to provide much income for a beginner. It suddenly dawned on the teacher how much she loved "appearing" in a class or workshop, making people laugh and appreciate her. When she first became a teacher, she had found teaching

ABILITY TO USE OR DEVELOP:

DATA SKILLS[5]

1. **Logical intelligence:** Think, observe, plan, analyze, evaluate, understand, solve problems. Put ideas and information together to deal with complex operations or to plan and organize work. Keep track of verbal and numerical information in an orderly way; make decisions using common sense based on "practical" experience.

2. **Intuitive intelligence:** Imagine, compare, see things "holistically," decide based on best guesses and "intuitive" common sense rather than rules or measurements. Use words, numbers, or symbols creatively, develop new ideas, new processes, new combinations.

3. **Verbal ability:** Use words to read, research, write, listen, record, discuss, direct, instruct, communicate, motivate.

4. **Numerical ability:** Use numbers and symbols to figure, calculate, estimate, keep books, budget, analyze. Measure, using instruments to determine such factors as length, mass, time, temperature, electric charge.

5. **Exactness with detail:** Follow directions exactly, make decisions based on set rules or measurements; attend to small details in proofreading words or numbers or examining lines and shapes of products.

6. **Facility with multidimensional forms:** Understand, visualize, relate, two- or three-dimensional lines or shapes, spaces, shadings—sometimes in color.

PEOPLE SKILLS

7. **Ability to carry on businesslike contact with people:** Manage, supervise, organize, motivate, entertain, train, serve, negotiate, cooperate with people.

8. **Ability to influence people:** Persuade/inspire others to think or behave in certain ways. Teach, exchange, interpret ideas/facts/feelings, help solve personal problems.

THING SKILLS

9. **Finger/hand agility:** Use fingers/hands to make, repair, process, test, assemble, operate various products/machines/tools using special, sometimes highly complex techniques.

10. **Whole-body agility:** Use the whole body to handle, carry, lift, move, balance, or coordinate itself or other physical objects.

difficult and, as a result, tended to either over- or under-discipline her classes. Confidence grew with the realization that she could teach and have fun doing it. Now she rarely misses a chance to talk with a group.

So instead of groaning at your "lack of talent," think of all the talents you've used in a life filled with data, people, and things. And because the majority of workers have only average skills—most workers can do *many* jobs. And that includes you! The question is, then, Of all the skills you possess, which do you enjoy using? And more important, which would you like to use in a work setting? Do you prefer to work primarily with data, people, or things? And of all the jobs you *can* do, which would you *like* to do?

> If you like what you are doing,
> you will excel at it!
> —*Ironworker Clif Signor*

All activities flow from just ten basic aptitudes or basic skills that can be grouped according to their interaction with data, people, and things. Though most people can operate in all these areas reasonably well, they will be more comfortable in some than in others based on their personality types.

As you can see, these ten skill areas range from almost invisible activities of the mind to very visible activities of the body. The interests you have been listing are usually a good clue to your skills. Most people acquire skills in areas they enjoy and tend to neglect other areas. If you like something, you spend time doing it, get better at it and like it more, and spend more time doing it. And it's comforting to remember that most jobs, by definition, require only average skills.

We came into this world already well equipped for action. Unless a serious defect exists, human growth and potential for growth are phenomenal. Look at a six-month-old and be amazed at the complexity of skills compared with those of a newborn infant. Compare with a six-year-old and be further astounded! Educator and author Peter Kline says that we are all budding "everyday geniuses" when we are born. But we express that genius in different ways.[6] Sometimes, somewhere along the line confidence and energy may begin to lag. Brain researcher Jean Houston says that by age seventeen we are using only 17 percent of our body's potential for flexible movement, compared to what we used at age three. She says that as the body goes, so does the mind. Houston finds that even the very elderly, with correct exercise, can "remake" their bodies in six months. Their mental and emotional powers are greatly enhanced.[7] "The true person is as yet a dream of the future."[8]

Dividing the self into "mind" and "body" is only an exercise about concepts that are very difficult to define. Because our educational system stresses mental activities, we sometimes infer that men and women who work with their hands are not "using their heads." In reality, the two cannot be separated; they can only be examined separately as two different modes of living and learning. Life experiences help us develop innumerable skills of both mind and body.

The Skills Trio

There are three kinds of skills: transferable, work specific, and personal responsibility skills.[9] The ten basic aptitudes and their related skills are called *transferable* skills because they can be used in many kinds of activities and transferred from one job to another. For example, planning, which draws on logical intelligence, can involve the following steps: (1) determine/establish objectives for a program; (2) set policies, procedures; (3) do long- and short-range forecasts; (4) schedule strategies; and (5) evaluate/revise the program. We learn to take these steps almost unconsciously when we make a decision to accomplish some task.

Every job requires transferable skills, with communications skills in writing and speaking highly important to many positions. For example, engineers must often write up and present proposals for projects and then report on their results. Perhaps 80 to 90 percent of the content of most jobs requires transferable skills—those you already have *to some degree.*

The other 10 to 20 percent may require on-the-job training (OJT), further formal education, or both. A general salesperson, for example, depends largely on transferable skills and can learn the needed *work-specific skills* quickly. *More and more* jobs require special training, especially in science, technical fields, and the arts. This special training develops work-specific skills, such as those used by electronics technicians, business managers, doctors, and ballerinas. But all these people need transferable skills, too.

Personal responsibility skills reflect the ways you manage *yourself* in relation to data, people, and things; they reflect the ways you express your transferable and work-specific skills. People usually begin to develop such skills at an early age, often independent of formal education. Common sense, responsibility, energy, dedication, willingness to learn and work hard, perseverance, acceptance of criticism, the ability to work well with people, promptness, good grooming: all are traits that can be learned and that develop with the help of both achievement and disappointment. (Employee recruiters often remark that the ability to get along with people is one skill they look for above all others.) Personal responsibility skills are the qualities that parents and teachers often stress. They are the traits that young people often learn well only by taking that first job and seeing it through, no matter how hard the work. Acquiring these skills is vital for career and life success.

You have survived modern life so far. Your physical, mental, emotional, social, and financial well-being have depended on your abilities. You must possess a good measure of skills in all areas *and can build on this foundation.*

You use your skills in four different modes called *work qualities:*

- **Repetition:** Duties involve a set way of doing things, sometimes over and over again.

- **Variety:** Duties change frequently, requiring a flexible response, different knowledge and skills.
- **Physical Risk:** Duties involve pressure in stressful, dangerous situations but sometimes provide adventure and excitement.
- **Status:** Duties involve recognition that you are someone important or in authority.

Getting an Edge on the Job Hunt Process

People often underestimate what they have done in life. Both job hunting and career searching require that you know what you have done so you can apply it to what you want to do. When a high school graduate was asked to make a list of her job activities in a drive-in, she replied that she had done nothing of importance. "All I did was make hamburgers." But speaking informally, she was able to describe what she did in more detail. That became her list. She then coded each activity with a P (dealing directly with people, T (dealing directly with things (material objects), or D (dealing with data): she noticed when supplies were running low, and ordered (D) and put them away (T). She took charge when the owners were away (D). She showed new clerks what to do (P). Sometimes she did minor repairs on kitchen equipment (T). She made all the sauces (T). She settled disagreements about orders (P). She could always tell when a new clerk wasn't going to work out (D).

After a great deal of work, her list was polished to read like this:

Human Relations (People, Data)
Worked well with customers/employers, coworkers
(good teamwork)
Oriented, trained, evaluated employees
Settled customer/employee disagreements

Materials Maintenance (Things, Data)
Inventoried, ordered, stored, prepared materials
Did maintenance/repair
Opened and closed business
Handled cash/cash register

Data without People or Things
Organized/scheduled work

Her job activities drew on many of the ten basic skills to a modest degree, especially logical intelligence, verbal ability, businesslike contact with people, finger/hand agility, and occasionally intuitive intelligence, numerical ability, and attention to detail. Her work had a great deal of the work quality *variety,* also. Knowing what she had done enabled her to make a better career decision.

A section of her résumé, developed for a management trainee position in a small restaurant, summarized her experience as a supervisor/cook: inventoried, ordered, prepared, and stocked food supplies. Settled employee and customer problems and complaints. Oriented/trained new employees, informally evaluated performance. Did minor repairs/maintenance. As occasional acting manager, opened and closed shop, handled cash/cash register.

A personal paragraph included the following: "Demonstrate good teamwork with customers, employees, and coworkers; notice and take care of details; am reliable." With her additional training in food and restaurant management, she was qualified for the position she was seeking.

> If you think you can't,
> You won't!
> If you think you can,
> You will!

Observe yourself. What skills do you want to acquire and develop to get where you would like to be? In what ways would you like to focus your transferable skills to gain more work-specific skills? If you have good finger dexterity, for example, would you prefer to become adept at the guitar, the computer keyboard, brain surgery, or all three? Are you willing to devote some time to further training and education to acquire these work-specific skills? Which personal responsibility skills are your strengths? Which will you work to improve? These are important questions to answer when you are making career decisions.

In this chapter, then, you've discovered your very own Personality Mosaic. You have identified skills that have motivated you to act success-fully in the past and will carry you into the future. And you are putting together some extremely valuable pieces of the career decision puzzle. In short, you have been gathering important words to describe the one and only YOU! In the next chapter we will relate this information to careers.

 Self-Assessment Exercises

1. Six Personality Types

Circle the personality types that describe you best: realistic, investigative, artistic, social, enterprising, conventional.

2. Data, People, Things Indicator

To determine your most important orientations in regard to data, people, and things consult the Activity Lists you have been working on from Chapter 1, Candid Camera 3-D. If they are now as long as you can make them, and if you have broken down your activities into specific component activities, and you have coded all these activities with a P, T, or D as follows:

P = interacting directly with people

T = interacting directly with things

D = using ideas and information (data) without interacting with
    people or things

Then check the following: (No check means "little or no involvement.")

Data: I want to get involved with data on my job:

_____ at a modest level with data that is easy to learn or that I simply keep track of while others direct my work.

_____ at a high level by putting ideas and information together to plan/orga-nize work and perhaps develop new ideas and way to do things.

People: I want to get involved with people on my job:

_____ at a modest level by being friendly and cooperative, greeting and serving them, discussing simple problems with them.

_____ at a high level by leading/influencing/organizing/motivating them, teaching/entertaining them, negotiating, or exchanging ideas with them, counseling them.

Things: I want to get involved with things on my job:

_____ at a modest level by following simple procedures set up by others.

_____ at a high level by working with more complex procedures/equipment that allow my own input.

3. Identifying Important Skill Areas

From your expanded activity list, star and then write ten to fifteen of your favorite activities in the Favorite Activities Chart. Be sure to state what you _did_ as specifically as possible. Then check (✓) the numbers of the basic skills you used to perform each favorite activity. For example, if you ordered supplies by phone, you would check 4, 5, and 7. If you arranged food attractively on a plate, you would check 6 and 9. The idea is to find those skills that you enjoy using the most.

4. The Key Qualities Indicator

- Check (✓) those qualities below that are important for you in your career. It is not necessary that the _entire_ description of each quality apply to you. (You may wish to circle those words that _do_ apply to you.)

- Now go back and place an H in front of those skills you want to use at a high level of ability. Place an M in front of those skills you want to use at a modest level of ability .

Data skills

_____ **Logical intelligence:** Think, observe, plan, analyze, evaluate, understand, solve problems; put ideas and information together to deal with complex operations; to plan and organize work; keep track of verbal and numerical information in an orderly way, make decisions using common sense based on "practical" experience.

_____ **Intuitive intelligence:** Imagine, compare, see things "holistically," decide based on best guesses and "intuitive" common sense rather

Activity	1. Logical intelligence	2. Intuitive intelligence	3. Verbal ability	4. Numerical ability	5. Exactness with detail	6. Facility with multidimensional forms	7. Businesslike contact with people	8. Influencing people	9. Finger/hand agility	10. Whole-body agility

Which of the basic ten activities do you like to do the most? _____

Favorite Activities Chart

than rules or measurements; use words, numbers, or symbols creatively; develop new ideas, new processes, new combinations.

_____ **Verbal ability:** Use words to read, research, write, listen, record, discuss, direct, instruct, communicate, motivate.

_____ **Numerical ability:** Use numbers and symbols to measure, figure, calculate, estimate, keep books, budget, analyze.

_____ **Exactness with detail:** Follow directions exactly; make decisions based on set rules or measurements; attend to small details in proofreading words, numbers, symbols, and/or diagrams or in examining lines and shapes of products.

_____ **Facility with multidimensional forms:** Understand, visualize, relate together two- or three-dimensional lines or shapes, spaces, shading— sometimes in color.

People skills

_____ **Businesslike contact with people:** Manage, supervise, organize, motivate, entertain, train, serve, negotiate with, cooperate with people.

_____ **Ability to influence people:** Persuade/inspire others to think or behave in certain ways; teach, exchange, interpret ideas/facts/feelings, help solve personal problems.

Thing skills

_____ **Finger/hand agility:** Use fingers/hands to make, repair, process, test, assemble, operate various products/machines/tools using special techniques—sometimes very complex.

_____ **Whole body agility:** Use the whole body to handle, carry, lift, move, balance, or coordinate itself or physical objects.

Work qualities

Circle the names of those qualities that are important for you in a job.

Repetition: Duties that involve a set way of doing things, sometimes over and over again.

Variety: Duties that change frequently, requiring a flexible response and different knowledge and skills.

Physical risk: Duties that involve pressure in stressful, dangerous situations but sometimes provide adventure and excitement.

Status: Duties that bring recognition that you are someone important or in authority.

5. *Personal Responsibility Skills*

Evaluate yourself and your ability to handle data, people, and things. Check
(✓) "Good" or "Could improve" after each statement.

■ **Evaluate YOURSELF**	*Good*	*Could improve*
I usually:		
work hard, with persistence	_____	_____
use common sense	_____	_____
show enthusiasm	_____	_____
have a sense of humor	_____	_____
handle my feelings well	_____	_____
dress appropriately for work	_____	_____

■ **Evaluate your interaction with PEOPLE**		
I usually:		
balance my needs and wants with those of others	_____	_____
respond with tact and courtesy	_____	_____
accept criticism without anger and learn from others	_____	_____
communicate assertively without attacking or blaming others	_____	_____
admit mistakes; apologize	_____	_____
respect and compliment the ideas and good work of others	_____	_____
share with and assist others; enjoy teamwork	_____	_____

■ **Evaluate your interaction with DATA and THINGS**		
I usually:		
follow rules and also work to make them more reasonable	_____	_____
am willing to learn, asking for help only when necessary	_____	_____

	Good	Could improve
am flexible, willing to try new and unfamiliar tasks	_____	_____
carry through with difficult or pressured work on time, without excuses	_____	_____
take care of property and equipment	_____	_____

6. Work-Specific Skills

List your work-specific skills—those acquired by education or training to do a particular job:

_____   _____

_____   _____

_____   _____

7. Sharing Your Discoveries

In the space that follows (or on a separate sheet of paper), write an enthusiastic paragraph or letter about yourself and your abilities to a potential employer (or friend). Use as many of the skill words as possible from this chapter to describe yourself and show that you would be an effective worker. Later you will be able to use the data gathered in this chapter to write an effective résumé.

3/

The Career Connection

Finding Your Job Satisfiers

 FOCUS

- Identify your satisfying job areas.

- Survey the entire U.S. job market.

- Learn to research jobs.

The data you collected on your personality and your skills in Chapter 2 will be helpful background for using the Job Chart Inventory that follows. This inventory will help you see which of the twelve major career interest areas[1] in the U.S. job market might suit you.

 ## CAREER FOCUS: Job Chart Inventory

Find satisfying interest areas by answering these questions about personality types in the job market. Circle Y (Yes) or N (No).

Realistic   Things/Body: The World of Matter

Interest areas = *Mechanical, Industrial, Nature, Protective, Physical Performance*

Y N   1. Do you like using your hands, e.g., to make, repair, "tinker with" physical objects?
Y N   2. Do you like being physically active?
Y N   3. Do you generally prefer working with physical objects rather than with people?
Y N   4. Do you like doing physically daring things?
Y N   5. Do you wish to explore *Realistic* Interest Areas (the world of matter)?

> NO = Go on to Mind: *Investigative and Artistic* Job Groups
> YES = Continue here

Jobs in the *Realistic* Interest Areas are involved with things, from simple to complex; they require little contact with people unless they involve supervising, teaching, or managing; use of data depends on complexity of the job. The skills needed are finger/hand to whole body agility, coordination, strength, along with moderate intelligence, some multidimensional awareness, and ability with numbers. The world of matter (or things) is associated with the realistic personality, which gravitates toward jobs that deal with mechanical systems; factory or production jobs; heavy outdoor work with nature; police work, firefighting, or other protective types of employment and activities requiring physical performance such as sports and acrobatics.

Answer the following to help select *Realistic* Interest Areas:

Mechanical
Y N   1. Do you like large, mechanical systems?
Y N   2. Do you like working with machines and tools?
Industrial
Y N   1. Do you like to use your hands doing factory-type production work?
Y N   2. Would you like being directly involved with large-scale production?
Nature
Y N   1. Do you like heavy, physical, outdoor work?
Y N   2. Do you like working with plants or animals?
Protective
Y N   1. Does protecting people's lives and properties interest you?
Y N   2. Would you like doing police work, firefighting, or other jobs to protect lives and property?
Physical Performance
Y N   1. Have you been actively involved in sports or other displays of physical ability?
Y N   2. Do you keep physically fit?

YES answers indicate interest in one or more of the *Realistic* Interest Areas.
NO answers indicate little or no interest in the five *Realistic* Interest Areas.
Regardless of your answers, do you wish to explore Job Groups in these areas?
YES = Explore *Realistic* Job Groups on the Job Group Chart.
NO = Goodbye *Realistic*! Go on to *Investigative* and *Artistic*.

Job Group Chart

R—REALISTIC JOB GROUPS

Column key:
1. Logical Intelligence
2. Intuitive Intelligence
3. Verbal Ability
4. Numerical Ability
5. Exactness with Detail
6. Facility with Multidimensional Forms
7. Businesslike Contact with People
8. Ability to Influence People
9. Finger/Hand Agility
10. Whole Body Agility
11. Repetition
12. Variety
13. Physical Risk
14. Status

MECHANICAL

#	Code	Job Group	1	2	3	4	5	6	7	8	9	10	11	12	13	14
1	05.01	Engineering: Applying research of science and math to design of new products and systems.	H	H	H	H	M	H	M	M	M			•		
2	05.02	Managerial Work–Mechanical: Managing technical plants or systems.	H	H	H	H	M	H	H	M	M			•		•
3	05.03	Engineering Technology: Collecting, recording, coordinating technical information.	H	H	M	H	H	H			H					
4	05.04	Air and Water Vehicle Operations: Operating planes/ships to carry freight/passengers.	H	H	H	H	H	H	H		M	M			•	•
5	05.05	Craft Technology: Doing highly skilled hand/machine custom work.	M	M		M	H	H			H	M		•		
6	05.06	Systems Operation: Caring for large, complicated mechanical systems like heating/power.	M		M	M	H	M	M		M			•		
7	05.07	Quality Control: Checking/testing materials/products in nonfactory situations.	M	M		M	H	M			M		•			
8	05.08	Land Vehicle Operation: Operating/driving vehicles that haul freight.	M			M	M				M	M	•			
9	05.09	Materials Control: Keeping records of flow/storage of materials and products.	M		M	M	H		M		M		•			
10	05.10	Skilled Hand and Machine Work: Doing moderately skilled hand/machine work.				M	H	M			M		•			
11	05.11	Equipment Operation: Operating/driving heavy equipment such as in construction, mining.	M				H	M			M	M	•			
12	05.12	Manual Labor–Mechanical: Doing nonfactory manual labor with machines, tools.					H	M			M	M	•			

INDUSTRIAL

#	Code	Job Group	1	2	3	4	5	6	7	8	9	10	11	12	13	14
13	06.01	Production Technology: Setting up/operating machines to produce goods in specific ways.	M			M	H	M	H		M					
14	06.02	Production Work: Doing hand/machine work to make a product: supervising/inspecting.	M			M	H	M	H		M			•		
15	06.03	Quality Control: Testing, weighing, inspecting, measuring products to meet standards.	M				H	M			M		•			
16	06.04	Manual Labor–Industrial: Basic manual labor in production requiring little training.						M			M	M	•			

NATURE

#	Code	Job Group	1	2	3	4	5	6	7	8	9	10	11	12	13	14
17	03.01	Managerial Work–Nature: Planning work for farming, fisheries, logging, horticulture.	H	H	M	M	M	M	M		M			•		
18	03.02	General Supervision–Nature: Supervising on farms, in forests, fisheries, nurseries, parks.	M	M	M	M	M	M	H		M			•		•
19	03.03	Animal Training/Care: Training, breeding, raising, showing, caring for nonfarm animals.	M	M	M			M	M			M	M	•	•	
20	03.04	Manual Labor–Nature: Doing basic physical labor related to farming, fishing, gardening.							M			M	M	•		

PROTECTIVE

#	Code	Job Group	1	2	3	4	5	6	7	8	9	10	11	12	13	14
21	04.01	Safety/Law Enforcement: Administration, enforcement of laws/regulations.	H	H	H		M	M	H	H	M			•	•	•
22	04.02	Security Services: Protecting people and property from crime, fire, other hazards.	M	M	M			M	M		M	M	•		•	

PHYSICAL PERFORMANCE

#	Code	Job Group	1	2	3	4	5	6	7	8	9	10	11	12	13	14
23	12.01	Sports: Of all sorts; playing, training, coaching, and officiating.	M	M	M		M	M	M	M	H	H			•	•
24	12.02	Physical Feats: Amusing/entertaining people with special physical skills/strengths.	M	M	M		M	H	M		H	H			•	•

Investigative and Artistic   Ideas/Intellect: The World of the Mind

Interest areas = *Scientific*/analytic and *Artistic*/intuitive.

Y N   1. Do you like to think or read about or discuss new ideas?
Y N   2. Do you like solving problems and puzzles?
Y N   3. Do you like to create new things?
Y N   4. Do you like to work alone?
Y N   3. Do you wish to explore *Investigative/Artistic* Interest Areas (the world of the mind)?

> NO = Go on to *People: Social and Enterprising Job Groups*
> YES = Continue

The *Mind* world attracts scientific/investigative people with a logical/rational personality who like to explore ideas; it also includes the artistic/intuitives who like to create them. These jobs usually involve high to medium use of data and little involvement with people (except in the field of medicine); they often require dealing with things or thinking about things and creating solutions to problems. Skills required are generally above-average logical and/or intuitive intelligence, good verbal skills and—in the scientific area—numerical ability; in some cases you will need a well-developed sense of multidimensional awareness and color.

Those investigative types who pursue the physical/biological sciences or engineering need to have some sense of the *Matter/Realistic* world. Purely investigative people with little interest in the physical world usually take their inquiring minds into areas such as theoretical math or they may research people, the arts, industry, or business—that is, any area that requires little direct interaction with things or people.

Artistic people are generally very intuitive and may find satisfaction in painting, sculpture, or crafts, if they have a facility with things. The more investigative artistic types deal with music and writing. Some artistic people with little specific "talent" give creative expression to their many ideas in a variety of other environments—for example, the innovative side of engineering or the innovative worlds of the classroom, the office, or the factory.

Answer the following to help select *Investigative* or *Artistic* Interest Areas:

Scientific
Y N   1. Do you enjoy using your mind to analyze or solve various kinds of problems?
Y N   2. Do you enjoy researching and exploring the physical world?
Artistic
Y N   1. Do you enjoy and have you been involved with the fine arts: art, drama, dance, music, or literature?
Y N   2. Would you be willing to make a long-term commitment to a fine arts area?

YES answers indicate interest in the *Investigative* or *Artistic* Interest Areas.
NO answers indicate little or no interest in the *Investigative* or *Artistic* Interest Areas.
Regardless of your answers, do you wish to explore the *Investigative* or *Artistic* Interest Areas further?
YES = Explore *Investigative/Scientific* and/or *Artistic* Job Groups on the Job Group Chart.
NO = Goodbye *Investigative/Artistic*!

I—INVESTIGATIVE JOB GROUPS

SCIENTIFIC/ANALYTIC

		1. Logical Intelligence	2. Intuitive Intelligence	3. Verbal Ability	4. Numerical Ability	5. Exactness with Detail	6. Facility with Multidimensional Forms	7. Businesslike Contact with People	8. Ability to Influence People	9. Finger/Hand Agility	10. Whole Body Agility	11. Repetition	12. Variety	13. Physical Risk	14. Status
25. 02.01	Physical Sciences: Research/development in physics, chemistry, geology, computer science.	H	H	H	H	M	H		M	M					
26. 02.02	Life Sciences: Studying functions of living things/ways they relate to environments.	H	H	H	H	M	H		M	H					
27. 02.03	Medical Sciences: Practicing medicine to prevent, diagnose, cure illnesses of people or animals.	H	H	H	H	M	M	H	M	H	H		•		•
(1) 05.01	Engineering: Applying research of science and math to design of new products and systems.	H	H	H	H	M	H	H	M	M	M		•		
28. 02.04	Laboratory Technology: Doing laboratory work to carry out studies of various researchers.	H			H	M	H			M					
29. 11.01	Mathematics/Statistics: Using numbers and computers to analyze and solve problems.	H	M	H	H	H	H	H	M	M	M				

A—ARTISTIC JOB GROUPS

ARTISTIC/CREATIVE

		1.	2.	3.	4.	5.	6.	7.	8.	9.	10.	11.	12.	13.	14.
30. 01.01	Literary Arts: Producing creative pieces from writing to publishing for print, TV, films.	H	H	H				M	M						•
31. 01.02	Visual Arts: Doing artistic work (paintings, designs, photographs) for sale or for media.	H	H				H	M	M	H					
32. 01.03	Performing Arts–Drama: Performing, directing, teaching for stage, radio, TV, film.	H	H	H				H	M		M				•
33. 01.04	Performing Arts–Music: Playing an instrument, singing, arranging, composing, conducting music.	H	H	H		H	H	H	M	H	H				•
34. 01.05	Performing Arts–Dance: Performing, teaching, choreographing dance routines.	H	H	M		M	H	H	M	H	H				•
35. 01.06	Craft Arts: Producing handcrafts, graphics, decorative products.	M	M			H	H			H					
36. 01.07	Amusement Arts: Entertaining/doing novel routines at carnivals, circuses, fairs.	M	M	M			M	H	M		M	•			
37. 01.08	Modeling: Posing for artists; displaying clothing, accessories, other products.	M							M		M	•			•

Social and Enterprising   Helping/Motivating: The World of People

Interest Areas = *Human services, Accommodating, Leading/influencing, Persuading/selling*

Y N   1. Do you enjoy having a friendly conversation with someone?
Y N   2. Do you like to talk people into doing a project and get them organized?
Y N   3. Are you concerned about the welfare of others?
Y N   4. Do you like to influence people and their opinions?
Y N   5. Do you wish to explore the *Social/Enterprising* People Helping/Motivating Interest Areas (the world of people)?

> NO = Go on to Paper: Conventional Job Groups
> YES = Continue

The world of *People* generally requires ongoing involvement with people; the level of data increases with complexity of the work; there is usually little or no involvement with things except in jobs requiring physical contact. Skills required are generally a range of "people skills": facility dealing with and communicating with people, solving people problems, and providing human services. The world of people includes four interest areas: (1) human services and (2) accommodating (the social personality), and (3) leading/influencing and (4) persuading (the enterprising personality). Jobs in these areas involve helping or motivating people. For career seekers who would love to work with people, opportunities range from waiter to psychiatrist, from manager to mortician! Such jobs involve being with people all day: greeting people, waiting on them, taking charge of a group, solving business or personal problems. These jobs often require leadership to organize groups, show people what to do, and direct projects. If you wish to work with people at a high level, consider earning a degree in business or one of the behavioral sciences. You will need creativity and intuition to work with people on any but the simplest level.

Answer the following to help select *Social* and/or *Enterprising* Interest Areas:

People Helping: *Human Services*
Y N   1. Do you wish to deal with people's personal concerns, their personal growth/care?
Y N   2. Do you like fairly steady involvement with people who have problems or needs?
People Helping: *Accommodating*
Y N   1. Do you enjoy waiting on people, serving them in some way?
Y N   2. Would you like dealing with the public in a nonpersonal way?
People Motivating: *Leading/Influencing*
Y N   1. Do you like to be a key person in a group?
Y N   2. Do you enjoy encouraging people to try new ways of thinking or doing things?
People Motivating: *Persuading/Selling*
Y N   1. Are you confident and persistent, with enough energy to get things done?
Y N   2. Do you enjoy persuading people to accept an idea, service, or product?

YES answers indicate an interest in the *Social* and *Enterprising* Interest Areas.
NO answers indicate little or no interest in the *Social* and *Enterprising* Interest Areas.
Regardless of your answers, do you wish to explore the *Social* and/or *Enterprising* Interest Areas further?

YES = Explore *Social* and/or *Enterprising* Job Groups on the Job Group Chart.
NO = Goodbye *Social* and/*Enterprising*! Continue.

S—SOCIAL JOB GROUPS

HUMAN SERVICES

#	Job Group	1. Logical Intelligence	2. Intuitive Intelligence	3. Verbal Ability	4. Numerical Ability	5. Exactness with Detail	6. Facility with Multidimensional Forms	7. Businesslike Contact with People	8. Ability to Influence People	9. Finger/Hand Agility	10. Whole Body Agility	11. Repetition	12. Variety	13. Physical Risk	14. Status
38. 10.01	Social Services: Helping people deal with personal, vocational, educational, religious concerns.	H	H	H	M			H	H				•		•
39. 10.02	Nursing/Therapy Services: Providing diagnosis and therapy to help people get well.	H	H	H	H	H	M	H	H	M	M		•		
40. 10.03	Child/Adult Care: Assisting with medical/physical care/services.	M	M	M		H		M	M	M	M	•	•		

ACCOMMODATING

#	Job Group	1.	2.	3.	4.	5.	6.	7.	8.	9.	10.	11.	12.	13.	14.
41. 09.01	Hospitality Services: Touring, guiding, greeting, serving people to help them feel comfortable.	M	M	M		M		H	M	M			•		•
42. 09.02	Barber/Beauty Services: Hair/skin care to help people with personal appearances.	M	M	M		M	H	M	M	H			•		
43. 09.03	Passenger Services: Transporting people by vehicle; also instructing/supervising.	M	M		M	M	M	M		M	M	•			
44. 09.04	Customer Services: Waiting on people in a routine way in business settings.	M		M	M	M		M		M		•			
45. 09.05	Attendant Services: Providing personal services to people at home or when traveling.	M		M				M		M	M	•			

S/E—SOCIAL/ENTERPRISING JOB GROUPS

LEADING/INFLUENCING

#	Job Group	1.	2.	3.	4.	5.	6.	7.	8.	9.	10.	11.	12.	13.	14
46. 11.02	Educational/Library Services: Teaching, providing library services.	H	H	H	M	H		H	H				•		•
47. 11.03	Social Research: Studying people of various backgrounds both past and present.	H	H	H	H	H			M				•		
48. 11.04	Law: Counseling, advising, representing people, businesses regarding legal matters.	H	H	H	H	M		H	H				•		•
49. 11.05	Business Administration: Designing procedures, solving problems, supervising people in business.	H	H	H	H	M		H	H				•		•
50. 11.06	Finance: Setting up financial systems; controlling, analyzing financial records.	H	H	H	H	H		H	M				•		
51. 11.07	Services Administration: Designing procedures, solving problems, supervising people in business.	H	H	H	M	M		H	H				•		•
52. 11.08	Communications: Writing, editing, translating information for media—radio, print, and TV.	H	H	H	M	M		M	M				•		
53. 11.09	Promotion: Advertising, fundraising, sales, and public relations.	H	H	H	M	M		H	H				•		•
54. 11.10	Regulations Enforcement: Checking/enforcing government regulations, company policies, procedures.	H	H	M	M	M	M	M	M				•		
55. 11.11	Business Management: Taking responsibility for operation and supervision of a business.	H	H	H	M	M	M	H					•		•
56. 11.12	Contracts and Claims: Negotiating contracts, investigating claims.	H	H	H	M	M		H	H				•		•

E—ENTERPRISING JOB GROUPS

PERSUADING

#	Job Group	1.	2.	3.	4.	5.	6.	7.	8.	9.	10.	11.	12.	13.	14.
57. 08.01	Sales Technology: Selling technical equipment or services including insurance. Also clerical work.	H	H	H	H	M	M	H	M						•
58. 08.02	General Sales: Selling goods and services, wholesale/retail to individuals, business, or industry.	M	M	M	M			H	M						
59. 08.03	Vending: Peddling, promoting items in public settings.				M			H	M	M		•			

Conventional   Words/Numbers/Symbols: The World of Paper/Data

Interest area = *Business detail*

Business Detail
Y N   1. Do you enjoy organizing papers, files, and notebooks?
Y N   2. Do you enjoy working with office machines?
Y N   3. Do you like to accomplish every detail of a task, generally on time?
Y N   4. Do you tend to be very accurate and orderly with detail?
Y N   5. Do you prefer to follow a set routine with established guidelines?

YES answers indicate interest in the Business Detail Interest Area.
NO answers indicate little or no interest in the *Conventional* Business Detail Interest Area.

Regardless of your answers, do you wish to explore Business Detail Job Groups further?
NO = Goodbye *Conventional* Business Detail! Now explore Combinations and Other Considerations
YES = Continue below, then explore *Conventional* Business Detail Job Groups on the Job Group Chart and then go on to Combinations and Other Considerations.

The *Paper* or *Conventional* World involves consistent use of data or business detail: words, numbers, and symbols; there is usually little involvement with people beyond what is required to process business details or other tasks; things dealt with are often office machines. Required skills are moderate intelligence in most cases; verbal and numerical ability; an eye for detail; and, in some cases, finger/hand agility. The world of *paper* (which now includes the video-screen world) attracts *Conventional* personalities who are careful about detail and valued for their contribution in keeping track of the many transactions that go on in any work setting. If your interests lie in the world of paper and your present job does not include this, look for ways to handle the data of your work environment.

C—CONVENTIONAL JOB GROUPS

BUSINESS DETAIL

	1. Logical Intelligence	2. Intuitive Intelligence	3. Verbal Ability	4. Numerical Ability	5. Exactness with Detail	6. Facility with Multidimensional Forms	7. Businesslike Contact with People	8. Ability to Influence People	9. Finger/Hand Agility	10. Whole Body Agility	11. Repetition	12. Variety	13. Physical Risk	14. Status
60. 07.01 Administrative Detail: Doing secretarial/technical clerical work.	H	H	H	M	H		H	M	M			•		
61. 07.02 Mathematical Detail: Keeping numerical records, doing basic figuring.	M		M	M	H		M		M		•			
62. 07.03 Financial Detail: Keeping track of money flow to and from the public.	M		M	M	H		M		M		•			
63. 07.04 Oral Communications: Giving information in person or by communication systems.	M		M	M	M		M	M	M		•	•		
64. 07.05 Records Processing: Putting records together and keeping them up to date.	M	·	M	M	H		M		M		•			
65. 07.06 Clerical Machine Operation: Using various machines to record, process, and compute data.	M				H		M		H		•			
66. 07.07 Clerical Handling: Keeping data in order by filing, copying, sorting, delivering.	M		M		M				M		•			

Some Combinations and Other Considerations

People are attracted to jobs for all sorts of reasons besides interest in the job itself. They want people to like them. They'd like to feel important. They want to avoid competition, to please parents, to look like the stereotypical successful male or female, to earn more money. We are all influenced by the convenience and availability of jobs. All of these reasons tap into our value system. But can you find long-term satisfaction in a career field that doesn't interest you? This all-important question must be answered in a way that is consistent with your values. If you pay attention to your strong interests, you will probably find that you have fewer conflicts with your value system. Also, people often have an interest in more than one area and would like a career that will use all or most of those interests. Although many jobs tend to reflect a single interest, most jobs, just like people, will have significant qualities in more than one interest area.

A person who enjoys physical activity and doesn't mind working with mechanical systems but would also like to work with people and follow set guidelines (the Realistic-Social-Conventional personality) may enjoy one of more than 300 careers in health care. A person who is mechanically adept and enjoys persuading people about a product may find technical sales or service an interesting area (the Realistic-Enterprising-Conventional personality) whereas the mechanically inclined person with an investigative bent may like research and development in industry (Realistic-Investigative personality). The Realistic-Conventional personality would find satisfiers in safety and time studies and other data-keeping tasks as well as with data processing equipment; the more creative person may enjoy product/process design, crafts, model building, and graphics (Realistic-Artistic personality).

The investigative person can also research and analyze people, the arts, and business—in fact, this individual can find satisfiers in almost any place. Likewise artistic/creative people can innovate new systems in many job settings that are flexible enough to allow for their creativity. And social personalities can find people to supervise, manage, train, and develop in almost any place they work.

Remember, many Social-Investigative-Artistic persons enjoy working with people to solve problems by creating new systems! This ability is important in just about every workplace.

Understanding these interests can sometimes save people from taking jobs in which they will feel quite uncomfortable. For example, realistic personalities with few social characteristics often find that a promotion to management status brings headaches they'd rather be without. And an artistic person may feel stifled doing routine work all day.

If none of those combinations and considerations seem to fit you, try some creative career ideas. If a career change is not in order, try some alternative work schedules and involvements. Also, consider

- the environment you might enjoy
- the product or service you might like to deal with
- the challenges that attract you
- an entry-level job in an enjoyable place that will allow you to advance

If you still feel uncertain about which interest area is of greatest importance to you, you might want to review this career focus material with a counselor or teacher. You may wish to explore the Job Group Chart in more detail by using the following material, or skip on to the section titled Library Research. Whichever you choose, your future career will turn up somewhere on this chart.[2]

Exploring the Job Chart Further

Just choosing one of the twelve major career interest areas is a significant step in choosing a career. It can help you zero in on an educational path or college major. Then if you wish, you can explore the sixty-six job groups or sub-divisions of these twelve interest areas in more detail. Next you will learn how to explore the 20,000 different occupations identified, defined, and arranged into these groups by the U.S. Department of Labor: twelve major interest areas representing sixty-six job groups with 20,000 jobs—there must be a job for you!

You may feel that you have already chosen a career and that you know exactly why that career fits you. It still can be an interesting exercise to learn something about the whole U.S. job market and how it attracts people from all backgrounds into jobs with such a wide variety of characteristics. You will be working with many different people over a lifetime. Understanding their personalities, interests, and skills can be a plus in most any field you choose.

Job Groups   The numbers 1 through 66 in the lefthand column refer to the sixty-six job groups identified by the Department of Labor. With some small exceptions, all jobs in a group have similar characteristics and call for similar preferences regarding the key qualities. They call for similar preferences regarding involvement with data, people, and things; they have the same key qualities; and they call for the same skills.

Decimal Code   Decimal numbers such as 05.01 refer to the numbered items in the Department of Labor's *Guide for Occupational Exploration,* available

"Your son has made a career choice, Mildred. He's going to win the lottery and travel a lot."

in many libraries and state employment offices. The first two digits, 01 through 12, designate the twelve interest areas.

Key Qualities In each of the fourteen columns following the job group, the symbol H means there is a need at a higher-than-average level and the symbol M means there is need for an average level of the key qualities in that particular group of jobs. A dot (•) means that the quality is needed, with no degree of need indicated.

Do you wish to explore your interest areas further on the Job Group Chart? NO = Goodbye Interest Areas and Job Group Chart! Continue on to Library Research. YES = Do the Following Activities.

Directions: Finding Your Satisfiers

1. Read the description of each job group in your top three or more interest areas. Circle the numbers of any groups that interest you.
2. If you wish to go further, locate the Key Qualities at the top of each column that match those you circled on the Key Qualities Indicator in Chapter 2, Exercise 4. Using a colored pencil, go down the columns and circle the symbols that indicate your satisfiers. For example, if you wish to use the skill "logical intelligence" at a modest level, circle the M's down the column in the interest areas you wish to explore further. When you have finished, you may discover job groups that have many of your satisfiers.
3. Study the Job Group Chart in your interest areas (or even throughout the whole chart) line by line to find groups that look interesting. Some of your

PEANUTS reprinted by permission of United Feature Syndicate, Inc.

satisfiers may be more important than others. Try to be as flexible as possible. Maybe you have indicated that physical activity related to whole-body agility is an important quality for you, but in looking at the other qualities that are required in such jobs, you find that most would not suit you.

4. Double star (**) any job group that has all your satisfiers. If you choose a job group that is not listed under any of your top three personality types, you may still be able to find ways to express your personality in some jobs in the group. Be aware that the Job Group Chart is an imperfect summary of the qualities to be found in thousands of jobs. An individual company can change a job title, alter the job duties at will, and come up with something that no job chart could describe in one line! It's important not to force the data about yourself to make it fit the Job Group Chart. It's also important to be open to possibilities that may be hidden there.

Most people are dismayed to find themselves definitely at sea in an ocean of many choices. If you don't have a nice, neat job title in hand by the time you finish this chapter much less this book, you may be tempted to give up. But if you keep searching, you will have a great chance to learn more about yourself and the work world. You may become more willing to explore important, supporting factors that go into a career choice, and you may also have the joy of learning that many enjoyable careers would suit you equally well. All in all, the career search process is a confidence builder. Even those with a clear-cut career choice need to learn about the job market and how to connect with it.

Library Research: Looking In

Library research enables you to survey the whole job market and eliminate those areas that would not work for you while you zero in on those that are important. Here are some resources to make that task easier. The Department of Labor has listed every job title in a monumental work called the *Dictionary of Occupational Titles* (DOT).[3] The book is a gold mine of information—if you know how to dig for the gold. Because there are sometimes several different titles for the same job, the 20,000 occupations result in about 40,000 listings. Job titles are listed both alphabetically and by industry. The alphabetical listings give the code number needed to find a short description of each job, located among descriptions grouped by occupational area.

The DOT supplement, the *Guide for Occupational Exploration*, is a much simpler book, classifying jobs into the same sixty-six job groups that you found on the Job Group Chart.[4] You can find these books in career centers, library reference rooms, and state employment offices.

Before you go to the library, list the job groups you would like to explore. Use the decimal code number from the Job Group Chart for easy reference. At the library, look up those numbers in the *Guide for Occupational Exploration*. As you explore the job groups, make a list of all the job titles included in each group of interest to you so that you can explore them further.

Suppose you are interested in Job Group 55, Business Management, code number 11.11. In the *Guide for Occupational Exploration* you will find this information:

> Workers in this group manage a business, such as a store or cemetery, a branch of a large company, such as a local office for a credit corporation, or a department within a company, such as a warehouse. They usually carry out operating policies and procedures determined by administration workers, such as presidents, vice-presidents, and directors. Some managers own their own businesses and are considered self-employed. Managers find employment in all kinds of businesses as well as government agencies.[5]

This paragraph is followed by answers to some important questions: What kind of work would you do as a business manager? What skills and abilities do you need for this kind of work? How do you know whether you would like or could learn to do this kind of work? How can you prepare for and enter this kind of work? What else should you consider about these jobs? This information is followed by a list of all the job categories in the Business Management group:

11.11.01   Lodging
11.11.02   Recreation and Amusement
11.11.03   Transportation
11.11.04   Services
11.11.05   Wholesale-Retail

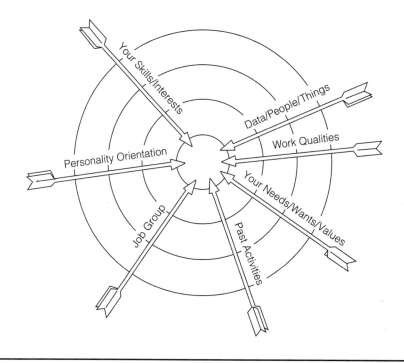

The Career Target

Each of these listings is subdivided into specific job titles and identified by a nine-digit number. Under Wholesale-Retail, for example, you will find Manager, Retail Store 185.167.046. If this particular job interests you, you can find a description of it in the *Dictionary of Occupational Titles* by looking up the nine-digit number: 185.167.046. The section includes other similar job titles so you can explore a variety of jobs with like characteristics.

Remember that titles for the same job may differ from one company to another. But if you know what general functions you want to perform, and if you spend enough time with these books, you will have an overview of your areas of interest in the job market and understand what you can do in it.

By now, if you've marked your areas of interest on the Job Chart, you have noticed which of the sixty-six job groups offer your most important satisfiers. Whenever many of your likes and skills point toward the same job group, you've hit the bullseye on the career target.

At this point you might be feeling a little scared, anxious, or confused. These are all normal feelings for anyone on the verge of a *great discovery!* Keep going! Don't be overwhelmed if you find that several jobs look good to you. Some people are comfortable in a number of areas. Sometimes a person needs more work experience before making a decision. Give yourself more time if you need it. Don't decide to decide without seeing clearly.

There are still other activities to help your decision along. Reflecting on the societal issues that will affect not only your career but also your life, and finding out about projected job market trends for your areas of interest can be helpful here. But one of the best ways to decide is to get some "inside information" through work experience, group tours of workplaces, or interviews with people who work in your area of interest. The rest of this book will give you some help with these concerns.

Making a good career decision is a growth process, and growth takes patience. You can't make a flower grow by pulling on it!

 ## Self-Assessment Exercises

1. Interest Areas

Rank the twelve interest areas in order of importance to you.

_____ 01 **Artistic** (Artistic Personality Type—Creative/Mind): An interest in creative expression of feelings /ideas

_____ 02 **Scientific** (Investigative Personality Type—Researching/Mind): An interest in discovering, collecting, and analyzing information about the natural world, and applying scientific research findings to problems in medicine, the life sciences, and the natural sciences

_____ 03 **Nature/Plants and Animals** (Realistic Personality Type—Outdoor/Matter): An interest in working with plants and animals, usually in an outdoor setting

_____ 04 **Protective** (Realistic Personality Type—Protecting People and Property/Matter): An interest in the use of authority to protect people and property

_____ 05 **Mechanical** (Realistic Personality Type—Machine/Matter): An interest in applying mechanical principles to practical situations by use of machines or tools

_____ 06 **Industrial** (Realistic Personality Type—Factory/Matter): An interest in repetitive, concrete, organized activities done in a factory setting

_____ 07 **Business detail** (Conventional Personality Type—Office/Paper): An interest in organized, clearly defined activities requiring accuracy and attention to details, primarily in an office setting

_____ 08 **Selling** (Enterprising Personality Type—Persuading/People): An interest in bringing others to a particular point of view by personal persuasion, using sales promotion techniques

____ 09 **Accommodating** (Social Personality Type—Serving/People): An interest in catering to the wants and needs of others, usually on a one-to-one basis

____ 10 **Human services** (Social Personality Type—Development/People): An interest in helping others with their mental, spiritual, social, physical, or vocational needs

____ 11 **Leading/influencing** (Enterprising/Social Personality Type—Leading, Influencing/People): An interest in leading and influencing others by using high-level verbal or numerical abilities

____ 12 **Physical performance** (Realistic Personality Type—Performance/Matter-Body): An interest in physical activities performed before an audience[6]

2. Job Groups Expanded

The following list of the sixty-six job groups and their subcategories may help you to further zero in on job groups of interest to you. They are in a somewhat different order than found in the Job Group Chart. Circle the ones you find appealing. Note those job groups with the most circles.

SUMMARY LIST OF INTEREST AREAS, JOB GROUPS, AND SUBGROUPS

01	**ARTISTIC/CREATIVE**		
		01.05	**Performing Arts: Dance**
01.01	**Literary Arts**	01.05-01	Instructing and Choreography
01.01-01	Editing	01.05-02	Performing
01.01-02	Creative Writing		
01.01-03	Critiquing	01.06	**Craft Arts**
		01.06-01	Graphic Arts and Related Crafts
01.02	**Visual Arts**	01.06-02	Arts and Crafts
01.02-01	Instructing and Appraising	01.06-03	Hand Lettering, Painting, and Decorating
01.02-02	Studio Art		
01.02-03	Commercial Art		
		01.07	**Elemental Arts**
01.03	**Performing Arts: Drama**	01.07-01	Psychic Science
01.03-01	Instructing and Directing	01.07-02	Announcing
01.03-02	Performing	01.07-03	Entertaining
01.03-03	Narrating and Announcing		
		01.08	**Modeling**
		01.08-01	Personal Appearance
01.04	**Performing Arts: Music**		
01.04-01	Instructing and Directing	02	**SCIENTIFIC/ANALYTIC**
01.04-02	Composing and Arranging		
01.04-03	Vocal Performing		
01.04-04	Instrumental Performing	02.01	**Physical Sciences**

02.01-01	Theoretical Research
02.01-02	Technology
02.02	**Life Sciences**
02.02-01	Animal Specialization
02.02-02	Plant Specialization
02.02-03	Plant and Animal Specialization
02.02-04	Food Research
02.03	**Medical Sciences**
02.03-01	Medicine and Surgery
02.03-02	Dentistry
02.03-03	Veterinary Medicine
02.03-04	Health Specialties
02.04	**Laboratory Technology**
02.04-01	Physical Sciences
02.04-02	Life Sciences
03	**NATURE (PLANTS, ANIMALS)**
03.01	**Managerial Work: Plants and Animals**
03.01-01	Farming

03.01-02 Specialty Breeding
03.01-03 Specialty Cropping
03.01-04 Forestry and Logging

**03.02   General Supervision:
            Plants and Animals**
03.02-01 Farming
03.02-02 Forestry and Logging
03.02-03 Nursery and
            Groundskeeping
03.02-04 Services

**03.03   Animal Training and
            Service**
03.03-01 Animal Training
03.03-02 Animal Service

**03.04   Elemental Work: Plants
            and Animals**
03.04-01 Farming
03.04-02 Forestry and Logging
03.04-03 Hunting and Fishing
03.04-04 Nursery and
            Groundskeeping
03.04-05 Services

04   PROTECTIVE

**04.01   Safety and Law
            Enforcement**
04.01-01 Managing
04.01-02 Investigating

04.02   Security Services
04.02-01 Detention
04.02-02 Property and People
04.02-03 Law and Order
04.02-04 Emergency Responding

05   MECHANICAL

05.01   Engineering
05.01-01 Research
05.01-02 Environmental
            Protection
05.01-03 Systems Design
05.01-04 Testing and Quality
            Control
05.01-05 Sales Engineering
05.01-06 Work Planing and
            Utilization
05.01-07 Design
05.01-08 General Engineering

**05.02   Managerial Work:
            Mechanical**
05.02-01 Systems

05.02-02 Maintenance and
            Construction
05.02-03 Processing and
            Manufacturing
05.02-04 Communications
05.02-05 Mining, Logging, and
            Petroleum Production
05.02-06 Services
05.02-07 Materials Handling

05.03   Engineering Technology
05.03-01 Surveying
05.03-02 Drafting
05.03-03 Expediting and
            Coordinating
05.03-04 Petroleum
05.03-05 Electrical Electronic
05.03-06 Industrial Safety
05.03-07 Mechanical
05.03-08 Environmental Control
05.03-09 Packaging and Storing

**05.04   Air and Water Vehicle
            Operation**
05.04-01 Air
05.04-02 Water

05.05   Craft Technology
05.05-01 Masonry, Stone, and
            Brick Work
05.05-02 Construction and
            Maintenance
05.05-03 Plumbing and
            Pipefitting
05.05-04 Painting, Plastering, and
            Paperhanging
05.05-05 Electrical Electronic
            Systems Installation
            and Repair
05.05-06 Metal Fabrication and
            Repair
05.05-07 Machining
05.05-08 Woodworking
05.05-09 Mechanical Work
05.05-10 Electrical Electronic
            Equipment Repair
05.05-11 Scientific, Medical, and
            Technical Equipment
            Fabrication and Repair
05.05-12 Musical Instrument
            Fabrication and Repair
05.05-13 Printing
05.05-14 Gem Cutting and
            Finishing
05.05-15 Custom Sewing:
            Tailoring, and
            Upholstering
05.05-16 Dyeing
05.05-17 Food Preparation

05.06   Systems Operation
05.06-01 Electricity Generation
            and Transmission
05.06-02 Stationary Engineering
05.06-03 Oil, Gas, and Water
            Distribution
05.06-04 Processing

05.07   Quality Control
05.07-01 Structural
05.07-02 Mechanical
05.07-03 Electrical
05.07-04 Environmental
05.07-05 Petroleum
05.07-06 Logging and Lumber

**05.08   Land and Water Vehicle
            Operating**
05.08-01 Truck Driving
05.08-02 Rail Vehicle Operating
05.08-03 Services Requiring
            Driving
05.08-04 Boat Operation

05.09   Materials Control
05.09-01 Shipping, Receiving, and
            Stock Checking
05.09-02 Estimating, Scheduling,
            and Record Keeping
05.09-03 Verifying, Recording,
            and Marking

05.10   Crafts
05.10.01 Structural
05.10.02 Mechanical
05.10.03 Electrical/Electronic
05.10.04 Structural/Mechanical/
            Electrical/Electronic
05.10.05 Reproduction
05.10.06 Blasting
05.10.07 Painting, Dyeing, and
            Coating
05.10.08 Food Preparation
05.10.09 Environmental

05.11   Equipment Operation
05.11.01 Construction
05.11.02 Mining and Quarrying
05.11.03 Drilling and Oil
            Exploration
05.11.04 Materials Handling

**05.12   Elemental Works:
            Mechanical**
05.12.01 Supervision
05.12.02 Mining, Quarrying,
            Drilling
05.12.03 Loading, Moving

(continued)

05	**MECHANICAL**
	(continued)
05.12.04	Hoisting, Conveying
05.12.05	Braking, Switching, and Coupling
05.12.06	Pumping
05.12.07	Crushing, Mixing, Separating, and Chipping
05.12.08	Lubricating
05.12.09	Masonry
05.12.10	Heating and Melting
05.12.11	Welding
05.12.12	Structural Work
05.12.13	Cutting and Finishing
05.12.14	Painting, Caulking, and Coating
05.12.15	Mechanical Work
05.12.16	Electrical Work
05.12.17	Food Preparation
05.12.18	Cleaning and Maintenance
05.12.19	Reproduction Services
05.12.20	Signaling

06	**INDUSTRIAL**
06.01	**Production Technology**
06.01-01	Supervision and Instruction
06.01-02	Machine Set-Up
06.01-03	Machine Set-Up and Operation
06.01-04	Precision Hand Work
06.01-05	Inspection

06.02	**Production Work**
06.02-01	Supervision
06.02-02	Machine Work, Metal and Plastics
06.02-03	Machine Work, Wood
06.02-04	Machine Work, Paper
06.02-05	Machine Work, Leather and Fabrics
06.02-06	Machine Work, Textiles
06.02-07	Machine Work, Rubber
06.02-08	Machine Work, Stone, Clay, and Glass
06.02-09	Machine Work, Assorted Materials
06.02-10	Equipment Operation, Metal Processing
06.02-11	Equipment Operation, Chemical Processing
06.02-12	Equipment Operation, Petroleum Processing

06.02-13	Equipment Operation, Rubber, Plastics, and Glass Processing
06.02-14	Equipment Operation, Paper and Paper Products Processing
06.02-15	Equipment Operation, Food Processing
06.02-16	Equipment Operation, Textile, Fabric, and Leather Processing
06.02-17	Equipment Operation, Clay and Coke Processing
06.02-18	Equipment Operation, Assorted Materials Processing
06.02-19	Equipment Operation, Welding, Brazing, and Soldering
06.02-20	Machine Assembling
06.02-21	Coating and Plating
06.02-22	Manual Work, Assembly Large Parts
06.02-23	Manual Work, Assembly Small Parts
06.02-24	Manual Work, Metal and Plastics
06.02-25	Manual Work, Wood
06.02-26	Manual Work, Paper
06.02-27	Manual Work, Textile, Fabric, and Leather
06.02-28	Manual Work, Food Processing
06.02-29	Manual Work, Rubber
06.02-30	Manual Work, Stone, Glass, and Clay
06.02-31	Manual Work, Laying Out and Marking
06.02-32	Manual Work, Assorted Materials

06.03	**Quality Control**
06.03-01	Inspecting, Testing, and Repairing
06.03-02	Inspecting, Grading, Sorting, Weighing, and Recording

06.04	**Elemental Work: Industrial**
06.04-01	Supervision
06.04-02	Machine Work, Metal and Plastics
06.04-03	Machine Work, Wood
06.04-04	Machine Work, Paper
06.04-05	Machine Work, Fabric and Leather
06.04-06	Machine Work, Textiles

06.04-07	Machine Work, Rubber
06.04-08	Machine Work, Stone, Glass, and Clay
06.04-09	Machine Work, Assorted Materials
06.04-10	Equipment Operation, Metal Processing
06.04-11	Equipment Operation, Chemical Processing
06.04-12	Equipment Operation, Petroleum, Gas, and Coal Processing
06.04-13	Equipment Operation, Rubber, Plastics, and Glass processing
06.04-14	Equipment Operation, Paper Making
06.04-15	Equipment Operation, Food Processing
06.04-16	Equipment Operation, Textile, Fabric, and Leather Processing
06.04-17	Equipment Operation, Clay Processing
06.04-18	Equipment Operation, Wood Processing
06.04-19	Equipment Operation, Assorted Materials Processing
06.04-20	Machine Assembly
06.04-21	Machine Work, Brushing, Spraying, and Coating
06.04-22	Manual Work, Assembly Large Parts
06.04-23	Manual Work, Assembly Small Parts
06.04-24	Manual Work, Metal and Plastics
06.04-25	Manual Work, Wood
06.04-26	Manual Work, Paper
06.04-27	Manual Work, Textile, Fabric, and Leather
06.04-28	Manual Work, Food Processing
06.04-29	Manual Work, Rubber
06.04-30	Manual Work, Stone, Glass, and Clay
06.04-31	Manual Work, Welding and Flame Cutting
06.04-32	Manual Work, Casting and Molding
06.04-33	Manual Work, Brushing, Spraying, and Coating
06.04-34	Manual Work, Assorted Materials
06.04-35	Laundering, Dry Cleaning

06.04-36 Filling
06.04-37 Manual Work,
          Stamping, Marking,
          Labeling, and
          Ticketing
06.04-38 Wrapping and Packing
06.04-39 Cleaning
06.04-40 Loading, Moving,
          Hoisting, and
          Conveying

07   BUSINESS DETAIL

07.01   Administrative Detail
07.01-01 Interviewing
07.01-02 Administration
07.01-03 Secretarial Work
07.01-04 Financial Work
07.01-05 Certifying
07.01-06 Investigating
07.01-07 Test Administration

07.02   Mathematical Detail
07.02-01 Bookkeeping and
          Auditing
07.02-02 Accounting
07.02-03 Statistical Reporting and
          Analysis
07.02-04 Billing and Rate
          Computation
07.02-05 Payroll and Timekeeping

07.03   Financial Detail
07.03-01 Paying and Receiving

07.04   Oral Communications
07.04-01 Interviewing
07.04-02 Order, Complaint, and
          Claims Handling
07.04-03 Registration
07.04-04 Reception and
          Information Giving
07.04-05 Information
          Transmitting and
          Receiving
07.04-06 Switchboard Services

07.05   Records Processing
07.05-01 Coordinating and
          Scheduling
07.05-02 Record Verification and
          Proofing
07.05-03 Record Preparation and
          Maintenance
07.05-04 Routing and
          Distribution

**07.06   Clerical Machine
            Operation**
07.06-01 Computer Operation
07.06-02 Keyboard Machine
          Operation

07.07   Clerical Handling
07.07-01 Filing
07.07-02 Sorting and Distribution
07.07-03 General Clerical Work

**08   PERSUADING/
            SELLING**

08.01   Sales Technology
08.01-01 Technical Sales
08.01-02 Intangible Sales
08.01-03 General Clerical Work

08.02   General Sales
08.02-01 Wholesale
08.02-02 Retail
08.02-03 Wholesale and Retail
08.02-04 Real Estate
08.02-05 Demonstration and Sales
08.02-06 Services
08.02-07 Driving/Selling
08.02-08 Soliciting, Selling

08.03   Vending
08.03-01 Peddling and Hawking
08.03-02 Promoting

09   ACCOMMODATING

09.01   Hospitality Services
09.01-01 Social and Recreational
          Activities
09.01-02 Guide Services
09.01-03 Food Services
09.01-04 Safety and Comfort
          Services

**09.02   Barber and Beauty
            Services**
09.02-01 Cosmetology
09.02-02 Barbering

09.03   Passenger Services
09.03-01 Group Transportation
09.03-02 Individual
          Transportation
09.03-03 Instruction and
          Supervision

09.04   Customer Services
09.04-01 Food Services
09.04-02 Sales Services

09.05   Attendant Services
09.05-01 Physical Conditioning
09.05-02 Food Services
09.05-03 Portering and Baggage
          Services
09.05-04 Doorkeeping Services
09.05-05 Card and Game Room
          Services
09.05-06 Individualized Services
09.05-07 General Wardrobe
          Services
09.05-08 Ticket Taking, Ushering

10   HUMAN SERVICES

10.01   Social Services
10.01-01 Religious
10.01-02 Counseling and Social
          Work

**10.02   Nursing, Therapy and
            Specialized Teaching
            Services**
10.02-01 Nursing
10.02-02 Therapy and
          Rehabilitation
10.02-03 Specialized Teaching

10.03   Child and Adult Care
10.03-01 Data Collection
10.03-02 Patient Care
10.03-03 Care of Others

**11   LEADING/
            INFLUENCING**

**11.01   Mathematics and
            Statistics**
11.01-01 Data Processing Design
11.01-02 Data Analysis

**11.02   Educational and Library
            Services**
11.02-01 Teaching and
          Instructing, General
11.02-02 Vocational and
          Industrial Teaching
11.02-03 Teaching Home
          Economics,
          Agriculture, and
          Related
11.02-04 Library Services

(continued)

11	LEADING/ INFLUENCING (continued)	11.06-03	Risk and Profit Analysis	11.10-05	Company Policy
		11.06-04	Brokering		
		11.06-05	Budget and Financial Control	**11.11**	**Business Management**
				11.11-01	Lodging
11.03	**Social Research**			11.11-02	Recreation and Amusement
11.03-01	Psychological	**11.07**	**Service Administration**		
11.03-02	Sociological	11.07-01	Social Services	11.11-03	Transportation
11.03-03	Historical	11.07-02	Health and Safety Services	11.11-04	Service
11.03-04	Occupational			11.11-05	Wholesale/Retail
11.03-05	Economic	11.07-03	Educational Services		
		11.07-04	Recreational Services	**11.12**	**Contracts and Claims**
11.04	**Law**			11.12-01	Claims Settlement
11.04-01	Justice Administration	**11.08**	**Communications**	11.12-02	Rental and Leasing
11.04-02	Legal Practice	11.08-01	Editing	11.12-03	Booking
11.04-03	Abstracting, Document Preparation	11.08-02	Writing	11.12-04	Procurement Negotiations
		11.08-03	Writing and Broadcasting		
11.05	**Business Administration**	11.08-04	Translating and Interpreting		
11.05-01	Management Services: Nongovernment				
		11.09	**Promotion**	**12**	**PHYSICAL PERFORMANCE**
11.05-02	Administrative Specialization	11.09-01	Sales		
		11.09-02	Funds and Membership Solicitation		
11.05-03	Management Services: Government			**12.01**	**Sports**
		11.09-03	Public Relations	12.01-01	Coaching and Instructing
11.05-04	Sales and Purchasing Management				
		11.10	**Regulations Enforcement**	12.01-02	Officiating
		11.10-01	Finance	12.01-03	Performing
11.06	**Finance**	11.10-02	Individual Rights		
11.06-01	Accounting and Auditing	11.10-03	Health and Safety	**12.02**	**Physical Feats**
11.06-02	Records Systems Analysis	11.10-04	Immigration and Customs	12.02-01	Performing

3. Job Group Choice

Now list your top three job group choices of the sixty-six job groups in order of importance. Use the four-digit number and name beginning with 01.01 Artistic :

1st _____ 2nd _____ 3rd _____

4. Match Analyzer

a. To further analyze your choice(s) above, fill in the following information about your top job group choice:

Number   Decimal code   Title

_____   _____   _____

b. Check below all the qualities from 1 to 14 required by that job group as they appear on the Job Group Chart. Then, using your colored pencil, circle the same qualities you circled in the Key Qualities Indicator in Chapter 2, Exercise 4, as being important to you. This will allow you to compare the qualities the job group requires and the qualities you would like in your job.

__ M __ H 1. Logical intelligence

__ M __ H 2. Intuitive intelligence

__ M __ H 3. Verbal ability

__ M __ H 4. Numerical ability

__ M __ H 5. Exactness with detail

__ M __ H 6. Facility with multi-dimensional forms

__ M __ H 7. Businesslike contact with people

__ M __ H 8. Ability to influence people

__ M __ H 9. Finger/hand agility

__ M __ H 10. Whole body agility

__ M __ H 11. Repetition

__ M __ H 12. Variety

__ M __ H 13. Physical risk

__ M __ H 14. Status

c. Is there a perfect match between qualities the job group requires and those you would like to use on the job? ____ Yes ____ No

d. Explain how you could overcome each quality that does not match.

_____

_____

_____

_____

e. You can repeat this analysis for any other job group of interest to you.

5. Researching a Job Group

Look up your top job group in the *Guide for Occupational Exploration.* Find the answers to the following questions.

■ Summarize the kind of work that you would do.

_____

_____

_____

Are you just drifting? Start gathering information about careers.

Are you swamped with information? It's time to start narrowing the choices.

Stay calm, stay on course, and you'll reach your destination.

Where Are You Now on the Career Choice Continuum?

■ Summarize the skills and abilities needed for this kind of work.

_____

_____

_____

_____

■ Summarize clues that tell whether you would like or could learn this work.

_____

_____

_____

_____

■ Summarize the training needed and the methods of entry into this field.

_____

_____

_____

_____

■ List job titles you'd like to explore further.

_____

_____

_____

_____

_____

6. Researching Job Titles

Identify one job title from your top job group. Look it up in the *Dictionary of Occupational Titles,* using the nine-digit number. Summarize what you find there.

Job Title: _____ Nine-digit code: _____

_____

_____

_____

_____

_____

7. Confirm Career Choice

If have already made your career choice, ask yourself these questions:

■ Is this career clearly your own choice?

■ Are you afraid to look at alternatives?

■ Are you willing to be open to important factors that may change your decision?

■ Can you support your choice with facts about your skills, interests, and values?

8. Blocks and Barriers

At this point, what could be holding you back from completing the career search process?

___ In too much of a hurry to explore

___ Have done some exercises (or pieces of the puzzle) but left others out

___ Experiencing personal/painful traumas

___ Afraid to look at myself; low/no self-confidence

___ Afraid to make a commitment

___What else? _____

9. *Filling in the Lines*

Discuss with a group or in writing the decisions you have made so far in regard to your career/life choices and how they feel to you.

4/

Roles and Realities

Sinking the Stereotypes

 FOCUS

- *Explore roles and understand stereotypes.*

- *Consider diversity and its impact in the workplace and life place.*

- *Examine changing themes.*

You have assessed your needs, wants, and most cherished values. You know your personality orientation and your interests and abilities. You have identified qualities that represent the unique person you are. And you have seen how, by identifying these qualities, you can find your satisfiers in the job market. Many people are so overjoyed after they have picked a job title or two that they can hardly wait to start job hunting. But sophisticated career searchers will first make sure they understand the society in which they plan to work. In this chapter you will examine the roles people play, the stereotypes about these roles, and the ever-increasing diversity of the United States, and you will examine some of the ways these factors affect personal life choices as well as life in the workplace. In the next chapter you will consider the challenges that influence the kind of work that society does and needs to do. The following chapter will deal with the inner workings of workplaces and workstyles.

Roles on the Life/Work Stage

When you assessed your personal qualities, you realized that you couldn't be described in terms of only six personality types or ten skills or four work qualities or lists of needs, wants, and values. Each set of assessments leaves out many shades and blends of color from your self-portrait. The same is true for titles used to describe the diverse roles you and others play on the life/work stage.

People play out roles for many reasons. Some roles they're born into and cannot change, such as racial or ethnic background; others they may feel pressured to assume, such as college student; and still others they may choose freely, such as marital status. Before people choose a career they usually imagine themselves in various job roles, wearing different outfits, doing all kinds of tasks. They see themselves in an office or in a classroom, on a plane or on a roof, behind a camera or under a car. Most people begin playing imaginary roles as children. Those dreams are an important part of the career/life planning process.

Motivated by your needs and wants and closely related to your values, your roles become deeply embedded in your being. They color the way you see yourself and other people. They affect your career and your life, sometimes fairly, sometimes not. When you choose a role, you choose membership in a group, yet we all play these roles in ways that are unique to us. Your task is to evaluate your roles and decide how you will act them out: male-female, married-single, parent-childless, person of color-white, native-immigrant, able-disabled, old-young, rich-poor, employed-unemployed, and career roles from top manager to lowly minion.

Sinking Stereotypes

Look again at the role pairs listed above: male-female, married-single, young-old, rich-poor. Each pair covers a broad continuum of behaviors. No single one of these roles is a complete picture; each person has qualities, talents, and experiences that blend across the roles and contribute to making a unique individual. We miss these characteristics when we simply label people and their roles based on unexamined opinions, a process called stereotyping.

Stereotyping *can* be a useful way of organizing information. Here are some obvious and helpful stereotypes: A doctor heals people; a carpenter repairs things. Therefore, a doctor can fix your sagging back, and a carpenter can fix your sagging door. But these simple statements fail to capture the full range of what and who a doctor and a carpenter are.

Negative stereotypes can label people unfairly. Consider some of the roles we examine in this chapter. Many of them have all-too-common stereotypes: Men aren't housekeepers. Women are passive. Immigrants take jobs from Americans. Old people aren't good workers. A disabled person can't do a job as well as someone who is not disabled.

One very pervasive stereotype from post–World War II days that still influences career and lifestyle choice is that of the "American Dream." This vision of success applied pretty evenly to everyone, although only a small percentage of the population ever achieved it. It consisted of an idyllic and affluent lifestyle in which young men and women married; the husband/father began his career early and worked full time; the housewife/mother raised two children in a house in the suburbs; and they were white.

This myth ignored such groups as single parents, the elderly, the disabled, gays, minorities, immigrants, and refugees. Many in these groups were poor and isolated from the mainstream of society—especially low-income women who have always worked outside the home, often in factory and service jobs. Geraldine Youcha notes in *Minding the Children* that as far back as 1930 there were more than three million female-headed households.[1] Even so, many in our society still believe the majority of people are living that dream or, with encouragement, will do so in the future.

People's dreams may not be the "American Dream," but it will be a version that suits their needs and longings. Our dreams and desires are what propel us. Groups who have traditionally been denied access to their dreams are more vigorously demanding—and getting—a position in the workplace, struggling with entrenched groups to gain full acceptance. Because we may be unfamiliar with them, the tendency is often to stereotype newcomers as a group before we know them as individuals. Many people, excluded from the mainstream by stereotyping, have been like foreigners in their own land.

> It is enough for someone to treat me like a foreigner for me to be one. If I am excluded, it is because someone has pushed me out. Therefore, it is my fault, too, if the other person is excluded, that is to say deprived of a feeling of security and of belonging, of a sense of identity. For it is up to me whether someone feels at home or not in our common world, and whether he feels tranquil or anxious when he looks around him.[2]
>
> —*Elie Wiesel, Nobel Peace Prize Winner and Andrew Mellon Professor of Humanities at Boston University*

As you read this chapter and examine diversity in the society and the workplace, think about stereotypes. Ask whether the information you learn about the groups and roles portrayed here causes you to rethink the labels they have so often been given. Flexible thinking can unlock the door to new information about the people we meet. As we open our minds, we will be free to see others and *ourselves* as we really are and not miss them because of stereotyping.

Diversity in Society and the Workplace

In the last quarter of the twentieth century, the complexion of the workplace changed dramatically. Not only did women and minorities enter in increasingly greater numbers, but the global economy brought us into contact with all the peoples of the world. No longer did we look at a "mass market" in which we can assume everyone looks the same way, thinks in the same ways, and wants the same things.

Everyone is learning new ways of doing business inside and outside their organizations; intolerance is no longer to be tolerated. "Only diversity-friendly and idea-friendly organizations will be competitive in the twenty-first century," according to Charles Powers, co-author of *Post Industrial Lives* and associate professor of sociology at Santa Clara University.[3] And at one of the Fortune 500's fasting-growing companies, Harry Pforzheimer, director of corporate communications, says, "The population here reflects the world population. That makes for an exciting melting pot of ideas. And I think it adds dramatically to our success."[4]

If we are to understand the changing world of work, we need to know the people who inhabit it as well as our stereotypes of them. Our examination begins close to home—with males and females.

Male/Female Roles

We know that human actions range from passive to aggressive. If we stereotype such behaviors as that of the fragile, fainting female or the mighty, macho male, we then expect women and men to behave in these opposite ways.

Passive people at one end of the male/female spectrum (the female stereotype) are easily frightened, cry at the drop of an eyebrow, are afraid of anger in themselves and others, and are often secretly angry. They tend to feel insecure, inhibited, and self-conscious; they are often hurt and overwhelmed by the harshness of others; they are dependent on the approval of those around them, and will often sacrifice satisfaction of their own needs to get it. If things do not work out, they may try to manipulate others or give up and withdraw. People tend to disregard or dominate them because they seem so uncertain of themselves and their opinions.

Aggressive people (the male stereotype), on the other end of the spectrum, like to appear powerful, all-knowing, and superior. They deny having tender feelings and try to appear rational, although they are often motivated by angry, explosive emotions and the need to control those around them. Rather than be "beaten," they attack first to get the edge; they are often reckless in "telling it like it is" without regard for the feelings of others. Underneath the anger, they are often secretly afraid and insecure. They are usually resented by others and feel bewildered and hurt when people isolate them and refuse to cooperate.

On the positive side, females are given credit for being sensitive, intuitive, flexible, and cooperative whereas males are viewed as strong, intellectual, logical, direct, and uninfluenced by emotion. But the reality is that everyone exhibits a wide range of behaviors from timid to tough. Few stay at either end of the timid/tough spectrum, yet people sometimes make career/life choices on the basis of gender stereotypes instead of their own strong points.

It's hard to believe that only a few short years ago it would have been considered extraordinary for a woman to become an astronaut or a zookeeper, to head a Fortune 500 company, or to venture into the world of venture capital. And it would have seemed just as extraordinary for a man to choose a significant share of housework and child care. Yet gender still influences societal attitudes. Almost before a baby takes its first breath, people ask, "Is it a boy or a girl?" Male/female roles are the most pervasive in our lives although. in the last few decades of the mid-twentieth century, they have become increasingly blurred. We can congratulate ourselves on how far our society has come in respecting and giving everyone equal opportunity, but we still have far to go. Let's look at some realities.

Gender Bender: Women   Researchers have found that *every* country treats women worse than men. According to a 1993 United Nations Human Development Report, throughout the world women are the neglected majority. Of thirty-three industrialized countries, Japan ranks first and the United States ranks ninth in the poor treatment of women.[5] Women are poorer, sicker, and less educated than the men living around them[6] and they work many more hours for a fraction of the pay a man would receive; they own little property. In many countries women still have almost no voice in government decision and policy making; in some they are virtually without any rights at all. According to Peggy McIntosh, associate director of the Wellesley College Center for Research on Women, the conclusion that follows is that men must be richer, healthier, and better educated than the women around them.[7]

U.S. Labor Secretary Robert Reich says that "subtle but pervasive patterns of discrimination dominate the public, private and nonprofit sectors of society because of a myopia on the part of many white male managers."[8] A large proportion of women continue to cluster in traditional clerical and personal services jobs, which are often low-paying, part-time, and dead end. The jobs lack security and often offer no benefits, pensions, union protection, or opportunities for advancement. Nearly half the women in these jobs are the family's primary wage earner.

Women still work in only tiny numbers as electricians, plumbers, and carpenters. Females in such skilled, lucrative, and nontraditional jobs (those that employ 75 percent or more men) earn 20 to 30 percent more than women in traditional occupations, but still make less than men.[9] In the nontraditional trades, they have few role models, limited experience with tools and mechanical operations, and often little support from family and friends. In this environment, they need a good measure of confidence and assertiveness to succeed.

In other traditionally male jobs, women have made inroads in increasing numbers, but overall they hold less than 5 percent of senior management positions in U.S. companies although they represent over half the work force. Many women who make it to top management do so in areas such as health and education that employ mainly women and do not pay as well as business and industry.[10] Forty percent of women in jobs listed as managerial earn less than $26,000 a year,[11] and they are still hitting that invisible barrier called the "glass ceiling." The glamorous career women pictured in slick magazines are a minority.

About 80 percent of working women are employed full time, and a fourth of those who work part time would prefer full-time work. Almost as many women as men hold more than one job.[12] And to make economic matters worse, studies show that women pay more for services than men do—for example, for haircuts, auto repair, dry cleaning, clothing alterations, and health care.[13] Most women recognize the danger to their future security of not having a high-paying job; yet juggling career and family is often a necessity, and they have little choice but to delay their career development.

Women still have not achieved equality in the workplace, but there are signs of improvement. Over the last sixty years, their wages have increased 20 percent more rapidly than men's. While wages are rising, occupational segregation is diminishing.[14] Women are making the greatest increases in nontraditional jobs in the professions, where their numbers grow each year.

On the educational scene, the picture for younger and college-educated women is brightening. Although many continue to avoid pursuing degrees in the sciences, math, and engineering, even though these are pathways to lucrative professions, the numbers of women enrolled in these courses are increasing. Those who study these disciplines tend to drop out at higher rates than men because they find the classes subtly or not so subtly oriented to males—unless they study at women's colleges, and enrollment in these schools increased 33 percent in the fall of 1994.[15]

For many women in the workplace, sexual harassment has been disturbing. Sexual harassment in any career can dim a woman's enthusiasm for her work. This behavior, however, is no longer ignored as it once was. Laws and policies are in place, and the message is out that sexual harassment of either women or men will no longer be tolerated.[16]

Gender Bender: Men   While women are trying to define new roles, men also face dilemmas. Over the past centuries, the male role has not evolved very much. While many more men now help with housework and child care, many others choose a career and plan to focus on it until retirement, with little deviation from the traditional path. But a man's future success isn't determined when he chooses a career, and the male manager doesn't always rise to the top in an easy, direct ascent, if he rises at all. Levinson writes in The Seasons of a Man's Life that many men experience traumatic crises as they make transitions in their thirties, forties (mid-life), and sixties. During these times, many men reevaluate and sometimes change at least two and possibly three components of their lifestyles.[17] Career is still an important life component to a man as a vehicle for contributing to society and fulfilling his dream about himself. Marriage and family are usually integral components of that dream, as are friendships/peer relationships, ethnicity/religion, and sometimes leisure—especially sports.

Decisions men make at these transition times are linked to values and are closely interrelated. Salary, prestige, commuting time, overtime, pressure, travel, and colleagues all have an impact, positive or negative, on personal and family life for men as well as for women.

While some men have been strongly socialized to see housework as very unmasculine, there are new expectations about a man's role in household care. Most people value a reasonably clean house and occasional home-cooked meals, although few people find it stimulating work. These facts can become friction in a family. However, researchers at the University of Maryland have found that men now perform about one-third of household chores and have been increasing their share.[18] They are also becoming more

involved in caring for their children, with one study showing 20 percent of preschool children being cared for by their fathers.[19] Another, however, finds that the average American father spends an average of fifty-four minutes a day with his children.[20]

Many men still feel that the major burden of family support is on their shoulders and they don't want the added chores of household/family care. Often these men feel threatened by the thought of a working wife, and others feel devalued if their wives are more successful than they are. But many husbands welcome the increased economic security that a wife's income provides. One man remarked that he "loves being dependently wealthy!" And Bess Myerson, a nationally prominent woman of many careers, once said, "When it comes to *machismo* versus mouths to feed, *machismo* is a luxury no family can afford."[21]

The results of the changes that many women have been making in their careers and personal lives have generally been positive for them: increased education, income, independence, and self-esteem. But these changes have forced men to change, not always in ways that are comfortable, not always in ways they would have chosen. For example, men now more frequently work with and are supervised by competent women with fewer promotions coming their way; the realities of family often force them into the unfamiliar role of house and child caretakers; divorce in this contemporary age, especially when children are involved, can leave conscientious men as well as women not only financially but emotionally drained. For men, approaching the final, settling-down years with a life that hasn't fulfilled their dreams can prove intolerable.[22] Trying to fit into new expectations about what they should do and how they should be is adding new layers of frustration and bewilderment to some men's lives. This is expecially so when they feel that they had their lives all figured out and are not sure what the new expectations really are and where these expectations will lead them. Often men come to a dead end where no more promotions are possible. Like many women, many men feel trapped in low-paying, monotonous, demanding, or demeaning jobs.

Much energy goes into the daily competition for success in the market-place. Those who have made it have to work hard to keep it. For men, mak-ing business contacts is as natural as breathing, or so we thought. The stereotype is that the "old boys' network" begins at age six with the soccer team and works its way up to the college/military fraternity. The hearty handshake and exchange of business cards isn't the road to success for every male, however, and images like these put needless pressure on many men to achieve, especially minorities with little access to the power structure. A study from the University of California, Los Angeles, noted that white males hold 95 percent of the positions of power in the United States, and minori-ties including black, Asian, and Hispanic men and women occupy only 1 percent of top corporate jobs.[23]

Unfortunately, career success does not prevent crisis. Some men and now women, achieve their long-sought goals only to ask, "Was it worth it?" Perhaps they have moved up and now find themselves in prestigious posi-tions they do not enjoy. Sometimes these jobs involve long hours, trips away from home, and frequent moving. The result may be alienation from family and friends, with a loss of nurturing that can be critical, especially in times of crisis. Many relationships don't survive this stress. Culturally conditioned to deny many feelings, men are taught that it is acceptable to get angry but not to show fears or tears. The successful man as well as the unsuccessful may be leading a life of quiet desperation. As Paul Tsongas, former U.S. senator from Massachusetts, said, "No man ever said on his deathbed, 'I wish I had spent more time with my business.'"[24]

Yet alternatives may seem frightening. Changing careers may mean stepping down, with a resulting loss of income and possibly a sense of defeat. Instead of retraining for a new line of work, the dissatisfied working man may go with the stereotype and decide to "stick it out" until retirement instead of risking a significant change. As mid-life approaches, the immedi-ate goal of many men and women is often not self-actualization. These mem-bers of the "sandwich generation," in addition to paying off the mortgage and children's college tuition, can expect to spend more time caring for aging parents than they did raising their children![25]

Men who have adjusted to the changes, however, often find that they are relieved at not having to prove themselves simply because they are males. They are finding freedom in just being themselves with the qualities that are unique to them regardless of stereotypes. Health care manager Jerry Pitts says that he finds it a relief to let other people shine as well, to be promoted,

---

SOME ECONOMIC REALITIES

- Women's income equals 71% of men's.
- Women with bachelor's degrees earn 73% of the income of men who have similar education.
- Eighty percent of working women earn less than $25,000 a year.[26]
- In the early 1990s, married couples had a median family income of $42,064.
- Woman-headed families earned $17,221.[27]
- Men earn about twenty-four cents an hour more for each year of experience; women earn seven cents.
- With four years of college, men average $50,000 a year; women average $30,000, about what high school graduates earn. With advanced degrees the gap narrows.[28]

---

and to find success. Many men are enjoying being closer to their spouses and children; feeling freer to express the softer feelings of affection, caring, and sadness; happy taking more time to relax with people instead of working nonstop.

> Don't let life
> discourage you;
> everyone who got where he is
> had to begin where he was.
> —*Richard L. Evans*

Family, Career, or Both?

By the last decades of the twentieth century, the definition of family had changed dramatically. Many more people are living alone; most of these are men until older age when women, who are likely to be widowed, become the majority. As many as six out of ten children will live in single-parent households some time while growing up[29] and the great majority of small children will attend day care or nursery school. Only about half of American children live in the so-called traditional families consisting of only a mother, father, and full brothers and sisters.[30]

The number of marriages in 1993 was the smallest since 1979 and many more couples are living together without marrying.[31] Now called domestic partners, the adults who manage a household are unlikely to be a stay-at-home wife and a working husband. They may both be working and married with or without children or remarried with part-time children, or not married; they may be two single mothers trying to make ends meet; they

A MAN SPEAKS

I followed all the rules this culture of the mid-twentieth century laid down for a man to follow. Many choices, many moves, many promotions, many set-backs later I faced divorce and starting over. Funds needed to get a business going well were absorbed in the settlement. The business and I struggled on for two years, finding the drastic and unwanted change of lifestyle almost too much. A rest, a reassessment, a different career, a new marriage bring me into the present. I am in my fifties and already the promotion brings new duties that are stressful. Major family problems and worry about retirement bring new levels of confusion.

I feel that a man over fifty is supposed to know everything and be there for everyone to lean on. My "shoulds" include the dictum that a man cannot show emotion, a man cannot cry, a man cannot be weak. These are my unwritten laws. They were molded into the framework of this growing man-child from birth. To change them is sacrilegious—unheard of. A man has unwritten laws hanging over his head, yet he has to learn how to cry and show emotion. He has to learn to deal with his anger. And most of all, a man has to learn to say, "I really don't know everything about that subject." It is not easy being a man in a man's world that is being *invaded* (emphasis added) by women. The rules have changed. To survive, a man must change.

—Leo L. Pavlovich

may be gay or lesbian partners. They are likely to have far fewer children than couples in preceding generations. *The Futurist* predicted in 1990 that in the twenty-first century only 4 percent of families will consist of the stereo-typical breadwinner husband, homemaker wife, and two children.[32] Yet despite our impressions from the media, as of March, 1989, more than 93 percent of Americans were or had been married at least once, and 60 per-cent of divorced persons had remarried.[33]

In the 1970s, "women's liberation" brought women from kitchen to classroom, from bedroom to boardroom in record numbers. There was an underlying assumption that somehow women could "have it all," both fam-ily and career. But more frequent divorce brought many single mothers to the brink of poverty, desperation, and the realization that taking care of children alone and making ends meet was often a huge, dismal, and lonely struggle. And dazzled by two incomes, trend-setting, successful working couples found themselves on the "trend-mill" toward a frenetic and hard-edged kind of success.

The 1990s began with bewilderment and a struggle to regroup. Some women who had chosen to forgo family felt cheated and lonely; those who chose family felt left out, sometimes deserted by spouse, and lonely; those who chose both career and family felt stretched to the breaking point. And many successful women who had succumbed to the illusion of wealth and power had become oblivious to those left behind. Despite hopes to the contrary, "unfortunately, there is no evidence that the system has grown any more compassionate since women have become a part of it."[34]

Some younger women are questioning the superwoman myth that a woman can raise a family and move up into a high-paced, high-paying job at the same time. Anne-Marie Foisy-Grusonik opted out of the work world after struggling with career and family concerns for some years. She says, "Frequently, after telling others about my family and my career, they would respond, 'It sounds like you have the best of both worlds.' But in my heart I felt I had the worst of both worlds, and they were constantly at odds." Someone gave her a coffee mug that said, "'I am a working woman. I take care of a house. I hold down a job. I am nuts.'" And she responded, "I was!"[35] Women who try to be the perfect housewife/mother/career woman in a Supermom T-shirt may well wear themselves out physically and emotionally. Journalist and producer of NBC's *Sports Journal,* Hilary Cosell asks, "Can we really do everything our mothers did, and everything our fathers did as well?"[36]

Everyone has to resolve basic questions about family and career while attempting to achieve success. Family life fulfills some of the deepest longings of men and women. It fulfills needs and wants on many levels for physical, emotional, intellectual, and altruistic/spiritual support and growth. Families are those people who, theoretically, see a person through the ups and downs of life and are enduringly present in a special way.

But the questions men and women ask are still vastly different. Women wonder if and how they can combine a family with a career. Men, remaining career oriented, wonder if they need a family, especially one that might include a very liberated wife. And each couple with children has to achieve rough parity between "the dirt work and the glory" of raising a family.[37]

If the budget allows, full-time family and community involvement can also be enriching. In some cases the costs of working, such as transportation, clothing, lunches, fast-food meals, child care, and income taxes, can make staying at home a bargain. Creative homemaking, generous volunteering, and meeting with like-minded people can be interesting and stimulating for some women, and men, too. Sometimes people find that the items they must sacrifice by not working or working part time are not as important as they once seemed. Many parents discover that sacrificing things to be at home with young children is definitely a rewarding trade-off. And for the woman finished with childrearing, the empty nest may be a delight of peace and quiet after years of mothering.

Child Care

For working parents who have *not* finished childrearing, however, finding someone to care for their children while the parents work is a difficult and often emotional task. Throughout almost all of history, most children were taken care of at home by relatives. The family worked at or close to home, and children quickly became integrated into adult work roles. In redeveloping* countries today, very small children work right alongside adults, their presence welcomed. According to their ages, they do child care, carry heavy burdens, and weed the garden. Only where factories and offices develop and transportation systems expand do parents start working outside and far from the home, necessitating non-family child care and now elder care as older people live longer.

As a nation, we don't care for our children very well. Over the last decade the United States has fared badly on five out of eight measures of the well-being of children. These five were child poverty, juvenile violence, imprisonment, death, and teen pregnancy. Child mortality and child death rates did decrease sharply, and the percentage of teens graduating from high school increased slightly.[38]

If you are considering marriage and family, the questions of who takes care of the children and how when both parents work is a crucial question. The family-leave law provides up to twelve weeks of unpaid leave for specific family and medical needs.[39] Although the law also covers men, in reality it is still not as acceptable for men as it is for women to stay home with children. Men who take leave for child care have a great deal of explaining to do, not only about their lack of "real work" but also about their ability to care for children competently.[40]

Day care in the United States, which was widespread as well as federally and industrially funded during World War II, is now available mostly in private centers. An increasing number of companies provide child care, flexible or part-time work schedules, and some form of family leave for their employees to care for children and elders—but often reluctantly. Sometimes a close friend or relative is willing to care for the children, or a live-in baby-sitter will exchange services in return for room and board. Some parents arrange for child care through help-wanted ads in company, school, or church newsletters. Whatever arrangements are made, dropping children off

---

*We speak of so-called Third World or developing nations as if they had no history or culture. They once had viable though limited economies. Here we will sometimes speak of them as redeveloping countries as they move their economies into the twenty-first century.

in the morning and picking them up from the child care center or sitter adds yet another chore in the work race for working parents.

And it doesn't help a parent feel secure to learn that those who do traditional women's work—child- and elder-care providers, teachers, and social workers—are among the least respected and lowest-paid workers in the nation. They often earn wages that keep them below the poverty level, with poor or nonexistent benefits and few opportunities for advancement, in positions unable to attract people of high skill. Our society gives the family and children little real support. Add in the trauma of the days when a child is sick, or school closes because of storms or special holidays, or a grandparent needs care, and working parents may find themselves at a loss as to what to do.

Generally, good child care in clean and safe facilities with nutritious meals, growth-promoting activities, and a caring environment is expensive, and subsidized day care is hard to find. Some parents have solved the problem by joining or setting up a co-op to share child care, if their schedules allow it.

Parents' needs for leisure on weekends and holidays should also be considered. Single mothers often have few ways to get the respite they need and many must struggle without child support from the children's father.

The question is whether women should feel free to choose full-time work, full-time motherhood, or whatever combination meets their needs. Should men feel free to be househusbands? Who should provide child care? And will we accept and value the varying contributions each person makes, regardless of the roles he or she chooses?

The Nontraditional Household

Household size fell from 2.8 persons in 1980 to 2.6 in 1990.[41]

Many companies provide some support for traditional families, but because not every American worker is part of a traditional family—and in fact most are not—the diversity of households is beginning to be acknowledged in the workplace. Single men and women, both with and without children, extended families, and gay couples are all a part of the real workplace world and need support through the unique life stresses that they encounter.

Some of these workers feel that married couples are given breaks they would like also, such as time off for personal emergencies. A woman or man may forgo marriage and children, opting for the challenge of a full-time career, and then be expected to pick up the extra work pieces for married colleagues. The struggle to "make it" is greater for women than for men in what is still largely a man's world. For the unmarried, working woman as well as the married woman without children, ambivalence about career versus family can last for years and undermine a serious commitment to a career. And the longer women put off the decision to marry and/or have children, the greater are the chances that marriage and parenting will not happen.

In many settings, strong feelings against gays and lesbians have led to prejudice and even violence. In some states, laws or ordinances have been passed making it illegal for them to be hired, get housing, and in short, to be accepted anywhere in society. Many gays and lesbians generally agree that they would not have chosen their orientation if they had had a choice. In spite of growing evidence that alternative sexual preference is genetically determined, many people feel that such a choice is deliberate, and morally wrong. As in most cases of disagreement where emotions run high, neither side listens with understanding to the other. But the human needs of this group are as great as those of any other. They have always lived among us and many have made extraordinary contributions. Now they ask for the chance to do so openly without fear.

Teenagers and Young Adults

Teenagers who have done well in high school are usually confident and college bound—but they are not the majority. Numbers of their peers have not yet learned necessary survival skills or experienced many feelings of achievement. They lack both the job skills and the sophistication needed to find work in a tight job market. Their sagging self-image is not improved when they are rejected by prospective employers who have neither the time nor the budget to train raw recruits.

For many young people, approaching the first rung of the ladder is the most difficult step in the entire lifetime career process. Statistics show that the unemployment rate for young adults is much higher than the rate for the remainder of the population.

Geographical locations add special constraints for young people. In rural areas, the upward-bound teen may have problems finding adequate higher education and good jobs. Inner cities may provide little support or career and educational opportunities for the ghetto teen. Often the need in these communities is not only skills training and support for the young person, but also a new way of viewing the economy of the area so that education and employment for all the people who live there can be enhanced. When businesses serve the community by addressing the basic needs of its members and fulfilling wants that really enrich them, including the desire for and need of employment, the lives of all the residents improve.

Even when employment for teenagers is available there are differences of opinion on its effect. Some people feel that for students to work while they are in school can be a valuable as well as a profitable experience, as long as their grades don't suffer. Such opportunities can help inexperienced workers step up onto the first rung of the career ladder and gain badly needed work experience. An opposing view is that too much work adds to the stress of adolescence and may even lead some teenagers to substance abuse; others believe that the low pay is not worth the sacrifice of time. Working can adversely affect students' grades and it generally encourages teenagers to buy unnecessary consumer goods. The percentage of students who work may even contribute to our loss of educational and economic standing in the world community. Some part-time and summer work *can* give young people confidence and help them develop work skills, but the benefits may not outweigh the risks. Young people also need some time for social life and relaxation, time to explore and become involved in a variety of activities, if their financial situation will allow it.

For both teenagers and young adults, the first venture into the world of work will often demonstrate to them sharply the necessity of being computer literate, as few businesses of any type function today without the support of computers. Many young people will have been exposed to computers in school from the early grades on; others will have had less experience with them. Job seekers who are knowledgeable and at ease with computers will have a major advantage over those who are not.

In addition to helping students acquire computer skills, schools can make the transition to work easier in other ways. Recognizing students' need to begin work, some high schools and colleges offer work experience, career and exploration programs, and internships. In one innovative program, a volunteer management consultant with the National Executive Service Corporation, Lynwood McDaniel, recruited Bronx High School students for summer jobs in labor-short Cape Cod. There were many obstacles, but these students who had been labeled inferior at school, learned rapidly and well over the summer.[42] In similar programs, people in businesses are getting actively involved with young people and in some cases promising them college scholarships if they stay in school.

A National Job Corps for young people has finally gotten off the drawing boards. Supervised community service can get others started. Such work helps the environment and the community; develops young workers' skills, experience, and confidence; and allow them to earn money.

A special case involves older young people, overeducated and underemployed, who are still living at home in delayed adulthood. Those who did leave home may bounce back into their parents' lives, sometimes divorced and with children, just as their parents have begun to settle into a childless lifestyle or are caring for their own elderly parents.

In our increasingly complex and changing society, young adults worry more than they used to about succeeding. Many parents seem to push their children onto the fast track early in life. With so many young people living in families struggling with poverty, they also worry about surviving. As Josh Salmons, a twelve-year-old from Elbert, Colorado, explains: "What happened to the homeless might happen to you. You're worried that if you don't get a job right after college, you're going to be in trouble later on."[43] Visions of becoming rich and the struggle for riches may simply be a way to see one-self secure from societal problems.

But despite the obstacles in launching a satisfying career, taking that first step, however small, can be a rewarding experience at any age. Many people feel that this stage of life is successful if young people have completed as much education as they are capable of and have acquired a job using their education and skills. For those with appropriate skills, entry into the job market should be easier in future years because there will be many fewer young people in the job-market pipe line over the next decade.

The Aging

People born today may well be alive in 2090 or 3000,
since many more people will live into their 90s and to 100 and over.

As the U.S. family shrinks in size, the overall population is growing older. In 1950 one person in twelve was over sixty-five;[44] by the year 2000, the ratio will be one in seven.[45] The average life expectancy is now 78.9 years for white women and 72 for white men, with blacks trailing behind by seven years.[46] These statistics indicate that there will be larger numbers of aging women. As the baby boom generation ages and fewer couples opt for children, the number of elderly people could outnumber the young.

Opportunities for rewarding work become fewer for both men and women as they grow older, especially after age forty. Many workers stay at jobs they've outgrown rather than face possible rejection in applying for a more challenging position. It seems that our youth-oriented, throwaway culture sees little value in older people. In playwright Lillian Hellman's words, they have "the wisdom that comes with age that we can't make use of."[47]

One out of every six elderly women lives in poverty with an annual income of less than $5,600. Even if women have worked and paid the same percentage of their wages into Social Security as have men, they may receive less in benefits as the system still reflects the days of the male wage earner with a nonworking wife. Only one in five women has a pension; many have no health insurance as they reach retirement age and are without union membership or a record of continuous employment in the same company. Divorce also is harder for older women, especially those who were married to men with moderate to low incomes. Fewer than half of all women over sixty-five are married. Being female, single, divorced, or widowed as a "senior" is often a ticket to poverty.[48] This picture is not true of all elderly, however.

There are many myths about the financial well-being of the older American population. When noncash income such as Medicare payments are included, only about 3 percent of seniors qualify as poor compared with 9.8 percent of the general population. A great deal of the federal budget goes to "senior citizens," some of whom may be classified as nonneedy.[49] A 1981 report by the White House Conference on Aging shows that as a group, older Americans are the "wealthiest, best-fed, best-housed, healthiest, most self-reliant older population in our history."[50] This statement is small comfort to those living below the poverty line on meager fixed incomes.

The increasing presence of older people in society will change the face of the workplace in many ways as businesses arise to accommodate their needs. As this segment of the population grows, they will require medical and support services, adult education, travel arrangements, and all the other goods and services appropriate to older, and often more affluent, active people.

Minorities/Immigrants/Refugees: The "Other"

In today's world, we encounter people whose appearance, language, customs and culture, abilities, education, social and economic background, interests, values, and just plain style can seem worlds apart from our own. Their roles challenge some of our deepest beliefs as well as our smallest concerns. And there is no doubt that as the twenty-first century rolls on, the workplace will include an even greater variety of people. When Jesse Jackson was running for president in 1988, he told supporters, "Most people in the world are yellow, black, brown—they're poor, female, non-Christian, and young—and they don't speak English!"[51] In the year 2000, the twenty largest cities in the world will have one thing in common: none will be in Europe or the United States.[52]

West Valley College Counselor Veronese Anderson sees the white, affluent, successful male at the top of our society. At the lower income levels, minorities are represented in numbers far out of proportion to their presence in the general population. For many years, mainstream leaders in the United States have been white males who reserved the right to vote, own property, take out bank loans, start businesses, and work at the more prestigious jobs. People of color and "foreigners" were also excluded from many neighborhoods, churches, schools, and jobs. In nineteenth-century Philadelphia, immigrants in the Globe Mills hired women to spin and weave at $2.62 per *week*. Today legal immigrant laborers make minimum wage (if they are lucky). Often, because they must work part time, they earn no benefits and must work extra hours or two jobs to make ends meet, often working *thirteen-hour days*. Even so, many are barely able to pay the rent.[53] Affirmative action programs attempted to level the playing field. Now some people feel that these laws have done their work and wish to get rid of them.

Because of past and present discrimination, many minorities get "stuck" in ghettos where the housing, education, and job opportunities are poor, adding to the struggle young people face in taking on adult responsibilities. Many are unable to begin careers because opportunities are limited or withheld, or because their basic skills are weak. Minorities have higher rates of unemployment and lower pay than majority whites. "The gap between blacks—by far the largest U.S. minority—and whites in everything from job opportunities to education continues to be wide. Overt racism is still a major hurdle."[54] The Urban Institute, a Washington, D.C., research organization, conducted experiments called employment audits in which carefully matched job applicants from targeted ethnic groups were sent to apply for advertised openings. The results showed that white, non-Hispanic applicants were typically three times more likely to receive favorable treatment during the application process than either African Americans or Hispanics.[55]

Another minority, Native Americans have suffered extraordinary discrimination over the years and in some parts of the United States are virtually invisible. Victims of a holocaust that most Americans would rather forget, many have been left out of the most important aspects of American life. Where their culture is visible, it is often trivialized; they rarely make the statistics. While they may have employment preference under U.S. law, they still have not been able to move into the mainstream to any extent. In some places native leaders are working to bring about respect for all cultures by hosting Indian markets, fairs, and peace and arts festivals that welcome and include everyone.[56]

Many minorities seldom have a chance to observe adult role models in successful positions because those who move up often move away. The young are left to find themselves, often in a hostile environment, cut off from the mainstream; hence, their expectations remain low. They watch others make decisions that affect them and find that it is these others and not themselves who get the lion's share of affluence. Minorities are just becoming visible in decision-making roles. While many of those who have moved into the mainstream find their careers blocked, over-all, minority women and men are slowly increasing their numbers in better paying jobs and positions of prestige.

Immigrants and refugees face added burdens. Never before in history have so many people migrated in fear and suffering during such a short period of time as these past decades. These migrations have been due in part, according to former President Jimmy Carter, "to the failure on the part of the world to live by principles of peace and human rights."[57] While people from stable countries may choose to emigrate for purely personal reasons, political persecution, war, economic collapse, and environmental devastation impel many to flee their countries unwillingly just to survive.

If the career search is demanding for everyone, imagine the added stress of coping with a new language in a new culture—and worrying about family, friends, and home left behind. Many immigrants feel caught in a bewildering whirl of low-status jobs, a mismatched work ethic, an ambiguous dress-for-success code, and a U.S. brand of go-for-it assertiveness.

The immigrant's first and most important task is to learn the language of the host country. While English-as-a-Second Language (ESL) classes help young people attending school and adults able to attend classes at community centers, many older people and those with family demands who work long hours often cannot go. People who feel unable to communicate are tempted to withdraw; some have never had any education. In the long run, this isolation is usually self-defeating although understandable. The younger the person, the more likely it is that he or she will learn English quickly; children often become translators for their parents. Additionally, women from many foreign cultures have to overcome years of economic, political, and social inequality.

Every group that has traditionally been out of the mainstream or that comes to a new country finds itself meeting attitudes based on stereotypes. Americans meet newcomers with emotions ranging from compassion and understanding, to resentment to ridicule to hatred. With their behaviors taking on larger-than-life-significance, immigrants are often labeled with negative—and sometimes contradictory—traits. We hear that they take away jobs from Americans; they refuse to work and go on welfare! They are lazy, aggressive, cowardly, violent, dirty, stupid, cunning, criminal . . . But can anyone say that they or their children haven't had days when they seemed to be some or all of the above? People are surprised when they find that individuals they get to know do not fulfill the stereotypes. We tend to forget that all our ancestors were either Native American or "boat people."

	Household Incomes 1992	Percent in Poverty
Asians/Pacific Isles	$38,153	12.5
White	$32,368	11.6
Non-Hispanic White	$33,388	9.6
Hispanics	$22,848	29.3
Blacks	$18,660	33.3[58]

As the pool of labor shrinks, minorities with some skills will have a better chance of finding satisfying work. And as each group settles in, more members find good opportunities. Hispanic-owned businesses, for example, have shown a healthy increase in recent years.[59] And many are entering untypical professions. Single mother Loretta Gallegos Mares earned her high school diploma after a head-on car collision left her in a half-body cast. By age twenty-six she was the president of a computer-consulting firm in that male-dominated world, and was slated to earn her first million dollars in revenues.[60]

The Disabled and Their Abilities

A humorous article by Adair Lara says that like the movie hero Forrest Gump, most people know how to do some things very well, and in the rest of life "kind of fake it."[61] While everyone has some limitations, people whose disabilities are more visible have been assumed to be incapable of doing *anything*. A silent minority, they were expected to stay in their place, a place of low expectations. They often struggled with poor self-images and feelings of inadequacy about making any contribution to society.

Society is finally recognizing that among people with unusual limitations there is a vast pool of valuable and important skills. These individuals now have more access to government, business, industry, education, and all phases of life. The Americans with Disabilities Act of 1992 made it illegal to discriminate in employing against anyone who has the skills, experience, education, and other requirements and can do the essential functions of the job with or without reasonable accommodations by the employer.[62] Old technologies like glasses have helped many people overcome the limitation of poor eyesight. And now high technology is bringing even greater wonders such as talking/braille computers for the visually impaired and robots to assist with physical tasks. But the best help has been the change in attitudes as people become more comfortable with the differences of others.

New Themes, Changing Attitudes

Everyone wants an enriched, successful, and balanced life with a chance to be successful in the community and to have a loving support system among family and friends. Perhaps most Americans agree, in theory if not in practice, that no one should be denied self-fulfillment because of sex, creed, color, nationality, disability, or age. The world needs to draw on the rich cultural diversity of all its people. Although discrimination still exists, there is growing evidence that despite well-publicized hate crimes and episodes of tension, racial harmony is growing.[63] Affirmative action, a changing population mix, and a realization that everyone, regardless of roles, can make a positive contribution, have brought a variety of people to visible positions in the workplace. Not only will you work with a greater variety of people, but you will be supplying goods or services to an increasingly diverse population with new and different ways of supplying their needs and wants. As trite as it sounds, no two people *are* alike. Yet beneath the surface qualities, each person has the same basic needs, the same yearnings. Seeing this diversity in terms of the roles people play without stereotyping can help you find common ground and smooth your work/life relationships as well as help you choose your own roles and behaviors wisely.

Changing Lifestyles

People are choosing more—and being more accepting of—diverse lifestyles. Women and minorities are more visible and willing to accept power and responsibility in the workplace. Women now represent more than half the work force in nearly a dozen industries, including the fast-growing health services, banking, legal services, insurance, and retail trade. Though in small numbers, women work in many jobs formerly held only by men. They are firefighters, pilots and navigators, crane and tower operators, professional athletes, police and detectives, fishers, auto mechanics, carpenters, electricians, plumbers, miners, fighting soldiers, and big rig drivers. Many women have moved into managerial and professional specialty occupations and overall their wages are becoming comparable to those of men. The largest business magazine in the country, ahead of *Business Week, Fortune,* and *Forbes* touts these successes: Its name? *Working Woman!* More women (67 percent) than men (58 percent) are going to college and they earn 54 percent of bachelor's degrees; they make up 59 percent of those in master's degree programs.[64] In any case, education increases the amount of money that both men and women earn.

In *The Second Stage,* Betty Friedan admits that one failure of the women's movement of the 1970s was a blind spot about the family, and she urged a revitalization and sharing of the traditional role of nurturer.[65] Dual-career couples are planning their career decisions together so that the needs for satisfying work of both are met, and childrearing is fitted into the picture, too. Career does not always take first priority. Many more men *are* taking parenting and household care more seriously as male roles are reevaluated. And now these men as well as women are experiencing first-hand the fact that, although difficult, raising children *does* have its rewards.

Many writers, like Marilyn Ferguson, applaud the emergence of what is called the "feminine principle" in society. Some say that such changes from dominance to nurturance will make possible the survival of the race and and even of the planet. Men are beginning to see that operating behind a shield of power is sometimes cowardly. Author Mark Gerzon says that men need new heroes;[66] they need to be liberated from old stereotypes. They are learning that "dis-illusionment" means seeing more clearly. Men are learning to provide nurturance for themselves as well as for children; they are breaking out of old patterns, going back to school, changing jobs more readily, start-

ing new careers and businesses, retiring earlier, and opting for more leisure time when possible. And women are sharing the financial burdens of the family. We see a slowing of the divorce rate and more parents taking time away from work for child care.

As men, who have had quite rigid and traditional workstyles, face these issues and *grow* through their crises, some develop a new, deeper, more mature outlook that restores their energy and vitality. Some are surprised to learn that they need better skills in human relations and communications instead of a new job or a new kind of work. The need to let go of the past to come closer to the real meaning of life is a common human experience. Not feeling that you should "have it all together," knowing that everyone needs support at difficult times, can be liberating.

The new corporate climate often requires more flexibility and teamwork. A study by Professor Judith B. Rosener of University of California, Irvine, reports that "decision-making in the international business arena needs to become decentralized and done at lower levels; women leaders who have a good share of the so-called feminine traits (though not all do) tend to share knowledge, power, and responsibility, and this may turn out to be a necessity in the new global economy." Contrary to the popular belief that women at the top earn less than men, she found that top executive women earn an average of $140,000, about the same salaries as men, who earn an average of $136,000. Sixty-eight percent of the women she studied were married.[67]

Opportunities for moving in and up in a large company may shrink, but many "seasoned citizens" begin successful small businesses, volunteer in satisfying activities, and stay active for many years. A national council reports that although they remain unemployed longer when seeking work, older men and women hunt harder for jobs, hold a job longer with less absenteeism, perform as well or better than younger people, and are more reliable and more willing to learn. One study showed that employee theft was much lower when companies hired retirees.[68] Older people are providing positive role models as they plow new ground in employment. Many are effectively handling retirement, finances, leisure, health care, increased longevity, loneliness, loss of independence, inflation, and productive involvement.

Employers are hiring older people in entry-level service jobs as the teen population diminishes. People don't lose ability and experience on the eve of their sixty-fifth or seventieth birthday any more than they grow up instantly at age twenty-one. And with a declining employee pool, older people will continue to find opportunities for satisfying employment. Elders are returning to school not only for enrichment but to learn new skills. It's a memorable experience to see a seventy-two-year-old grandmother receive a degree, cheered on by a group of balloon-waving grandchildren. A sixty-five-year-old who received her M.A. in psychonutrition (a self-designed major focused on the effect of nutrition on psychological well-being) was able to support herself by giving seminars and workshops.

Minorities also are moving up, becoming more visible in every area of life. The disabled are "mainstreaming" themselves by wheeling and whizzing and signing out of isolation and assertively speaking up about their needs. More than ever they feel a sense of energy and ability to change their lives.

For many, a transition time can be healing, a time for growth; a time to reorder priorities, build confidence, face areas of deficiency, and develop neglected segments of life, to befriend oneself by putting one's world into perspective; a time to ask, "What do I really want out of life?" An effective response to life requires flexible choices and behaviors appropriate to the situation.

Communicating through Adversity and Diversity

Although stressful situations and different backgrounds can add up to mighty misunderstandings, people are learning better techniques of communication. With one couple, for example, each reminds the other that there is a problem to solve and that anger is getting in the way. They recommend cooling-off periods. Two key elements of effective communications are these: *Take responsibility for your feelings. Change yourself, not others.* Listening, understanding, and accepting oneself and others signifies a growing person. The effort can bring a rewarding closeness.

Careful communication becomes ever more important in a workplace where workers of varied backgrounds must find common ground. Success in life comes best to those who are able to understand themselves in relationship to others and state their needs, feelings, beliefs, and expectations clearly and comfortably, without denying the needs, feelings, beliefs, and expectations of others—a definite plus in finding and improving a career. Communication courses can help sharpen interpersonal skills. With practice, these skills can be acquired by everyone. As people become more self-actualized, they replace acting out of anger or fear with *assertiveness,* a quality that makes communication much more effective and life much more enjoyable.

Assertive people are clear, direct, accepting, and open about feelings, with just the right amount of common sense. Acting with confidence, they feel they can stand shoulder to shoulder with anyone, that they are neither inferior nor superior to others. They are persistent, cooperative, and self-motivated. They are willing to negotiate and cooperate. Spontaneous, honest, strong, and buoyant, these humane humans of good humor are usually respected and accepted by others.

You might have moments when you feel timid or tough, when you under- or over-react. Getting to the reality of what you are feeling and what your motivations are takes time and thought. Suppose you feel angry at a meeting when someone speaks intelligently, expressing *your* idea that you couldn't put into words. Your anger may mask hurt. Your hurt may mask feelings of inferiority and insecurity, which in turn mask a profound fear of not being esteemed by others. If you learned to recognize the truth, you might say, "I really feel unesteemed when other people say things more clearly than I could." This statement puts you in touch with an absurdity and helps you to become aware of your esteem needs. You may then find ways to meet those needs. You may incidentally become aware that you seldom, if ever, compliment or grant esteem to others.

You can enhance relationships by sharing feelings with others when appropriate, in an honest and caring way, and by taking responsibility for those feelings without denial, without letting them overpower but rather strengthen you. Because feelings can so often get in the way of effective action, it is worth the effort to learn to change them. You have a choice. *You can actually select your feelings!* And that means that you can learn to select confidence over fear, compassion over anger. You can choose from a wide range of behaviors that will make you more effective and happier.

New Paradigms

Marilyn Ferguson speaks of a conspiracy of people beginning to "take charge of their lives," to make changes that deal with the transformation of the person and that could ultimately change society. Some of the changes she predicts could be described as becoming self-actualizing.[69]

Jean Houston's exciting brain/mind research asks, "What is the possible human?" and shows that we are on the verge of a giant step toward new forms of consciousness and fulfillment. She affirms that our human systems are vastly superior to anything technology could invent; we have only begun to plumb the depths of our inner selves. We may be reaching a "golden age of body/mind control that challenges us to a new humanity."[70] It's a time, then, for all of us to make thoughtful decisions about what we wish to be and what roles we want to play. Growing as a person means changing, adjusting to both inner and outer reality. It means expanding into new and exciting areas of life. Stereotypes about how we *should be* hold us back from becoming fully what we *could be.* That doesn't imply that change is simple and easy but rather that it is possible for people who are open-minded and open-hearted.

As we shall see, many people are beginning to take charge not only of their own lives but also of their local communities and economies as well. No longer waiting for business or industry or government to "bail them out," they are starting everything from banks to cooperative housing and neighborhood protection patrols.

It seems that in our society we have come to a time of decision about how we want to be. More aware of our fragile environment, our energy shortage, our waste of resources, we know that we can't have it all. It can be a good time for us if we act wisely, giving all of us a chance to develop more balanced lives and to free ourselves from stereotypes. To paraphrase Elizabeth Cady Stanton, "the true person is as yet a dream of the future."[71] Let's hope that that future is not too distant.

 ## Self-Assessment Exercises

The following exercises are designed to start you thinking about roles and considering their effects on successful life and work.

1. Thinking about Your Roles

a. List five roles that you play in life.

    1. _____   2. _____   3. _____   4. _____   5. _____

b. Do you live your roles as you choose or as others expect you to? Explain.

_____

_____

_____

2. The Timid/Tough Spectrum: Stereotypes

a. Do you tend to be more passive, aggressive, or assertive? Tell how.

_____

b. Write out a sincere compliment that you feel afraid to tell someone. Set a time when you will deliver it in person verbally. Describe how it felt to do this and how the other person reacted. Continue to practice positive assertiveness until you feel ready to deliver constructive criticism in a non-threatening way.

_____

_____

c. Briefly describe someone you know who fits each of the following types: a. the traditional, stereotypical female; b. a women who is the opposite; c. the traditional stereotypical male; d. a man who is the opposite.

_____

_____

3. Identifying Major Components of Your Life

a. Rank these components of your life in order of importance to you.

_____ Career   _____ Ethnic/national ties

_____ Marriage   _____ Religion/spiritual development

_____ Family   _____ Leisure

_____ Education   _____ What else?

b. Do the significant people in your life agree with your ranking?

Yes _____   No_____.   If no, explain: _____

c. What problems do you see in fitting each of these components into your life? Into the life of those around you?

_____

_____

_____

4. Planning For the Future

Describe the image of the successful you in terms of the roles you would like to play.

_____

_____

Group Discussion Questions

1. Describe a society where gender distinctions are still quite clearly marked. How do the expectations for men and for women differ? Do some of these expectations still exist in the United States? Besides obvious anatomical differences, are there real gender differences between men and women?

2. As a male, do you find it difficult to believe that women have been/are discriminated against? Explain. Have you observed sexual harrassment against any woman? Do you personally feel any dilemmas about your role as a male?

3. As a female, do you feel discriminated against? How? Do you feel that you have been the victim of sexual harrassment? Do you personally feel any dilemmas about your role in society as a female? How?

4. Describe yourself as an aging person facing retirement. How would you like retirement to be for you?

5. Gather information from an older family member about your ethnic background. Find out when your ancestors came to the United States and what the experience was like for them. Share the information with your group.

6. Is the American Dream for you? Explain.

7. Name two successful people that you admire. Tell why. Did the various roles they play influence your choices? How?

8. Do you feel that affirmative action programs have been successful enough that we no longer need them? Why?

9. Communications
   a. What problems do you have in communicating?
   b. What steps can you take to solve them?
   c. Share a positive, then a negative feeling with the group.

10. Discuss in class or write your answers to the following questions on a separate sheet of paper:
    a. What have you learned from this chapter?
    b. What stereotypes and prejudices would you like to change in yourself and in society?

5/

Work

Challenges, Options, and Opportunities

 FOCUS

- Reflect on the meaning of work.
- Explore societal challenges and options for the twenty-first century.
- Relate personality types to job market opportunities.

You have looked at some of the personal issues that will affect not only your career and your individual life but also your life in the context of a very diverse society. Before moving on to the great decision, wise career searchers will acquire a broader, deeper understanding of work in the global village of the twenty-first century. In this chapter you will explore some of the many positive and hopeful options and opportunities that exist in the context of work in response to societal challenges in three key areas: economics, environment, and ethics. You will look at ways in which people with your personality type can relate wisely to the job market in this fast-paced, fast-changing world as it rushes into the twenty-first century.

You'll also understand that the nontraditional/creative careers and lifestyles of today will be commonplace tomorrow. You will know that the functions of work do not change—only the content and the tools. You'll see the need to develop the skills necessary for living in this new world: flexibility, creativity, and the ability to learn, grow, and use information wisely. You'll see that the career you choose will fit in many workplaces and many jobs, both old and new. You'll also understand the need for a set of enduring values that will enable you to maintain a broad sense of direction without being swept away by trends or fads.

> The trouble with the future
> is that it arrives before we're ready for it.
> —*Andy Capp*

Charting the Future: Global 2000

Today we stand at the edge not only of a new century but also a new millennium. Turmoil and change seem to accelerate. We feel that an era as well as a millennium is ending and the new one can't seem to come into focus. And here you are, making a career decision and facing the job market at possibly the most uncertain time in history.

The speed of change is captured by John Peers, who has said, "We live three days in a day compared to the 1950s. We do in one day what couldn't be done in a week in 1900, in a lifetime in the 1600s."[1] Products can now be envisioned and drawn by computer. Overnight they can be turned into three-dimensional plastic prototypes. "Time-saving" devices fill a world where no one seems to have any of the time that was saved.

In our rush to the future, we have disrupted communities; used down centuries-old resources; polluted once-pristine air, water, and earth; and littered the world with our castoffs. Renowned "world watchers" Lester R. Brown, Christopher Flavin, and Sandra Postel write in "A Planet in Jeopardy" that we are as slow coming to grips with the potential disaster in earth functions as passengers on the Titanic. They feel that our real successes have been few and that we are destroying our very life-support systems.[2]

Jeremy Rifkin suggests as a motto for the twenty-first century, "Slow is beautiful."[3] It seems that we need to slow down and reflect very seriously, positively, and creatively on the future and how life and work choices can contribute in a positive way to that great adventure called life. If we rush to get ahead without clarifying our direction, we may be rushing behind!

> Nothing kills creativity like dread;
> nothing fosters it like delight.

A Global/Philosophic View of Work

An easy and uncomplicated definition of work might say that it is any activity that provides useful goods and services to others while providing some reward for the worker. But work is much more. For example, it can be rewarding, exciting, fulfilling, exasperating, exhausting, and dreadful—sometimes all at once. Work is often hard work!

Until relatively recently in human history, communities were largely self-sufficient. Labor was often brutally hard and controlled by tradition. The technical/industrial revolution changed all that. In democracies in this century, and in the United States in particular, the work and life choices have multiplied beyond anything our elders dreamed of. The "good life" became a reality for countless numbers of people.

But work still involves those activities that provide goods and services for people and, in reverse, it provides the means for workers to satisfy their needs and wants. What we think we need or want, or what we have been persuaded to think we need or want, decides what work will get done. Although the work world has become highly complex, the questions are the same as they were in 5000 B.C.: How much work must I do to fulfill my unique set of needs and wants? How will my work affect others? Work impacts not only your own life but the planet as well.

The Work Panorama

Day and night the world hums with the sounds of people and machines making goods and providing services for one another. Mines and forests, oceans and fields yield raw substances to make mountains of *things*. Wood and metal, coal and cotton, giant and motley masses of materials are baled and baked, pounded and pummeled, mixed and milled, cut and checked, piled and packed for delivery to the world. Trucks and trains, ships and planes move endlessly, huffing and hauling it all to factories and farms, stores, and homes. Things! They are bought, sold, used, recycled, worn out, and finally discarded to become heaps of debris—some of it to return to the earth, some of it to pollute and plague us.

Transactions, interactions, communications, deals, those intangible "services rendered," mingle with the flow of goods: orders are taken; food served; children taught; cases tried; patients treated. Many services that used to be done with modest training and common sense, now require more and more education and a continuous supply of information. For example, fire-fighters no longer just chop holes in buildings and pour water on fires. They have became explosives and toxics experts, bomb defusers, and structural engineers. They get degrees in fire science, chemistry, engineering, and human relations.

We are all becoming *information* mills. We create it, collect it, evaluate it, manipulate it, control it, and pass it on to the twenty-four-hour-a-day world. Circuits hum, screens glow, faxes drone, copiers blink, computers talk to computers, and digitized videos mix media. Vast webs of information "technet" around the world at the stroke of a key. New words come on line by the minute. We boot up, down-link, and scan our e-mail. We call all of this *work!*

Information that used to come every month now comes every day and the piles grow. People feel pushed to make decisions quickly and may some-times avoid them altogether. There is little time to do the reflection needed to consider all the angles. And sometimes it seems that the more information we have available, the less we know. According to youth advocate H. Stephen Glenn, "The world's information is doubling every twenty-two months today compared to 1940 when information only doubled every five-hundred years."[4]

Information is like a child's riddle: it's not only renewable but expand-able; it's never scarce, uses few resources, and takes little energy to produce; it can be kept while being given away. It has changed the way we live and work in ways we have barely begun to understand.

A century ago most jobs were visible. Forty percent of the work force were farmers; now less than 2 percent fit that classification.[5] Many other jobs were in construction, forestry, mining, and manufacturing. Today less than one-fifth of U.S. workers are employed in such industries.[6] Work became a mysterious shuffling of papers and now is also an even more mys-terious shuffling of electronic dots. The silicon chip is king, computers reign, and robots rule.

The service sector accounts for over four-fifths of workers and includes federal/state/local government, education, health services, law, entertain-ment/the arts, and repair services as well as wholesale/retail trade,

finance/banking, insurance, real estate, management, and marketing. It continues to grow rapidly.

Many new jobs are automated, low skill, and low paying. Priscilla Enriquez of the Food Institute feels that there is an unnecessary trend toward "downgrading of work." With automation, fast-food clerks, for example, hardly need to know any math or even how to read."[7] In a humorous vein, a University of Miami aeronautics professor described the aircraft of the year 2010 to the International Airline Pilots Association: "The crew will consist of one pilot and one dog. The pilot's job will be to nurture, care for, and feed the dog. The dog's job will be to bite the pilot if he tries to touch anything."[8]

Henry Ford once asked Walter Reuther of the United Auto Workers Union, "What are you going to do with your union when all of your men are replaced by robots?" Reuther answered: "Who are you going to sell your cars to, if nobody's working?"[9] Someone once suggested letting workers buy a share in the robots that replaced them and then collect the robot's pay!

> Work is the way that we tend the world,
> the way people connect.
> It is the most vigorous, vivid sign of life—
> in individuals and civilization.
> —*Lance Morrow*

Societal Perspectives: Challenges and Options

As a career seeker, you are told to find a need and fill it. Finding the needs is the easy part. The media are filled with overwhelming problems. But seeing these problems as *challenges* can be invigorating, especially when we begin to see that there are innumerable, real, hopeful, *and* socially responsible *options* for every challenge, not just *a* solution to *a* problem.

How do you fit yourself and your values into a world crowded with challenges and overflowing with options? The best way is to be true to yourself, know your strengths, accept your limits, and find those challenges, options, and opportunities that "charge you up." You will then make choices that will connect you with others like yourself. These people are likely to hire you, or do business with you, or start a business with you. Your wise choices and good example will definitely put you on the side of positive change. You can choose to be an artist or a zoologist and do it responsibly.

Here are ten major challenges that face us as we move into a new millennium. They center around economics, environment, and ethics, all challenges connected to work and lifestyle choices. The hopeful options that follow are only the tip of the iceberg of thousands of socially responsible activities being developed and actually being done as paid work around the globe. They are charting courses into the future job market, are certain to grow, and are designed to make the world a better place. As you read about the challenges of today's work world, think about your values and your job satisfiers. Ask yourself, "Where do I feel comfortable?"

Economic Challenges

As the twenty-first century comes into view, we find dramatic economic challenges facing us, but the major concern is the flow of money. In 1991 the richest fifth of the world's population had sixty-one times the wealth of the poor compared to thirty times in 1960. It is estimated that 84 percent of world trade wealth flows to the richest fifth of the world's population while less than 1 percent goes to the poorest.[10] In the United States the middle class seems to be shrinking as the ranks of the poor increase.

Although there are many things that money cannot buy—true friendship and love, good health, a sunrise on a pristine spring day—having enough money is essential. More and more people are using their time, energy, and talents to find careers in business or industry that promote a vital local community. Founder of the Institute for Community Economics, Chuck Matthei, writes:

There is nothing more personal than economics. It is, fundamentally, a moral and spiritual field, in a sense, the outward manifestation of our

Richest

Poorest

Each horizontal band
represents an equal fifth
of the world's people.

World Population Arranged by Income
Between 1960 and 1990, the richest 20 percent of the world's population increased
its share of world income from thirty times greater than the poorest to sixty times
greater. SOURCE: *United Nations Development Programme, Human Development Report
(New York: Oxford University Press, 1992).*

spiritual relationship, our moral and social relationships with one another.
If we look at how we respond to others economically, we will also find
out, despite our illusions and pretensions, how we really do regard one
another.[11]

Challenge 1: The Science/Tech Connection   Work, in the economies of the
industrialized nations, is tightly connected to the dramatic science/technolog-
ical explosion of the twentieth century. As this partnership between science
and technology creates marvels, it creates monsters as well. It saves us from
disease, it creates disease; it creates jobs, it eliminates jobs; it saves us from
tedious and boring work, it generates work that is tedious and boring; it
makes wealth and leaves many people in poverty; it preserves life, it destroys
life; it both cleans and pollutes; it saves time and consumes time; it discovers
new information, but often little wisdom. Science and technology seem to
proliferate almost on their own and we wonder who is in charge; even people who work with them all the time do not fully understand them; yet we
wait breathlessly to speed down the information superhighway.

José Ortega y Gassett wrote in *The Revolt of the Masses*, "Modern
man is becoming more primitive. He understands as little about the technology that serves him as primitive people understood about lightning and
air."[12] People feel that technology is creating a separate world—separated
from nature, separated from real life. And the push for profits, power, and
prestige has grown apace. No other species has been able to outwit nature

like the human being, but it seems as if nature is getting stretched to the limit. It may seem as though we have no choice except to continue on this path, but we *do*.

Taming Science and Technology for Human Need   Scientific and technological breakthroughs, many originating in the United States, have given us improved health, longer life, warmer homes, better clothes, marvels of transportation and communication, and innumerable "leisure-creating gadgets." There *is* greater consciousness of the need for pure water and other resources; for conservation and development; for industrial and transportation systems that pollute less, use less energy, and run on renewable energy; for healthy, vigorous soil and environmentally friendly food production; for biodegradable products and packaging; for hazardous waste cleanup; for shelter and clothing made of alternative and/or recycled materials.

Designer Buckminster Fuller realized very early that we are the first generation to be aware that we are affecting the universe with our every act. He was able to wed science and technology in practical, positive ways. He said that by the early 1970s we had the capability to produce and sustain, within ten years' time, a higher standard of living for all humanity than could be imagined earlier. We can learn how to do more using fewer resources and already existing technologies. Fuller carried out his dreams. He invented the energy-efficient geodesic dome along with a whole host of marvelous creations.[13] There is no doubt that science and technology with its many careers will play a major role in work in the coming century.

> The concerns for man and his destiny must always be
> the chief interest of all technical efforts.
> Never forget this among your diagrams and equations.
> —*Albert Einstein*[14]

Challenge 2: Industry and Business   The business of industry is the production of goods. The business of business is facilitating the movement of goods and services from manufacturer to entrepreneur to consumer. Jobs in industry and business make up a major part of the work world. In the twentieth century, America, built on science and technology, and driven by the vision of economic gain, became the world leader in industry and business. The American automobile, mass-produced by union labor on assembly lines, symbolized a dream of universal affluence. Today, people in the industrial/technical world are part of a global economic network that exchanges goods and services worldwide at a rapid pace.

We read that the largest single force in the world is multinational corporations with their networks of businesses, sometimes grown inflexible, often unregulated by any laws. People have begun to be suspicious of them—their perceived power to sway the political process; their impersonal quality, sometimes acting without regard for the well-being of their workers and their communities. Their use of the resources and labor of so many redeveloping countries, coupled with huge loans made to these countries by wealthier nations, have left the economies of the poorer states devastated.

Now, with some exceptions, nations do not invade other nations to build empires; instead they try to forge trade alliances. The new empires are economic. According to economics instructor Alan London, few well-known American corporations now remain "American," as companies such as Ford, Colgate-Palmolive, IBM, and Gillette conduct over 50 percent of their business overseas.[15]

Companies have struggled to remain "competitive" in the global economy. They have "downsized" with mixed results. Some businesses have seen that the loss of highly skilled people and the drop in employee morale have cut productivity and even damaged the corporate structure.[16] Even so, many businesses say that they will continue to downsize regularly and that additional jobs will be cut.[17] But the takeovers and makeovers have damaged millions of workers' lives.

Some people urge all sorts of questionable activities with the excuse that we must remain "competitive in today's market." And recent news articles tell us that we have regained our competitive edge in technology.[18] But Secretary of Labor Robert B. Reich asks, "What do we mean by 'competitiveness' anyway? Rarely has a term of public discourse gone so directly from obscurity to meaninglessness without any intervening period of coherence. Surely the ultimate test of competitiveness should be the standard of living of Americans." He urges a "new social contract between business, government, and citizens" that will help people survive downsizing, reengineering, and global competition.[19]

Many companies begin without real thought of their long-range effects on people and planet. Howell Hurst, principal of Strategic Asset Management in San Francisco, says, "To my mind, [they] . . . divert precious resources from the true needs of this country. . . . We face a multitude of social problems that cry out for creative business solutions . . . pollution that can be found in virtually every community. . . . homeless people who need training and jobs . . . many people who have yet to be integrated into our economic system. The industrial infrastructure is in desperate need of revitalization. The commercial waste will choke us if we don't figure out a way to recycle it. *I am interested in new businesses built on innovative concepts that contribute to the improvement of our society.*"[20]

Helena Norberg-Hodge, director of the International Society for Ecology and Culture, said that often "the emphasis has been on giving things up and making do with less, rather than recognizing how much we stand to gain. We forget that the price of never-ending economic growth and material prosperity has been spiritual and social impoverishment, psychological insecurity, and the loss of cultural vitality."[21]

Options: Restructuring/Refocusing A growing number of businesses are beginning to see that they can build a decent, affordable, vibrant society as well as make money. General Motors signed the CERES Principles, a corporate environmental code. Imagine a flexible workplace filled with workers looked on as and feeling like integral members of a team; with production line people, often highly educated, who are allowed access to the financial reports (open book management); for whom innovation, quality, and service are of utmost importance; who are proud of their workplace! And as Paul Hawken adds, human qualities will be even more important. Success will come to those able to provide outstanding goods and services. Ingenuity, intelligence, and craft will be essential, but so will consideration and compassion. In a high-tech society the premium on attributes like courtesy and friendliness will be great.[22] There are numerous examples of companies that provide honest, reliable, environmentally benign, appropriately priced, useful, and enriching goods and services.

Robert Rodale has trained groups of people to help regenerate towns that are in danger of economic failure. By working with the forces of nature instead of trying to overcome them, restoring nature instead of destroying it, and avoiding centralization and monopolization, a regenerated community uses local renewable resources and energy sources so that they do not need to be transported from far away. Cleaner, healthier, prosperous networks of caring neighborhoods develop. The arts as well as businesses flourish. The local economy becomes both self-generating and self-improving; the worker base is kept intact, and people's health and welfare count more than monetary wealth as a measure of success.[23] When companies do have to close, they search for new owners or help workers buy out the company or retrain for new jobs.

Raising capital to begin and continue a business is crucial. Some lenders are discovering that they can do well while doing good.[24] An ancient system was revitalized in recent years in one of the the poorest countries on earth: Bangladesh. Called the Grameen (or Village) Bank, it now has close to 1,000 branches and over $400 million on loan to over a million borrowers and has become a model for "micro-loan" lending all over the world. Borrowers, mostly very poor, are organized into circles of five who meet for orientation and planning. The group makes loan decisions, monitors and applies peer pressure for repayments, and supports its members.[25]

Using that model and determined to keep a bank open in a ghetto area, investors led by Ronald Grzywinski bought failing South Shore Bank in

Chicago. They found that people living in decent, affordable housing are a key ingredient in creating a vigorous business atmosphere. Their nonprofit housing corporation has assisted residents to rehabilitate a 265-square-block ghetto area, helping many residents to become first-time homeowners. Loan default rates run about 2 percent even though 60 percent of the community's households earn less than $25,000 a year.[26] South Shore Bank has gathered awards for its diverse workplace. Since 1973 its staff has financed over 8,000 multifamily units, placed 3,500 persons into jobs from its employment-training programs, and assisted over 156 new firms.[27]

The range of such economic institutions is from successful cooperative businesses in the poor Basque section of Spain to the Women's World Bank (WWB), started for poor women who have never had access to credit;[28] to Trickle Up (TUP) for low-income people in eighty-six countries worldwide;[29] to the nonprofit Institute for Community Economics in Springfield, Massachusetts. These groups were begun "to assist those who most need capital [sometimes loaned without interest], to engage those who have capital, to encourage and challenge by example, those who manage capital." They have grown dramatically with positive results.[30] U.S. banks and the World Bank are taking note and beginning to include similar projects for the very poor in their aid and loan programs.

> The poor need capital, not charity;
> a hand up, not a handout.
> —*Millard Fuller,*
> *Founder of*
> *Habitat for Humanity*

Challenge 3: Fire and Energy—Firing Up the Systems   All the economic systems that provide us with goods and services take energy. Since the industrial revolution, that energy has mainly come from nonrenewable fossil fuels like coal, oil, and natural gas. Over the twentieth century, the by-products from use of these fuels has done great harm to the environment all across the globe. Burning one gallon of gasoline, an oil derivative, produces twenty pounds of carbon dioxide, along with other pollutants. The emissions from burning fuels have caused serious human health problems, harm to plants and animals, ozone depletion, and acid rain. Most researchers agree that excessive amounts of carbon dioxide are creating the greenhouse effect that could result in a very harmful global warming trend. The mammoth insurance industry is on alert because of the dramatic increase in claims resulting from natural disasters, which some scientists attribute to global warming.[31] But companies have an enormous investment in fossil fuels, both in the United States and abroad, especially in the Middle East where wars are fought to protect fuel sources. Weaning ourselves from these fuels will be very difficult.

Nuclear power, touted earlier as a cheap and safe fuel source, is being phased out in many places worldwide. The costs of producing it have been astronomical, and the human and environmental damage it has created is extensive. Nuclear reactors become either unsafe or uneconomical to operate after thirty years of service; few have lasted that long. Shutting down a plant involves great cost and problems about how to deal with the facility's left-over radioactive material. High-level and highly-dangerous nuclear waste must be kept out of the biosphere until the year 12,000, almost 10,000 years from now! No safe ways of storing this waste have been found to date.[32]

Options: Cooling Down the Planet Over the past few decades and after a few energy crises, we are slowly coming to realize that we must change our habits and develop alternative and benign energy sources. No longer do companies find a source of oil and just move in and begin drilling. People and nations are much more aware of the consequences. Various bills were proposed in the early 1990s on Capitol Hill that would have required cars to have an average gas mileage of forty miles per gallon; that would save 2.8 million barrels of oil a day by 2005, even with several million more vehicles on the road. The saving represents about ten times the amount of oil that could be extracted from the Arctic National Wildlife Refuge and almost four times the amount of oil imported from Iraq and Kuwait prior to the Iraqi invasion of Kuwait in the early 1990s.[33]

One possible energy source that is more benign than oil is natural gas. It is abundant and "clean burning"; that is, it produces only carbon dioxide and water when burned. Although it is still not a perfect solution it could be seen as a "bridge fuel" until good, renewable sources are in place.

Hydrogen, earth's most abundant element, could be another nonpolluting source of fuel in its liquid state, producing only water as a by-product. Cars have been run with both hydrogen fuel cells and solar cells.

Hydroelectric and geothermal power are renewable, but construction and use of the necessary power plants and dams often cause environmental damage and hydropower ceases when there is a drought. These systems need to be carefully planned.

The United States has a considerable store of renewable and safe energy resources that could be tapped to our immense advantage both economically and environmentally. We are moving very slowly to adopt them. Japan and Germany, which use about half the amount of energy the United States does to do the same work, are working on key solar technologies that are likely to become major competitive industries in the future. In California there are 17,000 wind turbines in place, and the state gets a sizable amount of its electricity from renewable energy. Other states could supply their energy requirements with similar systems. Biomass—vegetable and animal by-products such as manure, corn husks, bagasse from sugar cane, and other decaying biological materials—is being converted into clean-burning fuels such as methane and alcohol.

Although utility companies are saving money by using some of these alternatives, the greatest saving and the safest energy source comes from conservation. Amory Lovins, director of the Rocky Mountain Institute, demonstrates that conservation can "create" dramatically high levels of energy at far less cost than building and maintaining power plants and other energy systems. "We could reduce energy use by seventy-five percent by the year 2000 just using the technology we have, with no sacrifice in our present lifestyle or standard of living."[34] He and his wife, Hunter, have briefed Congress and the military on ways to save energy. Some utilities now sell at discount or even give away energy-saving fluorescent light bulbs, light reflectors, insulation, water heater blankets, and other energy saving devices. If every family in the United States replaced their regular bulbs with fluorescent bulbs, we would save $30 billion a year, use 20 to 25 percent less electricity, and shut down 120 thousand-megawatt nuclear power plants. Everyone profits from these and other energy-saving appliances and processes. About 8 percent of the energy used in the country in 1992 came from renewable energy sources.[35] There is a great deal of room for expansion.

Some redeveloping countries are skipping the use of fossil fuels entirely and moving right to low-technology alternatives. Indonesia plans to bring electricity to 2,000 villages with solar power.[36]

Industries and businesses in the field of energy conservation create jobs and improve the quality of life for everyone. They can do well providing low-tech alternatives from bikes to bulbs around the globe. People manufacture, promote, and sell energy products such as energy conserving refrigerators, solar panels, fluorescent light bulbs, and photovoltaic cells. Utilities and businesses are hiring energy analysts. We haven't begun to see the many ways to conserve energy, live well, and still create more jobs than ever.

Some years ago, James Benson of the Council of Economic Priorities estimated that in the Nassau-Suffolk area of Long Island, New York, a low-cost energy package aimed at installing insulation, storm windows, and solar hot water systems could provide 270 percent more employment and 206 percent more energy over a thirty-year period than would the same amount of money spent to construct and maintain nuclear power plants. And for the individual homeowner, personally saving energy is like getting a raise in salary![37]

Challenge 4: Shelter/Created Environments Construction of places to live and work is an important part of the economy. In the last hundred years we have managed to cover enormous pieces of the earth with human-built structures. And still twenty-five percent of the present world population lack housing.[38]

The majority of the world's people will live in cities, including 60 percent of the world's poor, increasing the already heavy demand for services like water, sewage and garbage disposal, pollution controls, housing, and transportation, as well as jobs. Crime increases as people struggle to survive, and whole neighborhoods in the United States as well as worldwide have been left to decay. A vigorous world economy that includes everyone will need affordable shelters and viable cities in which to do business.

Options: Small and Efficient Is Beautiful   From cabins to condos, people have managed to create a wondrous array of shelters. Whether it's a home or a workplace, the best structure is one that gives its inhabitants a sense of belonging, a sense of safety. Building a human-scale community begins with this.

Former mayor of Davis, California, Michael Corbett not only wrote about a new "village" concept where people could walk or bike to work and shop in stores that were close by, but he also developed one in Davis. At Village Homes in that city, dwellings are energy efficient, the automobile is deemphasized, pollution is lessened, trees and gardens flourish, and rainwater moves naturally along streambeds to nourish the groundwater; community is strengthened.[39] Architects and developers have more such villages, even within cities, on the drawing boards, creating, as Sarah van Gelder calls them, "[places] of exuberance."[40]

Architect Mary Otis Stevens feels that because 25 percent of the nation's energy goes into maintaining buildings, it is important to develop structures that conserve energy. She is doing so. Many of her environmentally sound and surprisingly low-tech ideas are working their way into the mainstream: south-facing windows, solar-heated water storage systems, greenhouses, rainwater cisterns, plantings of shade trees, and nontoxic building materials.[41] Many old buildings are being "retro-fitted" for energy efficiency.

People are also looking into new and old housing systems such as cooperatives, shared housing, and a new concept called co-housing, where residents have a private space but share facilities such as play space, recreation, gardens, and laundry areas.

Land is a most valuable resource. But its escalating cost in many areas often makes building and buying homes and businesses unaffordable. This problem is avoided when municipalities or nonprofits buy land and keep it in a community land trust (CLT), only renting it for a small fee to the user or owner of the structure built on it.

Whole towns regenerate when people begin to look at the resources they already have, search for new ones, and then work together, building on their uniqueness and cultural diversity.

Designing and building safe, decent, affordable, and beautiful shelters, using environmentally friendly materials for the world's people is a career field that will always be necessary. Many support goods and services are needed for the construction industry. Also, living in a home that uses little energy and few resources, built on affordable land, is equivalent to another salary raise!

Challenge 5: Transportation—Moving People and Goods   Until the middle of the nineteenth century, humans could not travel on land faster than a horse could run. The railroad and then the automobile soon had people rushing around at the incredible speed of sixty miles per hour. Planes now make the trip across the United States in hours; spacecraft do it in minutes.

The automobile has been a mixed blessing. It has enabled people to move around in ways our forefathers and mothers could only dream about. Television commercials show new cars speeding to glamorous destinations down empty roads in beautiful settings. The reality is that numbers of people spend many prime-time hours a week sitting in their cars on gridlocked and often dismal freeways. Roads and bridges are in constant need of costly maintenance. About as many Americans die in auto crashes in a year as died in ten years of the Vietnam War, but somehow we do not complain; auto pollution contributes to epidemic levels of lung and heart disease, and threatens the stability of the climate itself. Cars leave no part of the environment untouched from the materials they use; the land taken for the roads they travel on and the places they park; or the pollutants they introduce to earth, air, and water. "Cars account for thirteen percent of the carbon dixoide entering the atmosphere."[42] And they can eat up as much as 25 percent of a family's yearly income.

Options: Connecting and Conserving   The technology already exists to create largely sustainable transportation systems that could move us away from dependence on automobiles. Auto transportation also is improving in many ways, most notably by safety improvements and lowered pollution. Businesses are instituting parking fees and rewarding workers for car pooling and using mass transit systems. When mass transit is clean, efficient, convenient, on time, and affordable, people will usually use it and enjoy it.

Rail systems around the world show that rail travel can be clean, comfortable, efficient, less energy consuming, and cheaper to use and to run than individual automobiles and the road systems that support them. Constructing a rail system costs as little as 10 percent of the price of freeway construction.[43] One two-track right of way for a rail system can carry as much traffic as sixteen lanes of highway. Per passenger mile, trains use one-third the energy of an airplane and one-sixth that of a driver-only auto.

Trains create little air pollution; stations are situated comfortably in convenient areas.[44] A number of innovative rail systems around the world could serve as models for similar systems to carry passengers in, around, and between U.S. cities.

In most countries of the world, bicycles are mostly for utilitarian purposes and are the principal means of transport other than walking.[45] Many more of them are produced worldwide than cars each year and their production is increasing. A growing number of people in the United States prefer bicycles to cars caught in freeway gridlock in places where traffic planning has provided safe bike lanes. Large tricycles are being used in New York for delivery and hauling.[46] Bike paths have been created in many communities; buses have bike-carrying racks; some train stations and workplaces have safe-bike parking.

People are always needed to work in the various transportation systems: as drivers and maintenance workers, as designers, as producers. As new transportation and road systems are created, so are jobs. The host of goods and services needed to support transportation systems make jobs in this sector a permanent part of the U.S. economy.

A type of nontransportation that is becoming popular is "telecommuting," communicating from home with work by computers and faxes instead of commuting physically to work and school. Telecommuting saves both transportation costs and personal energy. Air quality would improve, land use would be less, and a variety of costs could be reduced if more people telecommuted. And saving money on transportation costs is money in the bank!

Challenge 6: Health, Education, Military/Security—The Public Sector   The role of a government is to protect the health and well-being of its citizens, although there is disagreement over the extent to which government should involve itself in these areas. Government provides appropriate tax-supported infrastructure, goods, and services not easily provided by private companies in a way that makes them available to everyone. Roads and airports; dams, harbors, and bridges; schools; health protection and some health care; military protection; and other public facilities and services are some of the many government functions we have grown accustomed to.

Health   In many countries of the world, access to health care is almost nonexistent. Although many people in the United States have had difficulty obtaining health care at a cost they can afford, Americans have one of the best private health care systems in the world, with some of it supported by government. But it seems that just as one set of health problems is solved, others loom large. The AIDS (auto immune deficiency syndrome) epidemic, illness, injury, and death caused by pollution and by violence are examples.

Education   Society has changed so quickly that schools have been hard pressed to keep up. The technology of information has changed dramatically and quickly, giving schools computers, modems, copiers, television, video-cassette recorders—all with innumerable capabilities to access volumes of information. New methods are needed to teach people how to evaluate and deal with all this technology and its attendant deluge of data.

The function of education is changing, too, as more people need to be better prepared to help solve the world's problems. What place will education have in this scientific, high-tech information society?

As electronic media move into our lives, the boundaries that separate education, communication, and entertainment become less distinct. Television, for example, both educates and entertains; the use of video and self-paced computer programs in the classroom have given the student exciting alternatives. And in the broader sense, the values expressed by means of electronic media—videotapes, computer games, and television—are the values we "learn" simply from repeated exposure. We are told that information is the product and power of the future.

Military/Security   There are few places in the world where people leave their belongings unprotected. We want to secure them, protect the fruits of our labor, and enjoy them in peace and safety. We all know that some security is necessary. Our taxes pay police officers and fire fighters to protect our lives and property. We build more prisons. As costs escalate, especially the costs of maintaining our military, we try to decide how much is enough. According to the United Nations Center for Disarmament, in the early 1980s,

> the money required to provide adequate food, water, education, health and housing for everyone in the world has been estimated at about $18.5 billion a year. It is a huge sum of money . . . about as much as the world spends on arms every two weeks.[47] The U.S. share would be $2 billion per year—we spend that amount on beer *each month!*[48]

For years, military manufacturing industries in the United States were a highly profitable sector of the economy. Since the Cold War ended, the country has cut back on some defense industries causing a shift to peacetime manufacturing. But the government has not made significant cuts in the overall defense budget. Where the money will be spent and in what industries (and hence where the jobs will be) will be a political decision.

Health Options   In this century we have managed to prevent and cure diseases with wonder drugs and high-tech machines, with better food and healthier homes and workplaces. The population's longevity has increased dramatically.

We see people taking charge of their health in unprecedented ways. The publication *Take This Book to the Hospital with You, a Consumer Guide to Surviving Your Hospital Stay* tells people how to defend their rights when they go to the hospital.[49] People are questioning their doctors, asking for second opinions, and spending billions on alternative health care like relaxation techniques, herbal medicine, chiropractic, acupuncture, and homeopathy—more than on primary care physicians.[50] Whole industries have sprung up devoted to health maintenance—fitness spas and recreational sports among them. In-home health care is seen as a viable alternative to hospitals so that people can be born, live, and die at home.

People are reading health books, exercising, taking vitamins, and watching their cholesterol and fat intake; they are avoiding cigarettes, alcohol, and drugs. Most health experts believe that a healthier diet with fewer junk foods and more grains, fruits, and vegetables would go a long way toward preventing many health problems. The funky health-food stores of years past have become upscale markets with upscale profits as the food industry races to keep up with people's desire for good nutrition.

People are working out cost-containing health plans for businesses; others are becoming ombudspersons and inspectors to ensure proper care for patients in health care institutions; and others are opening health care centers. Protecting our health is the most cost-effective as well as "human-effective" health system.

Education Options   Students are told over and over that having an education is essential. But when they are sitting in a classroom on a lovely spring day, they realize that getting an education is hard work, the kind of work for which many young people have not learned the discipline. The truth is that people learn when and if they want to, and they must be motivated. One good motivator, costly and demanding, is to involve students more with the adult community so they will begin to see where education fits into the scheme of things. What if students could become apprentices in the careers they are thinking about? What if they could really do useful work in meaningful jobs? Students who have become involved with work experience or internships have usually found the results positive.

The education field is sure to grow as we produce more and more information to assess, organize, and pass along. The opportunities to inspire as well as to teach, to enrich as well as to inform are boundless: college degrees through distance learning, curricula for parents teaching children at home, computer-assisted instruction for everything from remedial arithmetic to non-hands-on dissections in biology. The content, delivery systems, marketing, and demonstration of the possible new products and methods are limited only by the imagination—and so are the jobs.

Military/Security Options   In this age of weapons of mass destruction, while mobilizing the military is sometimes necessary, we must search out ways to anticipate conflicts well before they happen and to resolve them before they reach the boiling point, to foster a "culture of nonviolence," as the editor of *Sojourners,* Jim Wallis, calls it. People are redefining national security, noting that individuals feel most secure when they and everyone around them have enough of the basic needs and enriching wants.

People find jobs counseling families with histories of violence and teach conflict resolution, the importance of self-esteem, the roles that drugs and alcohol play in violence. Others work to provide alternative activities for young people who are potential gang members and/or school and societal dropouts, all of which help to create a violence-free society.

Both Congress and groups in the private sector are looking at "economic conversion," the smooth transition from weapons production to a full-employment peace economy. Former Stanford University Assistant Dean Michael Closson directs the Center for Economic Conversion in Mountain View, California. His group has been working with businesses, industries, and various institutions for over twenty years in conversion projects. In the Naugatuck Valley, Connecticut, groups developed one of the largest democratically controlled industrial firms in the nation.[51] A team of rotor blade engineers who worked for the attack helicopter industry joined United States Windpower to make rotor blades for electricity-generating wind farms.[52]

The truth is that "while producing arms for export generates jobs, spending an equivalent sum of money on civilian industry generates more of them. In the United States, spending $1 billion (in 1992 dollars) creates about 11,000 jobs in guided missile production or 17,000 jobs in military aircraft production. But the same amount spent on manufacturing pollution control equipment yields roughly 20,000 jobs and on local transit programs some 26,000 jobs."[53] Weapons industries create far fewer jobs than would the same amount of investment in other areas.

No one is suggesting that we stop minding the store. There is always a need to be prudent and to follow safety procedures. Police officers, fire fighters, guards, as well as the military will no doubt always be necessary. The question is how to find the balance and set priorities fairly. The answers will determine which careers will employ great numbers of people in the next economy. Staying healthy, getting a good education, and resolving conflicts peacefully are all ways for individuals and nations to get a raise in salary!

The Environmental Perspective

The old axiom says that money makes the world go 'round and it *is* certainly a giant motivator, but money pays for less than half of all the work that is done in society. The money part of the economy includes the private sector which rests on and depends on the tax-generated money of the public sector. It is surprising to find that over half our production, consumption, and investment consists of unpaid activities such as volunteering, community work, family gardening, and child and elder care. Futurist Hazel Henderson says this "layer cake" of private, public, and nonmonetized sectors rests and depends on Mother Nature for all its resources.[54]

And Mother Nature will not be ignored! "A new computer model developed by the Hadley Centre for Climate Prediction and Research at the Meteorological Office in Bracknell, England, has succeeded in showing that average global temperatures have been on the rise since the onset of industrialization in the 1860s. The model predicts a net warming of around 4 degrees F over the next century if greenhouse gas emissions continue at curent rates. The Hadley breakthrough opens the way for governments to override the objections about scientific uncertainty that have been used by skeptics to impede immediate action for reducing emissions worldwide.[55]

Additionally, almost 35 percent of the earth's land is degraded, and this proportion is increasing and largely irreversible; almost 55 percent of the world's richest species habitat, the tropical forest, has already been destroyed and the rate of species extinction is estimated at between 5,000 to 150,000 per year.[56] In the 68 million years prior to the industrial age it took 10,000 years for 50,000 species to disappear.[57] Today, many fish that once served as a low-cost food are becoming scarce. Scientists are observing large numbers of birds and frogs dying off. These disappearances are more than warnings of serious danger; they signal the presence of real planetary degradation.[58]

A computer simulation of the Sahel in Africa showed that improper stewardship of the land, such as clearing forests, reduces humidity and favorable winds. As a result, fewer clouds form, cutting rainfall below expectations.[59] We are barely beginning to understand the role of air and water in the overall ecology of the planet and the relationship among the water, land, air, and weather patterns; but it seems that our activities are changing them dramatically.

Challenge 7: Air and Water—Breathing and Drinking Life   It is apparent that clean, clear, fresh air and sparkling pure water, our most basic needs, are in short supply. The lakes, rivers, and seas, once thought to be infinitely capable of getting rid of our waste, are filling up with pollutants.

Because of the expense of pollution control and water conservation systems, business and industry often resist implementing them; many people are afraid that jobs will be lost as a result of environmental protection measures, which can be costly and complex. But air and water pollution is robbing us of clean supplies. And agriculture and industry use by far the lion's share of available water. Cleaning up pollution and conserving water have become political, economic, and social issues.

As we enter a new millenium, most Americans find themselves enmeshed in wasteful consumption habits. Lance Morrow once wrote in *Time* Magazine that "whole nations could live comfortably on [our] leftovers."[60] Our technology has become a basic human need. It is a world of possibilities, hopes, and hazards that reaches into every corner of life.

Options: Cleansing the System   Ever since the first astronauts on the moon looked back at earth, our global consciousness, or awareness of the interconnectedness of life on this planet, has grown. Viewing the earth from space, astronaut Russell Schweickart said:

> It is so small and so fragile, such a precious little spot in the universe . . . you realize that everything that means anything to you—all of history and art and death and birth and love, tears and joys, all of it—is on that little blue and white spot out there which you can cover with your thumb.[61]

Our communications network shows us more and more to be inhabitants of a global village, all breathing the same air and drinking the same water, all drawing sustenance from food, fiber, and fuel. And this "precious little spot" is all that we have to provide us with that sustenance. We must protect it.

Already we know many ways to use technology without causing undue harm to the earth. The Office of Technology Assessment, the analytical arm of the U.S. Congress, as well as many other government and private groups, has identified hundreds of earth-friendly options in the areas of buildings, transportation, manufacturing, electricity generation, forestry, and food. Although these options are sometimes expensive in initial outlay, they require no major technological breakthroughs. We already know how to do them, and the savings far outweigh the expense. With technologies and methods available today, industry and agriculture could cut air and water pollution significantly. Farmers could cut water needs 10 to 50 percent, industries by 40 to 90 percent, and cities by 33 percent—with no sacrifice of economic output or quality of life.[62]

There are natural ways to purify and use waste water. Rather than throw away valuable nutrients, some cities are using partially purified waste water as fertilizer and saving money on chemical and polluting materials. New projects that use "sewage-eating" plants or bacteria to clean grease, soap, and toxic chemicals from water represent a remarkable advance. John Todd, founder of the Center for the Restoration of Waters at Ocean Arks International uses organisms he calls "living machines" to bring sewage water back to pristine purity.[63] Industries are beginning to recycle water and even to use the heat in industrial water for co-generation of energy. When agricultural water is measured and not subsidized, its use drops considerably, as conservation rather than use is rewarded.

Solutions will come drop by drop. Water-saving programs and products are coming on line: drip irrigation that delivers tiny amounts of water directly to plant roots; soil that is built up to hold water; water-saving shower heads; low-flush and composting toilets. Desalinization plants, though expensive, are being developed in water-short coastal areas. New water-miser crops are being considered. A project in Chile "waters the desert" using huge nets to catch fog. The catch is considerable and a six-kilometer pipeline to a nearby village of 450 people could provide each of them with twenty liters of water per day.[64]

There are many careers that support, maintain, improve, and educate people about conserving and purifying air and water. Saving air and water will put money in the bank for all of us.

Challenge 8: Earth Systems—Land's End Land and soil are the life of a nation and of the world. In the United States, we lose six billion acres of soil a year through erosion and the building of roads and shopping malls, although we have enough retail stores to service almost double our population.[65]

We pollute the land with pesticides, toxic and hazardous wastes, and just plain junk. Thousands of chemicals mix together in combinations that science cannot keep up with, much less tell us how they will affect the human system. As landfills overflow, we try to hide our garbage, often pushing it off into poor neighborhoods, onto Indian reservations, into redeveloping countries. Surely no one wants waste in his or her own backyard!

Trees/Wildlife Spotted owls! Who needs them? In reality, we all do. The truth is that we are all environmentalists, at least those of us who breathe, eat and drink, wear clothing, live in shelters. We all depend on the earth. The loss of the spotted owl signals the loss of an entire ecosystem, and the irreparable loss of old growth forests that house a vast array of plant and animal species. We often destroy a system before we understand it.

But slowly we are beginning to see connections among all the species of the earth. This knowledge is beginning to change us in surprising ways. Though Alaska Governor Walter J. Hickel said, "You just can't let nature run wild,"[66] not everyone would agree!

Food/Farming The farther people live away from the land, the less important it often seems. But even synthetics began life as earth vegetation, eventually becoming the fossil fuels so prized in the twentieth century.

Since World War II, farming has been revolutionized by the development of synthetic fertilizers and pesticides making farming seem "fail safe." But in the 1960s, Rachel Carson touched off a giant controversy that still rages in a landmark book, *Silent Spring*. She called attention to the potential for serious damage to earth systems that could be caused by synthetic soil amendments.

Today in much of the world, land is controlled by agribusiness and nonfood conglomerates, corporations, governments, and wealthy, often-absent landowners from other countries. They are seldom the best stewards. As land ownership is consolidated in a few hands, rural people move to urban areas where water, food, shelter, jobs, and their community support systems are often in short supply. For people who have lived on and nurtured the land for centuries, its loss means loss of sustenance.

Still, in the industrialized world especially, food, like information, travels around the world in an amazing and abundant network. It is often processed and packaged miles from its origin. Even so, 65,000 human beings will die from starvation every twenty-four hours.[67] Famine is often the result of poverty as much as poor farming methods, bad weather, military buildups, war, inadequate transportation, politics, and ecological devastation but rarely because of lack of food.

> Although its strictly economic implications
> have still not been worked out,
> it should be clear:
> an exhausted planet is an exhausted economy.
> —*Thomas Berry*[68]

Options: Regenerate, Recycle, Respect the Earth and Its Creatures   We simply are not certain as to how much earth change will finally be too much for the ecosystem to carry. It is difficult to alter the ways in which we do business when the systems apparently are working so well. But careers are growing in all areas of planet protection. Some people work directly on issues of concern. Thus, a group dedicated to preserving or bringing some areas back to a wilderness state have begun a publication called *Wild Earth*.[69] Others may work far from the wilderness, but by their ecological awareness can make a dramatic difference in the way business does business on the planet.

Options: Trees and Wildlife Give Us Life   When one person plants one tree, it will eventually remove twenty-six pounds of carbon dioxide from the air every year.[70] Urban trees can cool our overheated cities and save Americans $4 billion a year in air-conditioning expenses.[71] Trees refresh and bring beauty to a landscape, while supplying us with many resources such as for building, for food, and for medicine.

Lislott Harberts is founder of a lumber company in North Carolina called Forest Care. Loggers call and ask to work for her because she has developed very careful logging methods. She says that the biggest problem in the logging industry is that loggers have never really had any basic skills training to enable them to plan a job well.[72] Although her method is more expensive than clearcutting all the trees, in the long run the forest that is logged this way will be healthier.

If people indigenous to tropical rainforests are left to harvest them and if they are encouraged by new markets, they *and* the forests can survive well. Harvesting quick-growing and sturdy jungle vines for wicker for furniture, and domesticating animals for food (thus saving the wild variety) are two examples of viable businesses that can help preserve the natural environment.[73] Rubber tapper Chico Mendes, who was murdered while working to save an area of rainforests in Brazil, said, "A rubber tree can live up to one hundred years if you tap it right, *affectionately.*"[74] (italics mine)

Jobs are opening that bring people to better appreciation of natural and beautiful areas as they also work to repair them. David Packard, co-founder of Hewlett-Packard Company in Silicon Valley, has helped to fund the impressive Monterey Bay Aquarium and Research Center. He has also contributed to establishing Elkhorn Ranch, a native plant project to repair damage to overused agricultural lands and return them to their function as part of a wetlands ecosystem. Some groups take people on "eco-vacations" to help them appreciate such places as the rainforests in Costa Rica.

As we become more aware of the interconnectedness of all living things, our appreciation grows for animals—both wild and domestic. Any number of organizations are involved in training animals to help disabled people or in doing "pet therapy" for people in hospitals, psychiatric wards, prisons, abuse shelters, and retirement homes. Says president Rich Avanzino of the San Francisco Society for the Prevention of Cruelty to Animals, "This program keeps us focused on what's important—the compassion, understanding, forgiveness, and acceptance of all things. Animals have a way of reaching our spirit, our nature, that cannot be duplicated in any other way."[75]

Options: Food/Farming: Planting the Planet   If we are to conserve our topsoil and reduce agricultural pollution, we must move toward more methods that are healthier for the planet, finding less harmful ways to farm. Large-scale agribusiness resists major changes that might be less damaging to the ecosystem because these operations have so much invested in their present methods of farming. Farmers with middle-sized acreage have more flexibility, are often more productive, and can be more careful of soil and water, but they also have a much smaller financial cushion to tide them over transition times, making them wary of trying totally new ways to farm. Also, sustainable farming methods are more labor intensive and thus can be costly. In spite of these negatives, little by little we are moving toward more sustainable farming methods.

Rodale Research Institute in Pennsylvania has been promoting organic gardening and farming since the 1940s. Now the U.S. Department of Agriculture listens to them and has greatly increased funding for research in organic farming methods. The people at Rodale have shown that crops grow well and pest free in healthy soil that has been built up over the years with organic compost and natural fertilizers. The savings that result from not using artificial fertilizers and pesticides usually offset labor costs, and the increasing demand for organic produce provides a good market. The number of certified organic farms tripled between 1988 and 1990. Some companies are researching, developing, and selling organic pesticides.

Like Robert Rodale, Paul Keene has been an organic farmer in Pennsylvania since the early 1940s. His business, now run by his sons, is called Walnut Acres and grosses more than $5 million annually through local and catalog sales.[76] And Dennis Tamura, a graduate of the Agricology Program at the University of California, Santa Cruz, farms over ten acres of land "never touched by pesticides" in Corralitos, California. He sells elegant "Blue Heron" produce in the San Francisco Bay Area.

Rooftop gardens, driveway gardens, prosperous greenhouses in the ghetto, gardening without soil, gardening in gravel or even gardening in a bed of crushed soft drink cans—it's all been done successfully. According to the National Gardening Association, twenty-nine million households across the country are gardening, supplying a great deal of their own food, saving energy, water, and lessening or eliminating pesticide use.[77] Businesses in support of these activities are also growing.

The earth can supply us with a wealth of materials beyond food. Henry Ford developed a prototype of a car in 1941 made largely out of cellulose from soybeans and other farm crops. He believed that autos could be made "sustainably" and his "chemurgists" thought that renewables made good sense. They invented a number of products from plants. One of his auto plants used wind-generated electricity and recycled almost everything; but cheap oil, that became available after World War II, put us on a chemical course toward synthetic materials.[78]

Since the 1970s, however, the public has rediscovered natural products and is showing increasing preference for these over synthetic ones. Smith & Vandiver manufactures personal care products using such natural substances as almond meal, apricots, honey, sea salt, sesame oil, and mint. It employs ninety people, markets around the world to 6,000 stores in fourteen countries, and recorded $8.5 million in sales in 1993. The company's founder/owner Alida Stevens would use more local agricultural products if more were available.[79] There are many such "green companies" building a new economy based on environmental consciousness.

People produce, market, and use jewelry, art, and furniture that does not exploit forests, wildlife, or people. They work for nurseries, the forest service, and city planning departments. They become landscape architects who promote water-conserving native plants. They are travel agents, bankers, and others in industry and businesses of all sorts working within environmental guidelines.

Encouraged by environmental groups, local governments are setting up systems enabling mainstream Americans to recycle. Many communities have curbside pickup to recycle cans, bottles, newspapers, and cardboard. Companies are springing up to make treasures out of trash; others to find use for and market these treasures. In Naperville, Illinois, a company turns plastic milk bottles into building and fencing material that looks like wood and can be sawed and nailed and used where wood would rot—good for decks and fenceposts. Plastic bottles turn into warm sweaters, jackets, and blankets. Recycled asphalt as well as the millions of old tires (and even old ceramic toilets) discarded every year can be ground up and mixed with new asphalt to become an excellent road surface. Composting the nation's garbage is even being looked into by the United States Department of Agriculture.[80]

Garbage—getting rid of it and finding ways to reuse it—is becoming a multimillion-dollar industry. But recycling still costs money. Buying only what is needed with the least possible packaging is the best way to solve the waste problem. Companies are marketing environmentally safe products, using recyclables, developing biodegradable packaging in ever-greater numbers, and creating jobs in the process. Japan and German are the leaders in multibillion-dollar environmental products and processes industries. Composting is becoming mainstream as municipalities look for ways to reduce material for their landfills.

On the land, U.S. farmers cut excessive soil erosion by one-third in the five years from 1985 to 1990 as the result of the 1985 Food Security Act; they may increase that to as much as two-thirds by 1995. Planting wind breaks, multicropping, using mulch, planting marginal land with grass or trees or letting it return to a native state, and contour plowing will continue to help if farmers don't revert to former methods, lured by the world market. The Worldwatch Institute provides a yearly report on progress toward a sustainable society, and their research shows innumerable ways to chart a path to a sustainable future.

Challenge 9: Increasing and Multiplying—Planet People The world population has passed the five billion mark with six billion on the horizon for the year 2000. Some estimates predict an increase to ten or eleven billion sometime after the mid-twenty-first century.[81] "Current trends indicate the world's over-all population will nearly double to nine billion by 2030."[82] Six billion people—to say nothing of nine or eleven billion— will impose heavy demands on the earth's natural resources.

Many of the world's people are living in dire and miserable poverty, numbers of them as refugees. "The expanding cornucopia of globally distributed goods is largely irrelevant to the basic needs of most people in the world —of the 5.4 billion people on earth, almost 3.6 billion have neither the cash nor credit to buy much of anything."[83]

Options: Preserving People   Evidence shows that as women become more educated and as families feel more financially secure, they have fewer children. Authors of *Earth Day 2030* say that it's possible the world of 2030 could have a population of eight billion people that's heading downward to a number the earth can support comfortably.[84] The options for making life better for all have never been more abundant.

People are doing positive work in all the options, responding to the challenges that face the inhabitants of planet earth. They work in ghettos, prisons, hospitals, farms, factories, and offices. An example is Delancey Street in San Francisco—a beautiful home and business complex built by residents with donations of money and material from the business community. Their elegant restaurant with a view of the bay nets $1 million each year; their moving company earns $3 million. Other businesses they've developed and run, such as printing and catering, add more. These five hundred, well-dressed and well-mannered men and women were all headed for prison terms, many because of having committed violent crimes! With the support of the self-help, no-nonsense program, with *no* government funding, and lots of hard work, they are able to turn their lives around, help those coming after them, and move on to a respectable life.[85] The concept has spread to several other parts of the country.

The Ethical Perspective

We've come to realize that people need guidelines regarding *physical* well-being. Thus the surgeon general scolds us for smoking, states clamp down on drunk driving, and we are urged to eat less fat. With access to enormous amounts of information, the best education and health care, excellent food, and stores full of wonderful gadgets, we ask, "Are we wiser and better people for all this?"

Challenge 10: Evil Work—Time for a Change   We seem to be facing an ethics crisis. With the help of the media, the corruption of people in high and low places is brought to our attention daily. At an international conference, "The Future of Intellectual Property Protection for Biotechnology," an eminent speaker said he hoped others would not have to face "environmentalists and those who would bring ethics and other irrational considerations to the table."[86] But most people think that ethics is a very rational subject and that the Golden Rule is still a good one: "Do unto others as you would have them do unto you," or its variant, "Bring no harm to anyone." But in a complex society, the lines become blurred because people can use loopholes in laws to cover what really does harm, and large institutions make decisions far from the places where the decisions will be implemented. People can say, "That's business!" But the question is this: Is what is legal and profitable always ethical?

Lending institutions, the guardians of our money supply, were a startling example of poor ethical decisions in the 1970s and 1980s. They overextended themselves on loans, especially to foreign governments and helped to mastermind financially shaky buyouts. In some cases, downright fraud resulted in closures, loss of people's investments, government intervention, and legal prosecution. Heads of corporations have gone to prison for disregarding public safety, and high government officials have joined them for fraud and dishonesty.

Options: Being Good—Ethics for a New Age   Arthur Morgan wrote in 1928, "When starting for the West at nineteen, I determined never to do a day's work for pay where the normal and natural results of that day's work would not be of human value, and I never quite starved on that program. I realized that to live wisely by such a standard, one's ideas of values must include the whole range of legitimate human needs, both the practical and material and the so-called 'impractical' hungers of human nature. My failures have been due to living not closely enough in accordance with my convictions and in not using ordinary common sense in applying them in specific cases. Good will is only potent when associated with intelligence."[87]

People are finding that ethics is good business. Some industries are hiring ethics consultants. Business schools are reinstating ethics courses. There is a growing awareness that choices have consequences, whether they are made by private individuals or by people acting as businesses.

Alida Stevens of Smith & Vandiver also says that her company and its products are based on solid values that express respect for customers. Her company uses a team-management approach to instill in workers a sense of ownership and pride; and each employee gets to work in just about every area of the company. Workers may shut down the production line any time they see something that doesn't look right. Her products are animal-free, that is, they neither use nor are they tested on animals. She doesn't go with fads but rather hopes that her customers will stay "for life."[88]

Being socially responsible, however, doesn't mean being stupid. To use good social practices does not make businesses competition proof. They still must be wise and prudent. And sometimes, these practices are not enough and a business fails. As difficult as such times are, owners and workers must be ready to move on to other jobs and other careers in the global economy.

We make ethical choices within the borders of our own jobs and lives, and those decisions, that often seem so small, will have an impact on ourselves and on everyone whose lives we touch. In fact, they will touch many whom we will never see. There is no question that economics meets ethics and the environment at the factory gate and the office door.

The opposite of social responsibility is social irresponsibility.

Global Consciousness: New Ways to Think

Albert Einstein wrote, "The unleashed power of the atom has changed everything except our way of thinking." And never underestimate how difficult it is for people to change how they think. Even the "experts," positive they are right, are sometimes wrong. In 1865, an editorial in the *Boston Post* assured its readers that "it is impossible to transmit the voice over wires and that were it possible to do so, the thing would be of no practical value." Early in the 1900s, Simon Newcomb said, "No possible combination of known substances, known forms of machinery and known forms of force can be united in a practical machine by which men shall fly long distances through the air." And Dr. Richard van der Riet Wolley, British Astronomer Royal, stated in 1956: "Space travel is utter bilge!"[89]

We tend to resist strongly those people who give us unpleasant messages about changing our attitudes and our ways. We say they do not understand the environment or the economic systems or ethics in the real world. But such visionaries are often proven correct in the long run. People predicted all sorts of dire results to the economy if the slaves were freed or women could vote and own property and businesses. Since those events have happened, the United States has become an economic giant!

One argument, often presented to avoid different ways of doing things, is that such changes will take away jobs; but a letter from *Friends of the Earth* says that recycling produces more jobs per ton of solid waste than either landfills or incinerators; public transit and light rail investments produce 50 percent more jobs per dollar spent than new highway construction; increasing the recycling rate of aluminum to 75 percent would create 350,000 new jobs. Some two million Americans in over 65,000 companies earn their living doing some kind of environmental clean-up work.[90] Urban Ore, a recycling company in Berkeley, California, contributes over $300,000 to the local tax base each year by salvaging, cleaning, repairing, and reselling items from the municipal waste.[91]

Recycling *is* becoming mainstream; people *are* conserving water. Meat consumption has seen a 14 percent reduction, down from seventy-nine pounds per person per year in 1986 to sixty-eight pounds four years later.[92] U.S. infant mortality is reduced. Worldwide, bicycle production is outpacing car production; military spending fell from $1.03 trillion in 1987 to $934 billion in 1990; nuclear stockpiles have dropped considerably along with production of ozone-depleting chemicals; energy-conserving power use is up significantly; cigarette smoking is down.[93]

In a period of six months, four historic agreements were signed by world governments: the Law of the Sea, the Biodiversity Convention, the Climate Convention, and the Ban on Hazardous Waste Exports.[94] And thoughtful people are discussing these ideas from the World Bank to the local city governments; from captains of industry to citizens on the street.

The Organization for Economic Cooperation and Development estimates that the worldwide market for environmental goods and services in 1990 was some $200 billion—nearly equivalent to the gross national product of Belgium. This figure is projected to grow 50 percent by the year 2000, making environment-related businesses one of the world's fastest-growing sectors.

U.S. government programs gave *Green Lights* awards to 300 companies that installed more efficient lighting. These businesses reduced their electricity bills by at least 60 percent within five years or less, thus covering the cost of installing new light fixtures and saving energy while reducing pollution. A *Golden Carrot* award and a $30-million market was in the offing for a company that invented a refrigerator that did not use chlorofluorocarbons. *Energy Star* encouraged U.S. computer makers to cut energy requirements of desktop models by more than 50 percent. *33/50* encouraged chemical makers to reduce their emissions of seventeen highly toxic chemicals by one-half by the end of 1995.[95]

The King of Sweden challenges his country to adopt a program called "The Natural Step," which was conceived and implemented by leading cancer researcher Karl-Henrick Robért. The astounding results are that everyone from King Carl XVI down to grade schoolers—and including business-people and politicians—knows that "(1) life can continue only if natural processes are allowed to recycle waste into new resources; (2) current industrial society is producing too much non-recyclable waste too fast!"[96]

Bob Berkebile, a principal in one of Kansas City's leading architectural firms, says that "we are waking up to the fact that our buildings and our communities are part of nature rather than an environment apart."[97]

An idea whose time has come—a newsletter called the *Tightwad Gazette* that helps people live frugally and sustainably—was launched from a kitchen table in 1990 at $12 per year for a monthly copy. In twenty months subscriptions rose to 50,000![98] If we continue to change our ways, we can find an energy-saving, comfortable life in the future with pure air and water; fresh, unpolluted food; good housing; accessible transportation; and a more relaxed lifestyle, using only the technology that we already have.

> Never doubt that a small group of
> thoughtful committed citizens can change the world;
> indeed, it's the only thing that ever has.
> —*Margaret Mead*

Work: Looking at Realities/Finding Balance

Despite images to the contrary and the general affluence of this country, a major concern for most people is to make enough money to live on at any job they can live with. It has been that way in the past, and there are no indications that it will be much different in the future. But people are still searching for work that fits their values, even though they may have to compromise for the moment. Ethical, satisfying work does not have to be a luxury for the lucky few!

It is a time of reassessment from the excesses on both ends of the spectrum: working as we please and working out of need. To find work that helps everyone live more lightly on the earth does not necessarily mean starting a new business or working for such low wages that you are barely able to survive. With your values in place, you can find businesses that match them.

Ask yourself: Which of the ten challenges captures my attention, my energy, my caring? Which options seem to speak to my personality type, to my values? Remember, the content of work remains basically the same

"I had the dream about meaningful employment again last night."

Drawing by W.B. Park; © 1994 The New Yorker Magazine, Inc.

whether you are helping to create more problems for the world or finding solutions. You can manage, repair, compute, sell, or create in almost any type of workplace.

No matter what your career is, you will be working in an economy that affects the environment and is guided by ethics. The challenges are formidable, but the options are exciting. We need to see ourselves as dynamic pioneers moving into a new century. There is no longer room for petty self-interest, depression, or complaining. A father used to tell his children, "The person who is all wrapped up in himself is overdressed."

What once sounded strange and unworkable to many people—social responsibility, appropriate technology, economic democracy, sustainable ecology—is now becoming a part of the culture. As an old Chinese proverb tells us,

> Person who says it cannot be done
> should not interrupt person doing it!

Job Market Outlook and Opportunities[99]

During your career search, you may often find yourself wondering, "Who needs me out there?" The truth is that there is no way to predict the future needs of the job market with absolute certainty.

While change is here to stay and predictions hard to make, those who research and weigh trends honestly will not be very surprised by the future. The Department of Labor makes job market predictions regularly, and generally is able to give us a handle on what to expect from these "guesstimates." However, every prediction of job availability carries with it a "yes, but" set of possible exceptions.

For example, the health fields are slated to grow; therefore, you might say, people need dentists. Dentistry, however, is one health care area that is slowing down because of improving preventive care and large numbers of available dentists. The very best way to research job availability is to talk to people in your own area. A dentist who relocated from a busy city to a semi-rural place says that if he had chosen a site just five or ten miles away, he wouldn't have had enough business to sustain him, but *he* is doing quite well despite the odds!

So the availability of jobs is affected by geographical limitations, educational requirements, experience, the state of the national and even international economy, and the personal decisions of many individuals. Jobs that have a high salary potential and few openings will always have stiff competition even though their numbers are growing. Your state employment office can supply information on the dynamics of your local job market. It is important to remember that even career categories that are expected to decline dramatically will no doubt still need some workers somewhere, and you could be one of those. All *you* need is that one opportunity—yours!

The U.S. population, always a microcosm of the world, has become even more diverse. The number of Americans in the work force is expected to grow. Women, minorities, and elders who decide to work past age sixty-five are among those adding to the labor pool. Immigration brings more people into the mainstream with opportunities to share their varied cultures in new ways.

But we are told that fewer new recruits will be job hunting into the twenty-first century.[100] And fewer than 10 percent of the next generation of workers born on this planet will be born in an industrialized country.[101] So the pool of available workers seems to be shrinking—good news for young job seekers.

The new global millennium will no doubt require more cooperation with varied cultures, world governments, and organizations such as the United Nations. People who can learn to forge foreign policies and business contracts, who can learn to work with others equitably, who have the vision to see where the world is going, will no doubt be valuable. And with computers inserting themselves into our lives almost everywhere, computer capability will be a plus for most job seekers.

Overall, projections show an economy using smart machines and thus fewer *resources,* an economy short on the *capital* necessary to build businesses, and an increasing shortage of *skilled labor,* the third essential component in employment. This combination should add up to a good outlook for specially skilled job seekers.

With computers extending the capacity of our brains and robots giving us brawn, the work of the future could be ideal. Many boring and repetitious tasks, and dangerous and dirty tasks have already been taken over by smart machines; these "steel-collar" workers are being monitored by "gray-collar" or technical workers. More people will wear white collars and use creativity in their jobs.

> We are confronted by
> insurmountable opportunities!
> —*Pogo*[102]

In the adjacent box are listed some of the jobs predicted by the Department of Labor to be among the fastest growing between 1992 and 2005. These jobs sometimes employ very small numbers of workers overall and they are not always the jobs the Department tells us have the largest growth—that is, the largest number of jobs overall (and which tend to be lower-skilled and less well-paid). "Fastest growing" does not always mean easy to get.

THE FASTEST GROWING JOBS 1992–2005

REALISTIC

Aircraft pilots (competition)

Construction contractors/managers

Correction officers and guards

Data processing equipment repairers

Food/counter preparation workers

Gardeners/groundskeepers

General maintenance mechanics

Janitors, cleaners, and supervisors

General maintenance workers

INVESTIGATIVE

Computer scientists

Computer systems analysts

Operations research analysts

ARTISTIC

Actors, directors, producers
(competition for few jobs)

SOCIAL

Dental hygienists

Flight attendants (competition)

Home health aides

Human services workers

Licensed practical nurses

Nursing/psychiatric aides

Occupational/physical therapists

Physical and corrective therapy
assistants

SOCIAL (*continued*)

Physical therapists

Preschool workers

Psychologists (Ph.D.s)

Registered nurses

Respiratory therapists

Special education teachers

Speech/language
pathologists/audiologists

Teacher aides

Technicians: electroencephalo-
gram, nuclear, radiologic,
surgical

**ENTERPRISING AND
SOCIAL/ENTERPRISING**

General managers/top
executives

Health services managers

Management analysts/
consultants

Travel agents

CONVENTIONAL

Bill/account collectors

Insurance adjusters/examiners/
investigators

Medical assistants/records
technicians

Paralegals

Well-qualified secretaries

SOURCE: United States Department of Labor, Bureau of Labor Statistics, *Occupational Outlook Quarterly,* Spring 1994, pp. 10–45,47.

Because of the large number of people working in some job classifications and in some of these, because of high turnover, there will be many openings even though the category is not necessarily growing. These include cashiers, file clerks, mail clerks, office clerks, record and bookkeeping clerks, retail sales clerks, and truck drivers.

Personality Types in the Job Market

Realistic Type   Realistic personalities provide food, clothing, shelter, transportation, repair, and maintenance—jobs that are basic, necessary, and highly visible. They are also at home in the world of physical performance. Careers in sports, of course, are extremely competitive and limited to the most talented. Increased automation and cheap imports have cut employment for many realistic jobs. Large-scale farming, fishing, and forestry now use technologies and fewer workers. Mining has decreased because of resource depletion, cheaper imports, and use of alternative materials. The employment outlook in specialized areas is good, however, especially for workers who are service oriented or do highly skilled and specialized work.

You might consider indoor or outdoor jobs in industry or with public utility companies. Vocational training, on-the-job training, or an apprenticeship in a construction union is sometimes necessary. With increased emphasis on protection against crime, providing security to companies, their computers, and individuals is a growing possibility. Government cutbacks have limited the number of outdoor jobs available to people who like to work with nature, but ecological awareness is helping to slow that trend and even create such jobs in the industrial area. Realistic persons are valuable because they can handle the practical needs of any workplace. Further training can be a plus.

Investigative Type   Most investigative jobs, except for some technical areas, require at least a four-year college degree. Many jobs in the sciences are not "productive" because they deal with "pure research," so funding is limited even though research is necessary for future development. The growth of "the information society" is tailor-made for the person who is investigative: new kinds of artificial intelligence and new ways of putting information together are there to challenge the mind person. Vast amounts of data that formerly took years to work with can now be crunched in seconds. Computers can tell marketers the likes, dislikes, and activities of just about anyone. Engineers and medical researchers who research "practical problems" find jobs more available and are generally well paid because their work earns company profits. Because few women and minorities go into math and science, those who do should find jobs readily available in gender- and race-neutral workplaces.

With its electronic network, the information world provides service jobs for multimedia content developers, services marketers, and all sorts of computer specialists, systems analysts, and software programmers. In general, the investigative job outlook (except scientific research) is good. Investigative types who are not scientifically or technologically oriented can apply their investigative talents to other areas. Many work settings can profit from the research and analytical skills of the investigative person.

Artistic Type   Most jobs for the artistic type require special talent along with special training. They tend to be highly competitive, so the artistic type should plan alternatives. Although the work of the artistic person enriches everyone, Americans generally do not place high value on the arts and artists in their lives.

New developments in electronic media will provide opportunities for some creative people. And packaging information using computerized lay-outs can be a rewarding outlet for the creative person. Technical writing would fit the scientifically minded creative person, and that area is growing. Decision makers in many businesses and industries are slowly realizing that workers on the front line often have better ideas about how to do their jobs than the people in the front offices. Creativity is useful in just about every career and workplace.

Social Type   Social personality careers involve caring for people. There is great need here, especially in social service jobs, often in government; but these most often are still underfunded and thus scarce. Workers in some settings are drained by responsibility for large numbers of clients, many of whom have serious and chronic problems. With little support, few resources, and yards of red tape, a worker needs strong motivation to succeed. People with good business sense and enough funding sometimes start private practices or community organizations. Because our society is committed to building many more prisons, prison work is a growing field.

The health care industry is experiencing significant restructuring, with certain careers showing promise. Fewer people are using hospitals, as out-patient care offers a cheaper and often more desirable alternative, and healthier lifestyles are becoming mainstream. There have been dramatic breakthroughs such as imaging techniques, transplants, and genetic discoveries. While there are periodic shortages of workers, admissions to training programs are often limited. With the growing population of the elderly, geriatric care managers and physical therapists should be able to find a well-paying niche. Although they are not paid well, home health aides, medical assistants, and child care workers will be in demand.

Employee assistance programs are growing as industry sees the need to help its workers with personal problems and human-resources managers guide employees through the maze of personnel demands. The desire to share some of their profits with nonprofit organizations has prompted some companies to hire "planned-giving officers" who review proposals from the community and fund those that meet certain criteria. Teachers such as those in special education are on almost every state's critical shortage list. People with social concerns find that their special talents can be used in a variety of settings, however, because all employers hire people and need to solve employee and customer problems.

Enterprising Type Enterprising personalities have the inner drive to "connect" with the people and events that help them get involved, though they do not always see that in themselves. And there is always a need to organize and sell goods and services in the world of things and data. Marketing financial services and doing financial planning with investors are two "hot" career areas. Hotel managers, tourism promoters, law-firm marketers, paralegal/legal assistants, labor/employment lawyers, intellectual property lawyers, and environmental attorneys and engineers are other professionals whose jobs are likely to be satisfying for the enterprising person.

The most effective person for an enterprising job achieves a balance between courage and confidence and commitment to people's concerns. Enterprising jobs are mostly high-data jobs, requiring intelligence and good verbal skills; they are readily available for the go-getter.

Conventional Type Conventional personality careers require steadiness, order, and tolerance for paperwork; at times they involve business contact with people and the use of office machines. Experience may build the conventional person's confidence and the courage to advance, but generally such types prefer supportive roles.

Now that we have become a nation of datakeepers and processors, jobs in this area are abundant, visible, usually easy to find, and can pay well in the right setting.

Social-Investigative-Artistic and Other Combinations: The Hard Cases The realistic, conventional, and enterprising types and various combinations of these have the easiest time choosing careers: the realistic, because their jobs are concrete and visible; the conventional, because they tend to follow established patterns; and the enterprising, because they are willing to take risks. Generally speaking, the SIA personalities—social, investigative, artistic, or some combination of these—have a harder time choosing and launching a career. People who work with ideas or feelings have no tangible product to show their employers.

SIA personalities gravitate toward work in which they can deal with people to solve problems by creating new systems, a need that may arise in just about any work setting. Information systems require these SIA qualities: intelligence, analytical and communication skills, autonomy, responsibility, commitment, flexibility, and creativity.

Satisfying jobs in this area are usually on a highly competitive, professional level, with a college education almost a must. Some supporting work-specific skills that relate to the workplace will help SIAs get started. They should plan to get a four-year liberal arts or specialized degree, take electives in such subjects as business, computer technology, or health, or obtain a two-year vocational certificate and complete transfer requirements at a community college before going on to a four-year college.

The social and investigative person who is conventional enjoys working with people to solve problems by following established guidelines such as those in human resources, labor relations, probation and law enforcement, health care, and sales.

Individuals who represent the enterprising and social combination have both drive and good people skills. Those who have or can develop both traits will usually be successful with people in business and public service administration. Often, the SIA personality has enough enterprising skills to work happily in many of the social/enterprising areas. Teachers, for example, must organize and motivate people and must serve as key figures in a group, in addition to using their investigative and creative qualities. Be clear on the main function that your highest personality components enable you to perform with enjoyment:

Realistic: Do the practical, physical work required

Investigative: Gather information (research) and solve problems

Artistic: Create fine arts, but also create systems in many settings

Social: Help people resolve problems

Enterprising: Initiate the work/project to be done

Conventional: Follow the guidelines of others to get the work done

When you can state what it is you wish to *do,* finding a place to do it will be much easier.

Back to the Future

Regardless of your personality type, analyzing your transferable skills in depth and zeroing in on your strengths are important steps in choosing a career. No one can guarantee you a job after you have invested many years and dollars training for it. How much are you willing to risk? How motivated are you? Have you looked for ways to use your training in alternate choices?

If you need some help in being your own futurist, you will find that the *Occupational Outlook Handbook,* published by the U.S. Department of Labor and generally available in any library, is one of the best beginning references in which to explore projected needs for over 80 percent or 250 of the most popular careers in the United States. It outlines the nature of the work, average earnings, training requirements, and places to write for further information, along with the projected employment outlook.

The world we live in depends on the input of all personality types, on all the talent that we can bring to the challenges that face us as we enter the twenty-first century. The realistic personality can show us how to deal with the physical world capably. The investigative person will carefully explore, analyze, and critique various options. The artistic or creative person will keep us from staying with options that no longer work. They will be out there way ahead of the rest of us, trying new ones. The social person will be concerned with the effects of new systems on people and will urge us to consider ways to care for the planet and its creatures. The enterprising person will take the risks necessary to begin and move enterprises that will take us into a new century. The conventional person will keep us moving in the right direction and will keep track of the data, urging us not to advance too quickly lest we lose artifacts and ideas of value. You, with your special qualities, will contribute to the future.

 ## Self-Assessment Exercises

- Circle the following areas of challenge that capture your attention. Tell why.

  Science and technology   Health, education, military/security

  Industry and business   Earth/land

  Shelter/created environment   Planet people

  Transportation   Air and water

  Energy   Ethics

  _____

  _____

  _____

- Which options might you use to respond to those challenges?

  _____

  _____

- Look up your first job choice in the *Occupational Outlook Handbook* and summarize what it says under "Job Outlook" about the possibility of future job openings.

  _____

  _____

- What are your beliefs about the future?[103]

  Circle all the items you agree with.

  1. I have no control over my own future, much less the future of the world.
  2. We can keep world conflicts within reasonable bounds.

3. We will be able to keep conflicts from becoming nuclear wars.
4. Conservation will become an acceptable way of life almost everywhere.
5. Luck or chance, rather than our choices, causes the outcome of events.
6. We can learn to live peacefully on earth.
7. Enough people will learn to be careful of resources to save us from destruction.
8. The future is created, more so than not, by choices that people make.
9. We can do little about overconsumption and the waste that causes excess pollution.
10. It is possible for me to influence the direction of my future.
11. I believe that the future will be shaped by forces outside my control.
12. Soon we will not have enough of anything.
13. There are enough people making good choices to keep the world from destruction.
14. Researching and planning ahead can make my future turn out well.
15. There may be shortages, but generally we will get through the coming years well enough.
16. The world is consuming, polluting, and populating itself to death.
17. The world's resources are abundant enough to provide food, raw materials, and energy for everyone.
18. Most of our energy sources will be renewable and nonpolluting in the not-too-distant future.
19. It is largely up to people to determine the options to be taken.
20. The future will happen no matter what a person does.
21. We can rely on most people to make wise choices.
22. I look forward to the future with hope and enthusiasm.
23. People are swept along by forces over which they have little control.
24. In a few years we will begin to see declining population, rising levels of affluence, and a world of plenty.

Scoring: Circle the same numbers here that you circled above to get an idea about how optimistic or pessimistic you feel about your future and how much control you feel that you have. Where do you feel you stand on the Pessimistic/Optimistic Spectrum?

Doomsday/Pessimistic—Little Control: 1, 5, 9, 11, 12, 16, 20, 23

Muddle Through—Some Control: 2, 3, 7, 8, 10, 13, 15, 19

Bright Future/Optimistic—Much Control: 4, 6, 14, 17, 18, 21, 22, 24

Pessimistic	Midpoint	Optimistic

Group Discussion Questions

1. What does John Peers mean when he says, "We live three days in one compared to the 1950s. We do in one day what couldn't be done in a week in 1900, in a lifetime in the 1600s?" Give examples. Do you feel busy? Why or why not?

2. Describe your classroom, your community, your home, and your lifestyle as if you lived in 1890.

3. Community checkup: Note a challenge in your area that relates to your personality type and find an innovative option. Interview someone who is working to build a better community. Report to the class.

4. Some people feel that all necessary work could be accomplished in perhaps two days a week. How would people use their time off? How would you?

5. Define economics, environment, and ethics and then describe how they relate to one another.

6. What does it mean "to vote at the checkstand of the supermarket"?

7. Discuss your views on world population growth. What is your stand on birth control, abortion, immigration, the death penalty, welfare?

8. Describe a practice that is legal but that you consider unethical. How many ethical principles can the group collect and agree on?

9. How do your new ideas affect others? How do theirs affect you? What does Alvin Toffler mean when he says, "Social decay is the compost bed of the new civilization"?

10. Describe your ideal world.

6/

Workplaces and Workstyles

Scanning the Subtleties

 FOCUS

- *Connect personality types with the seven categories of workplaces.*

- *Look at the rewards offered in various work settings.*

- *Explore and evaluate workplaces, workplace values, and workstyles.*

*D*eciding on a career is a big step. But even with a job title in mind, you first need to decide on the type of workplace where you can do what you enjoy and the workstyle that will suit you best. You may be surprised to learn that workplaces can be divided into just seven categories: business, industry, education, communication/entertainment, health, government, and military. Each of these categories has hundreds and some even thousands of jobs, many of which have similar characteristics. If you're unable to choose a job title, just being able to pick one of these seven categories is a huge step in narrowing down your choices. Let's look at each of them.

Seven Categories of Workplaces

Business

The category of business includes every desk, from an executive suite to a space in the back of an auto repair shop. And business is not limited only to desks; it occurs wherever two or more people get together to trade goods and services. Business workers range from the retail clerks in your neighborhood sport shop to the shipping tycoon who has offices around the world; from one person preparing taxes in an office at home to traders in the international stock market network. Labor relations, human resources, contract negotiations, accounting, marketing, consulting in all areas, and hundreds of other functions make up the work of the business world and its many support systems.

The enterprising and conventional types are most at home in business, but all types can find expression there: the social person in dealing with people and their problems, the artistic person in creating or advertising new designs, the realistic person in managing products and production, and the investigative person in research and problem solving. Choosing business, then, will narrow down your choices and still leave the door open to a variety of careers.

To facilitate the flow of goods and services in business involves both paper data and mind data. The classification, *paper data,* includes reading, writing, using computer data, and filing information; *mind data* encompass researching, organizing, analyzing, and teaching. General clerical skills enable you to enter the field of business as a data entry clerk or shipping clerk. When you feel the need for more training, you can attend workshops and seminars or take college courses at the Associate in Arts (AA) or Bachelor of Arts (BA) level. Or you might go directly to college to earn a BA in business in a field such as accounting or marketing. Even with a BA or an MBA degree (Master of Business Administration), most people must start near the bottom of the ladder and work up—unless a serious shortage of personnel exists or you have special expertise or experience.

Industry

Industry can be defined loosely as a concern with products and with services that involve physical objects, not with people or paper (if you exclude the "business end" of industry). Repairing cars, flying planes, pouring concrete, and raising wheat are industries in this sense, along with manufacturing, testing, quality control, and quality assurance of products and services. Even the artist making clay pots at home is involved in industry. Working with machines and tools and tangible materials attracts the realistic person to industries of all kinds. Those realistic individuals with an investigative bent will enjoy scientific and engineering research directed toward practical problems. The ones with a conventional side will appreciate seeing that the jobs are done correctly and with care, following all the rules; realistic people with an artistic slant will enjoy inventing and creating; those with an enterprising side will find satisfaction in demonstrating products for sale; social/realistic people will do well in technical supervision.

To enter jobs in this area, take related high school and community college or adult education courses. And look into on-the-job training (OJT) in industry as well as apprenticeship programs through trades such as carpentry or cement working.

Education

Many careers besides teaching in schools and colleges are available in the field of education. Corporations hire specialists to develop basic learning programs, and business and industry carry on employee training programs. People who teach various skills or crafts at home or at community centers also participate in the field of education.

The enterprising and social personalities enjoy the task- or people-oriented interactions of teaching, leading, and motivating others. Those with a realistic bent enjoy teaching such subjects as physical education, military arts, and shop, whereas the artistic types drift toward humanities and fine arts, crafts, and design classes. Investigative interests are needed for scholarship and research and for teaching the liberal arts and sciences, whereas conventional personalities do well in teaching the basics. In fact, all personality types can be found in education—it helps to be a jack-of-all-trades to teach.

Communication/Entertainment

In the communication/entertainment arena, the workplace ranges from circus tents to TV studios, but opportunities tend to be more limited than those in any other area because these "glamour" fields are generally highly competitive. To succeed here, you need exceptional ability, great quantities of luck, and lots of courage and perseverance. Artistic personalities who may be attracted to communication and entertainment may find success elusive, unless they possess some of the qualities of the enterprising type (or possibly a good agent). The electronic media continue to grow erratically, and sometimes positions for creative people with enterprising, conventional, realistic, or investigative sides can be found in the marketing, business administration, clerical, engineering, and research areas of media. Because creative people usually like to work alone or in unstructured settings, many find it difficult to do routine work, even though the workplace may deal with a creative product.

Realistic types who are creative may enjoy careers such as industrial design, whereas conventional/artistic types may do well in such areas as computer-assisted drafting. Enterprising artistic people may open their own galleries or become book publicists. With the incredible rise of the information society, opportunities will open up for the creative person who is technically talented, word-wise, or number-nimble.

Health

When they think of the health care field, many people see jobs in a hospital or doctor's office, but in fact health care workers also find employment in business, industry, education, and military settings. Specialization and technological advances have expanded the health profession rapidly, but growth slows when recession and unemployment pinch health care budgets. The investigative person with a good social orientation will enjoy the challenge of helping people solve their health care problems, whereas conventional/social persons will like the established systems found in some health care facilities. There may be a great deal of physical work, which may be attractive to the realistic person who likes to work with people. Several hundred job titles are associated with health care delivery.

Government

People of all types find employment with government in every setting from agricultural stations to hospitals, from prisons to the great outdoors. You must usually pass a test to become employed at the federal level (and often at state and county levels, too). The test may combine an oral interview and possibly a written examination; job applicants often receive additional credit for years of education, military service, and past work experience that can give them preference in the hiring process. Any type of personality can find satisfiers as one of the great variety of government workers that includes narcotics agents, food program specialists, museum curators, and public health workers. Your state and other employment offices have information about these and other civil service jobs.

Traditionally, a government job has implied security but low pay. In past years, the pay increased along with the number of jobs, but growing tax-payer concern about government spending has brought lower pay and inse-curity for many government employees. You need persistence to obtain these jobs, but many are still there for the person who is willing to try for them.

Military

Realistic and conventional personalities are attracted most readily to military operations and procedures, but here also people of all types can find oppor-tunities—from cooking to hospital laboratory work to sophisticated indus-trial research and design, along with frontline fighting. Like other government workplaces, the military is "downsizing" in certain areas for budgetary reasons, so many in military jobs are moving to other employment fields. Even so, new recruits may still apply and be accepted. For those so inclined, the military provides a very structured working and living situation, training in a variety of skills, and good benefits, offset by the chances of being assigned to undesirable duties or locations, or having to participate in wars or "peace actions."

As you review these categories, begin visualizing the size of workplace you might enjoy. This process will also help focus your choice even more. Is a multinational corporation for you, or a tiny business at home? A modest-sized company in a nearby city, or a cooperative venture in your neighbor-hood? Gather job titles that would work in these places.

Then, before you discard some job titles, be sure you aren't stereotyp-ing them in a way that distorts their possibilities. Food services might seem to mean frying hamburgers, but if you stop there, you miss management at local, regional, and corporate levels, finance, accounting, marketing, plan-ning, and all the functions of any corporation. The possible work settings include industry, schools, hospitals, airlines, and even executive dining rooms, where highly professional food service personnel work a five-day week serving upper management and their guests.[1] And consider engineering. Engineering students at the Massachusetts Institute of Technology (MIT) found a great project by working out a faster, more economical system to put the hard candy coating on M&Ms. The company sent them 1,500 pounds of M&Ms, not all of which went into the experiment! The students and profes-sors grew in wisdom and weight and found that the food industry has "tremendous engineering prospects."[2]

Choosing a category of workplace focuses your career exploration and can even get you started on a basic college curriculum or training program.

Keep in mind the main functions your personality combination enjoys and imagine the sort of place where you would feel comfortable:

R: working with things   S: helping people

I: solving problems   E: initiating projects

A: creating new systems   C: following guidelines

Wanted: Rewards on All Levels

While your career choice puts you on a path to certain rewards, the workplace you choose can enhance or subtract from them. Robert Levering and Milton Moskowitz say that "most companies offer dreadful work environments."[3] As we watch the frantic activity in the work world we've created, a disturbing question arises. What is happening to the individual in the workplace? Many work situations prove far from ideal on the personal level.

First, subtle changes have removed us from the natural world where our ancestors worked. We drive and park along heavily concreted wastelands. Many people work in buildings without windows, far from sunlight and breezes. They work in cyberspace—a not-always-amusing theme park of virtual unreality. They have little say about what happens to their souls and bodies during the workday and on what schedule. What are some of the rewards to look for in these workplaces of the twenty-first century?

Workplaces provide a paycheck, which satisfies some basic physical/survival needs such as food, clothing, and shelter and some of the enriching wants on your agenda. In the last three decades of this century, we have seen the buying power of worker wages decline, jobs disappear, and new but lower-paying jobs come on line. A new upper-middle class of "knowledge workers" has developed, wielding power and influence, as many poorly skilled people fall into poverty.

But also consider the areas of reward that go beyond a paycheck and that may in the long run bring added satisfaction to your work: opportunities for climbing the career ladder, fringe benefits, and subtle emotional satisfiers, such as a supportive atmosphere, autonomy, and compatible values.

Career Ladders

You may find it helpful to match your satisfiers with one of the levels in Career Ladders and to be aware of other closely related factors such as size and complexity, and settings both indoor and outdoor. There are four major levels on any career ladder: entry, supervisory/technical,

THE CAREER LADDER

Position	Responsibility	Education	Support Staff
TOP LEVEL			
Top management and professionals, such as Presidents Board members Doctors Lawyers	The decision makers: responsible for nearly everything. There is more independence at this level.	PhD, DD, MD, MBA, etc. Technical and professional expertise	
MIDDLE LEVEL			
Middle management and professionals, such as Department heads Engineers Nurses Teachers Product managers	Share responsibility with the top level and enjoy some independence.	MA, MBA, MS, BS, BA, etc. Middle-level expertise	Operate at all levels to provide auxiliary services such as Personnel Finance Communications/ Graphics Legal counsel Research Purchasing Marketing Data processing Secretarial/Clerical Maintenance
LOWER LEVEL			
Lower management and technicians, such as Supervisors Lead persons Legal assistants LVNs	Are responsible for a small part of decision making. May supervise others.	AA, AS, vocational, or on-the-job training	
THE WORKERS			
Basic production and service work, such as Trades, crafts Assemblers Machinists Waiters/Waitress	Are responsible for a particular function. Entry-level jobs; often repetitive work.	High school, apprenticeship. Usually *some* training or experience is needed.	

mid-management, and top management. These are often divided into sub-levels. Each level includes some support services such as human resources, purchasing, secretarial/clerical, and maintenance. Some companies are trying to group employees into a few broad job categories ("broadbanding" them) rather than naming them with the dozens of titles found in traditional systems. And many are shortening the ladder so that there are fewer managers. Moving up is still as difficult a climb with the short ladder! In some of these companies, moving over instead of up can be a good career strategy if the lateral move will help you gain new skills and confidence.[4]

In some settings, such as the military, the structure is rigid. In others, the structure is less formal and less evident. In large workplaces, the very size increases the complexity. But no matter what size they are, all workplaces— lawyer's offices, large catering services, hospitals, or international manufacturing corporations—have similar structures, sometimes repeated over and over in various divisions. A small staff might consist of the boss, who has many management functions, and one assistant, who does the rest.

Julie Martin-Pitts was a medical assistant in a doctor's office. Her job included billing, data entry, personnel, a little family counseling, public relations, tax work, research, and even interior decorating. Many days brought surprises to her work and interesting employment opportunities. At one time she consulted for a doctor who wanted a more efficient management system for her office. Now a consultant, Julie helps people deal with the complexities and traumas involved in using the health care system.

In a larger workplace, entry-level workers can expect to do more limited and specialized jobs, such as putting lettuce leaves on a thousand sandwiches, soldering links in a thousand electronic circuits, or data processing a thousand letters. Possibilities for change, however, including moving both up and over, are greater in a larger than a smaller work environment. Research shows that small and mid-size companies often outperform huge corporations, create many more jobs, are usually more flexible and innovative, and often grow dramatically to become huge corporations, which tend to lose flexibility, productivity, and creativity!

In a smaller workplace, tasks may be more varied and responsibility greater, but options for advancement are narrowed. Small businesses employing fewer than twenty people make up 89 percent of U.S. firms.[5] So size and complexity as well as type of workplace can be very important factors in career ladder opportunities. But in this fast-paced world, the companies that survive will be those of any size that maintain flexibility, productivity, and creativity.

Generally, the higher you climb on the career ladder, the higher your salary will be. Some people begin at the bottom and, with additional training, degrees, and experience, rise to the top. One young woman started as a nurses' aide, moved up to registered nurse (RN) with a BS in nursing, and then went on to earn an MS in nursing so that she could teach. She could also have gone into hospital administration. Where do you want to fit in this scheme of things? How far up the ladder do you want to be? (It may be lonely at the top, but it's also exciting and challenging—but not everyone can get there. It may seem more comfortable at the bottom but often not so lucrative or so interesting!) You may want to move up the ladder within a career area but not to a higher level that requires more education and career commitment. If you know where you want to be in a few years, you will make use of present opportunities and not choose dead-end jobs.

Setting is another related factor. Some people like their career ladder in the outdoors where the structure is usually simpler; others like to be more on their own or on the road where they feel more autonomy; others like a mix in which an office is their base but they move around inside the same plant, on the road, or outdoors; and still others like to be indoors in one spot on the spot. Such choices may move a person either farther away or closer to the center of decision-making power in a company. This in turn may enhance or delay progress up the career ladder.

Don't Overlook Benefits

Generally, salary is the prime consideration most people look for. But fringe benefits are not just a minor attraction. These perquisites or "perks" represent a considerable, if hidden, part of your pay and if carefully considered can result in larger paychecks and long-term savings, as well as enriching activities off the job. Health care, for example, can include dental and vision care in addition to medical/hospital care. Many companies, especially smaller ones, find it a struggle to offer health benefits. As the cost of health care skyrockets, medical expenses can put someone without insurance deep into debt. Also consider a company's record in career "pathing" or career development and the quality of their employee training programs, for these can lead to better-paying jobs.

Paid holidays and vacations, child care and education subsidies, use of a company car, expense accounts, and even such executive perks as use of vacation resorts are just a few of the benefits offered by some companies. Some give raises when workers acquire and broaden their skills; some provide sabbaticals, during which time an employee who has worked for them for some years can take several months off with pay for enrichment. Some offer "cafeteria style" benefits and allow employees to choose whichever combination suits them.

Although retirement can seem eons away, it's never too early to look at various options and plan accordingly. For some people, the opportunity to work after age sixty-five is most welcome. To others, retirement (as early as possible) means liberation. There are many retirement plans, some that can lead to considerable income. Several, like Individual Retirement Accounts, or IRAs, involve reduced or deferred income taxes. Some people manage to save and invest wisely enough to make their retirement free from financial worry. Many are taking better care of their health and finding enriching involvements or even new career areas. With some creative planning, "retirement" could be on your career agenda sooner than you think.

Many companies are offering fringe benefits that help with the complex business of *living*, a term that refers to the endless but absolutely necessary tasks each person must perform in regard to (1) financial matters, such as banking, taxes, insurance, real estate, and other investments; (2) medical/ dental care; (3) personal care including food, clothing, and shelter; (4) child care; and (5) education—keeping up with your field. Companies are becoming more aware that when employees are frustrated and concerned about such problems, their energy and productivity are drained. Businesses are now beginning to provide child care and recreation facilities, counseling, short-term health consultation, financial services, and educational courses for work or personal improvement. As a job hunter, you benefit by knowing which benefits you would like and which you think are absolutely necessary.

Staff Support: The Emotional Contract

Work also brings intangible rewards on many levels. Self-esteem, prestige, rewarding relationships, and opportunities to actualize your unique potential are powerful motivators. Many people find pleasure in working and would continue some kind of work involvement even if they were wealthy. As you search out information about workplaces, try to find those ingredients that would draw your loyalty and make you feel that you are a part of its activities over the long haul.

You will find that workplaces have personalities just as people do. Some are austere, rigid, demanding; others are lavish, casual, easygoing. They reflect various combinations of the six personality types and tend to attract people who enjoy being together. And bosses vary in their treatment of employees, too.

Most workers want to feel they are valued not only for the work they do but also for themselves. When you are hired, you agree to an unspoken, unwritten emotional contract that can seem almost as real as a legal document. This contract pertains to the way you will be cared about and respected, how personally supportive the atmosphere is (for many people, praise is a great motivator), how fairly you will be treated, how much you are trusted, and yes, even how sensitive the company is to employee feelings during times of cutbacks in personnel. Some companies bend over backward to keep staff on, letting "downsizing" occur through attrition—that is, as people move on to other jobs or retirement. Severe morale problems are created when employees experience prolonged uncertainty about their job security; productivity suffers.

You can often pick up a company's attitude toward employees intuitively from people who work there and from the environment, suggesting that emotional rewards will be forthcoming. You are tapping into the corporate culture or climate. "Corporate culture" can be defined as a common and shared set of beliefs that shape attitudes and behavior, and make for reduced conflict and greater efficiency. Your work life will be more satisfying if you choose an environment with just enough support for you.

As time goes by, the interpersonal characteristics of all jobs change. One newly divorced mother enjoyed working in a small savings and loan office. An older woman gave her support and understanding, the boss was great, and the younger workers were delightful. But the boss, who had decided to work harder at moving up, began to be more restrictive, even to the point of pressuring workers to stay overtime without pay. The older woman was phased out when the company decided to hire a security guard/teller. The work atmosphere of the job changed from fun to funk—but later it became fun again when the now-experienced working mother became the manager.

James Kouzes and Santa Clara University professor Barry Posner made the following observation in *Credibility,* a book they co-authored: "Leaders we admire do not place themselves at the center; they place others there. They do not seek the attention of people; they give it to others." The authors contend that generally "we will work harder and more effectively for people we like and we will like them in direct proportion to how they help make us feel." In their research they found that people felt *valued, motivated, enthusiastic, challenged, inspired, capable, supported, powerful, respected,* and *proud* when they had leaders they valued. Yet they also found that less than half the employees surveyed by the Opinion Research Corporation could say that their companies treated them with dignity and respect.[6]

No matter how carefully you plan your career, at some time you are likely to have a job that does not satisfy all your needs and wants. Some people have exaggerated expectations about the role the workplace and coworkers should play in their lives. For example, some people hope for more emotional support from work friendships than their coworkers are prepared to supply. Cultivating a reasonable amount of independence and a moderately strong skin can protect you against the ups and downs of the work world; unfortunately, "'It would be a kind thing to do' is rarely if ever considered a sufficient reason for doing anything in the business world."[7] At the same time, be aware of your particular needs and aim for a match.

Workplaces are valued not only for the way in which they treat workers but how they treat their local community. They are good neighbors when they use local people and resources as much as possible, enhancing community life by positive participation, not depleting it by adding to its problems.

Autonomy Dimensions: Who's Boss?

Old industrial-style management techniques gave bosses complete authority over employees with whom they shared little about the business. But authors Levering and Moskowitz assert, "The authoritarian work style . . . has failed."[8] The information age is bringing marked changes. Many workers are taking responsibility for their own decisions based on access to data formerly reserved for management. Managers use their computers to write letters and file data, once the task of secretaries. Some businesses have an "open book" policy and share financial information with workers, which often increases productivity.[9] The lines between levels of workers are changing and in some cases becoming quite blurred as more people gain autonomy in the workplace. Management is learning that the more involved workers feel in their jobs, the more energy they will bring to their work and the more enjoyment they will derive from it.

An attitude of responsibility and trust between employer and employee generally increases autonomy and decreases alienation. In a workplace characterized by such an attitude, a positive atmosphere develops that often causes an increase in productivity. Some autonomy can do a lot to ease systems at all levels, global to personal. Sometimes minor management decisions over who can use the copier, when, and how much, can upset personnel more than major decisions over restructuring company finances. The majority of workers will be touched more by the types of decisions that affect them personally every day than by those in that less sensitive spot called the long run.

Erving Goffman wrote in *Asylums* that simply by reason of sheer numbers, institutions tend to become dehumanizing.[10] But large size doesn't always mean depersonalization. Within many large organizations, you can discover companies within companies and/or small, cohesive, caring groups of people looking out for each other's interests. This kind of support would be missing in a small business run by a tyrant.

Barbara Garson studied three workplaces in New York. She reported that two well-known companies had extremely restrictive policies for workers: no talking to other employees during work time, no personal phone calls about family emergencies, and other rigid rules. In contrast, the report described the accounting office of a community college where five older women worked very hard, often staying late to complete their tasks. They also managed to fit in noon parties, trips to the hospital to visit sick family members, and other personal ventures.[11] Want ads and job descriptions don't tell about these kinds of fringe benefits or perks.

Because the number of workers with college degrees is increasing, and because these workers are often underemployed, they are likely to challenge old-style management techniques. If their survival needs and material wants are fulfilled, they often focus on their emotional needs for self-esteem, prestige, and recognition as well as the intellectual and artistic needs to use their minds creatively. Often they become altruistically more aware of the needs of people and planet, and they work to make changes in their workplace.

Autonomy requires workers to assume greater individual responsibility. Many feel that the resulting freedom is worth it. Others will prefer a more structured workplace. If autonomy is important for you, zero in on workplaces that encourage it.

"INSPECTORS, ROBINSON, DO NOT EXPRESS OPINIONS."

Workplace Values: Ethics 101

What would you do if you found your employer involved in some illegal, unethical, or immoral actions? Suppose you further found that you were expected to participate, either actively or by keeping quiet? Work is value laden, but not everyone agrees on what ethical/moral behavior is in practice. We can say, however, that people are ethical when they are honestly and consistently trying to behave according to their values without shirking their responsibilities to society. If the conduct of individuals is not in harmony with their values, they will experience painful conflict.

You can often avoid serious ethical dilemmas in the workplace by doing a little research ahead of time. More and more companies are being evaluated for their level of social responsibility, a concern not only to workers but also to investors. A social screen was developed by U.S. Trust Company of Boston to advise concerned investors who do not want to put their money into companies that make faulty products, pollute the environment, treat employees poorly, or practice fraud.[12] Socially responsible investors have already diverted over $610 *billion* away from corporations whose policies they didn't support, and 80 percent of American consumers say that environmental concerns have led them to switch brands of the products they buy.[13] An expanded version of the social screen is presented below. You can use it to help you determine a given firm's level of social responsibility:

- Do they produce and market safe, high-quality products that are as beautiful as possible?

- Do they sell products and services that affordably fulfill basic needs or enriching wants of their target markets?

- Do they respect and preserve the natural environment wherever they operate?

- Do they practice energy conservation, recycling, and use of renewable energy where possible?

- Do they provide a safe, healthy, humane work environment?

- Do they provide equal employment opportunities for women, men, and minorities?

- Do they have fair labor practices?

- Do they provide workers with information, tools, and an environment that encourages high performance?

- Do they support workplace democracy, encouraging and teaching worker participation by cooperation instead of confrontation?

- Do they contribute to the community where they operate without overwhelming its political, economic, and social life, while understanding the problems their workers face in meeting their needs there?

- Are they honest and fair in their business dealings on both the national and international levels, without exploiting others?

- Do they make an effort to learn the history, language, and culture of international business partners, trying to understand their needs and worldviews?

- Do they operate under and depend on repressive governments?

- Do they depend on military weapons contracts?

- Are they willing to disclose information that gives us answers to all these questions?

Many companies struggle valiantly to get high marks on all the above, but few are perfect. They do have to meet expenses; they do have mountains of governmental regulations to follow that sometimes hinder rather than help them; they may be in a period of difficult transition. Being socially responsible doesn't mean being impractical—for example, giving such lavish benefits that the company fails. But the bottom line is always a business's efforts to consider the needs of its employees and the larger community.

Workers also have ethical responsibilities to do their jobs well, to be honest, and to respect others. The personal responsibility skills you assessed in Chapter 3 will help you make yours a "high-performance" workplace where everyone profits. No amount of legislation or rules can take the place of the ethical behavior of individuals in a society. For both individuals and companies, "Free market competition works not because it is unfettered, but because of the moral dimension we each bring to it. Without these internalized social bonds, efficient competition becomes destructive chaos."[14]

Some companies with a poor track record are trying to present themselves as socially responsible, but their honesty is questionable; some are pretending to be grassroots organizations looking out for people's interests. You can be more confident in your assessment of companies if you do some research and ask questions about what they really stand for. If you have reason to suspect a company of unethical practices, do library research, including a review of the business section of newspapers and magazines. This kind of research can turn up a great deal of information. And ask around. You can be amazed at how much employees know about the ethics of their own company. The question, "Can a company do well when doing good?" (can it be both ethical *and* profitable) is being answered with a resounding "yes!" It's important to find a company whose values match yours. A group called Student Citizens for Social Responsibility at California's Humboldt State University initiated a pledge for graduates whereby they promised "to investigate thoroughly and take into account the social and environmental consequences of any job opportunity I consider." Their pledge is spreading to other campuses.[15]

Buyouts and Sellouts

One way to ensure that a company's value system matches yours is to buy it! We don't envision an untested recruit buying out a company single-handedly, but in the event of plant closings, seasoned workers are beginning to consider the option of buying the company and in some cases are making it work for them. United Zipper Company in Woodland, North Carolina, became an employee-owned reality after months of hard, persistent work following near panic when the factory closed. And in 1994, 54,000 United Airlines employees sported buttons that declare, "You are talking to the owner!" After seven years of difficult times and red ink, the airline worker-owners reported profits more than double the earnings of the previous year.[16] You might consider what it would be like to work in one of these companies.

WORKPLACE TAKE-CHARGE GROUPS

These groups—each with a different focus—provide ideas and support for workplace owners and workers to cooperate to effect positive change. They encourage businesses to show greater fairness toward employees and customers. They show companies ways to improve their relationships with their physical environment and with their host communities. Write for information if you are interested.

ACCESS: Networking in the Public Interest
Publishes *Community Jobs*
50 Beacon St.
Boston, MA 02108

The Alternatives Center
Education Resources and Consultation for
Democratic Organizations
1740 Walnut
Berkeley, CA 94709

Center for Economic Conversion
222 C View Street
Mountain View, CA 94041

Clearinghouse for Community Economic
Development
University of Missouri, 628 Clark Hall
Columbia, MO 65211

CO-OP America
1612 K Street N.W. #600
Washington, DC 20006

Earth Work, magazine of conservation
careers
P.O. Box 550
Charlestown, NH 03603

Environmental Career Organization
Publishes the *Complete Guide to
Environmental Careers*
286 Congress Street
Boston, MA 02210

Environmental Opportunities
P.O. Box 4957
Arcata, CA 95521

Essential Information
Publishes *Good Works: A Guide to Careers
in Social Change*
P.O. Box 19405
Washington, DC 20036

Good Money, newsletter for socially
concerned investors
Box 363
Worcester, VT 05682

ICA Community Economic Development
Program
Suite 1127 Statler Building
20 Park Plaza
Boston, MA 02116

Job Seeker, a listing of national
environmental jobs
Rt. 2, Box 16
Warren, WI 54666

Minority Environmental Internship
Program
1001 Connecticut Avenue, NW
Suite 827
Washington, DC 20036

National Center for Employee
Ownership
1201 Martin Luther King Way
Oakland, CA 94612

New Ways to Work
785 Market Street, Suite 950
San Francisco, CA 94103

North American Students of
Cooperation
Publishes *Guide to Cooperative Careers*
P.O. Box 7715
Ann Arbor, MI 48107
313-663-0889

Opportunities in Public Affairs
1100 Connecticut Avenue, NW
Suite 700
Washington, DC 20036

People who considered themselves ordinary workers have to rethink their abilities and to realize that they can take responsibility, learn, and grow. If a worker-owned company is to succeed, business plans need to be formulated, market research done (sometimes just canvassing the neighborhood), legal and financial help sought, loans acquired, and careful overall guidance sought.

A surprising alternative to the buyout is the sellout. Some small company owners, overwhelmed with data management or other tasks that take away from the products or services they wish to provide, are terminating their employees (and sometimes themselves) and letting them be rehired by a rent-a-staff (RAS) business. The RAS business then leases back the workers, taking responsibilty for the management tasks that are so time-consuming, and freeing the workers to do what they do best: create a product or service. The advantages may include computerized payroll management and filling out and filing government forms, credit union access, wellness programs, and cheaper health insurance resulting from grouping with other companies.[17] Flexibility and more independence from the company can also result when employees are leased back to their companies by an agency that has taken over all hiring of permanent employees. You may find work with an RAS. You may begin a small business using RAS services. You may even begin an RAS. Many work-at-home people provide one or more services to established businesses.

Alternatives to Nine-to-Five: Workstyles/Time Styles

Many of us work according to schedules that don't match our natural rhythms. We are continually caught in a time bind in an increasingly complex world of ever-longer commutes, more complicated personal business transactions, and more involved maintenance of homes and gadgets. Most people work on a rigid schedule with little leeway for personal needs.

For example, most employers are fearful of letting people leave early when they finish their work. Workers in a state office in a small midwestern town report that when they occasionally finish all their assigned work at 4:00 or 4:30, they don their hats and coats and sit in their darkened offices until 5:00.

Work occupies prime time. For the past fifty years, the forty-hour week and the 2,000-hour, fifty-week year have been the center of life, virtually set in concrete and further regulated by professional and union rules about who does what when. In the 1980s, the work week for many workers grew well beyond forty hours. Corporate cutbacks can force remaining workers to work more hours or lose their jobs. Many people are working two or three jobs just to make ends meet (though some are also stretching those "ends" beyond what is necessary). With regard to the expanding work week, editor Ruth Walker writes, "The number of women working two or more jobs has quintupled in 20 years."[18] And then there are those folks who are in constant touch with work by beepers, phones, fax machines, and computer link-ups even when they are driving down the freeway! Work plus the demands of family and the business of living leave many people with little time for other enriched choices.

Workplace stress has become a concern as companies downsize, move away, and otherwise squeeze their employees to produce more, with the threat of unemployment often only a paycheck away. Many Americans are juggling six things at a time not just to succeed but to survive. Stress in great enough quantities can cause exhaustion, illness, and even death.[19] Stress is magnified by the pace of innovation and the necessity to beat competitors to the market with new products. A difficult boss can be a source of stress as well as a hindrance to productivity. Lack of time to relax with family and friends and simply have fun creates a life out of balance. Stress results when the demands of life become too great.

In the early 1980s, studies of some Silicon Valley, California, firms disclosed a higher divorce rate among their employees than for the United States as a whole; high rates of sexual and physical abuse of children; frequent drug use by children of families employed in high-tech firms; high numbers of strokes at work; and families living beyond their means.[20] Our biology can't catch up with our technology. We have yet to learn to blend with technology without losing our identities or our health. Yet many people hate to look like they are not busy, so caught are Americans in the Puritan work ethic (or so afraid their bosses will give them more work if they seem idle!). People brag that they haven't had a vacation in years, almost as if this is a mark of excellence. Some become so used to working that they can't turn off their minds if the opportunity presents itself, and then they fill the air with radio and TV chatter. Yet those who opt for less work and hence less pay might be enjoying life more!

Here is a checklist to help you decide whether you are overstressed, with some tips for changes you can make to reduce your stress level:

- Are you very unhappy with your life or your work? It's time to reevaluate each life component to pinpoint and resolve the problem. Learning to accept yourself and appreciate your good points can be an important first step. Sometimes the changes needed may be very small.

- Are you feeling excessively fatigued and overworked? Get someone to take over for you at home or at work for a couple of days while you spend time sorting out your priorities. What can you eliminate? How can you get the help you need? Sometimes a good friend or colleague can help. Plan regular meetings, with a friend or fellow worker to talk over your progress in keeping a balanced schedule.

- Are you spending too much time working? Find some enjoyable activity outside of work that will give you new energy. Exercise, for example, can actually be energizing. Watch funny movies because humor is a great stress reliever, and even tears can help. Meditate, do yoga, play soothing music, enjoy a romp with the dog or brush your cat. Take a mini-vacation—for example, a weekend at home doing nothing but soaking up leisure, letting other people deal with distractions. Alternate with a friend, providing such respite care for each other.

- Do you feel regularly stressed? There are stress-reduction workshops available at many community centers, conferences, and health care centers, and many companies teach simple relaxation techniques that can become a habit.

Leisure, for many, is hard won. John Kenneth Galbraith says, "Only if an individual has a choice as to the length of his working week or year, along with the option of taking unpaid leave for longer periods, does he or she have an effective choice between income and leisure."[21] Studs Terkel quotes a steelworker who says, "If I had a twenty-hour work week, I'd get to know my kids better, my wife better. Some kid invited me to go on a college campus. On a Saturday. It was summertime. Hell, if I have a choice of taking my wife and kids to a picnic or going to a college campus, it's gonna be the picnic. But if I worked a twenty-hour week, I could do both. Don't you think with that extra twenty hours people could really expand?"[22] And if more people were able to work fewer hours, there would be less unemployment. Humans have always dreamed of a world without work or at least with less work. In *BREAKTIME, Living without Work in a Nine to Five World*, Bernard Lefkowitz discusses some alternatives to "work."[23]

Many more workers could be employed if some people worked fewer than forty hours a week, fifty weeks a year. The loss of income might be offset in many ways (even financially): saving energy and resources, enjoying a more enriched life, having more time for the business of living. Many people with special needs such as parents, the elderly, and the handicapped are able to work when they are provided with a shorter schedule. Writer and philosopher Tony Shively felt that with a shorter work schedule people might be more efficient. He once remarked in conversation with the author, "Society often demands more of a person's nature than it can give."

Flexible Workstyles

Although the nine-to-five routine fits many people quite well, others find it constricting. They may search for a workplace that is more flexible. To provide alternatives, new time styles such as job sharing and flextime have come on line. Temporary and part-time work can also be used to ease aching schedules.

Job Sharing   Sharing one job allows two qualified people to work at the same position, in any combination of time schedules they can work out with their employer. One person might work mornings, the other in the afternoon. They work out a system for sharing information.

Flextime   Flextime allows employees to work any eight hours between specified times, such as 7 A.M. to 6 P.M. Workers on flextime can take care of the business of living in their off hours, when others are still at work to serve them. Compressed work schedules, such as four ten-hour days per week, are a variation on flextime. Some companies are even experimenting with three twelve-hour shifts, enabling college students to work three weekend nights and still attend classes, or working parents to share child care. Some employers allow employees to choose which holidays they will take off; some allow them to accumulate and use sick leave as paid time off. Some allow full-time employees to reduce work hours for a period of time in exchange for reduced compensation. Instead of laying off large numbers of people, companies sometimes ask all employees to work fewer hours at a reduced salary.

The Bechtel Group, a worldwide engineering company based in San Francisco, felt that they would have an edge in recruiting valuable workers if they offered their people a nine-hour day, four days a week, with every other Friday off and the alternate Friday an eight-hour day. Their employees now look forward to twenty-six three-day weekends a year![24]

Such flexibility may add to the work and cost of management, but research shows that absenteeism drops and productivity rises when companies adopt less rigid work hours. Businesses find that they benefit from the flexibility and the ability to change workers' hours and utilize work stations more efficiently.

Telecommuting   Working at home by a computer linked to the workplace, called telecommuting, is an alternative, especially in some areas where physical commuting is so time-consuming. Recent major earthquakes closed so many California roads and slowed traffic for so long that companies were forced to consider alternatives. According to New Ways to Work, an organization that helps people explore alternative work schedules, Pacific Gas and Electric experimented with a wide variety of schedules and commute methods, including van pooling, commute-hour shuttles, ride matching, telecommuting, flexible schedules, and compressed work weeks. The results were highly favorable.[25] Besides being attractive to employees, telecommuting in particular has enormous potential for unclogging roads and saving energy. A Small Business Administration report found that setting up a home office with computer, printer, telephone, and fax machine costs about $5,000. The report said that not all telecommuters chose this method because they had children at home; most of these workers said that they did not feel isolated from peers; they took only moderate time off for breaks; and they smoked, drank, and took drugs less than regular nine-to-five, office-bound workers. Other research found that telecommuting workers were about 20 percent more productive than regular office workers.[26] About half of telecommuters are men.[27] As we move into a skilled labor shortage, companies may find that offering such benefits will make them more desirable places to work.

Contingent Work   Today we see a growing "contingent workforce" of part-time, just-in-time, temporary, or leased workers and independent contractors. Twenty-two million Americans hold contingent jobs all across the employment spectrum, many of them part time, a number that has been growing three times faster than the labor force as a whole. Only half the new jobs created in 1992 were full-time jobs.[28] Yet studies show that contingent workers are often far less productive than permanent employees because they do not have the same commitment to the company, because they do not have the time to learn well the techniques required by the company, and because when the temporary workers are managers, they do not get to know the workers well.[29] Still, two-thirds of Americans, regardless of gender, marital status, occupation, industry, education, or geographic location say they would be willing to sacrifice pay just to have one or two days off each week.[30] On the other side of this picture are the many unemployed people and those who work part time and who want full-time jobs. Manpower, Inc., the largest temporary agency in the United States, is now the nation's largest employer with 560,000 employees, most of whom are women. They work for much lower pay than workers in regular jobs, usually without medical coverage or other benefits.[31]

Temporary Work   A growing variation of contingent work is temporary work. This involves full-time but time-limited jobs. Such work is available in many areas: office, technical, professional, industrial, and medical. All these fields require a wide variety of skills for trained or trainable workers. Some people find that working full time at intervals is quite to their liking; they may learn new skills and find access to jobs that are often available to those inside the company. In a survey of temporary workers, 38 percent said they were offered full-time employment by a company they entered on a temporary assignment.[32] Some temporary agencies even provide a variety of benefits. Some people contract their services to businesses directly on a temporary basis, part time. The trend toward part-time and temporary work seems to be emerging as a major feature in employment.

There are disadvantages to part-time and temporary work. When a worker is classified as part time or temporary, he or she will generally get less pay, no benefits or pension rights, and little security. The U.S. Office of Personnel Management has issued regulations to limit the amount of time federal agencies can keep employees in temporary jobs.[33] The continual uprooting of workers due to the greater ease with which employers can hire and fire affects both the workplace and the community. Part-time and temporary workers are often considered expendable as companies struggle to make business more profitable. But to many who choose to work this way, the time flexibility is worth the job uncertainty.

Work of One's Own

Susan Meeker-Lowry, founder of Catalyst and author of *Economics as if the Earth Really Mattered*, says, "Many, if not most, Americans are dissatisfied with their jobs, simply 'putting in time.' . . . It is rare to find someone who is doing what s/he loves *and* earning a decent living at it. As a result, it is not surprising that we feel we should at least be able to 'have' luxuries and conveniences as rewards for our servitude . . . [but] the daily grind reasserts itself . . . . We feel out of control—and we often are." She continues, "Cooperative businesses and worker-ownership are two of the most promising tools we have to regain control over our work lives *and* to revive our communities."[34]

People all over the world are asking for more rights and responsibilities, including greater democracy. And in fact there are many ways to create the community and autonomy that have been lost in this century's development and expansion. One of these ways is the worker cooperative, in which a group gets together to begin a business and sometimes to share the work and profits with their customers.

Other ways include shared ownership by workers, democratic decision making, profit-and-loss sharing, skills sharing/job rotation, and education in job and cooperative skills. All of these display social responsibility along with profit making and community involvement. Cooperative ventures, or co-ops, can be businesses ranging from grocery markets to print shops, from forestry trusts to sewing operations.[35] For example, food co-ops sometimes sell memberships to individuals who agree to work a certain number of hours a week in exchange for lower-cost food. Nonprofit groups work with businesses to develop a new and more cooperative, ecologically concerned economy.[36] "The social sector is the fastest growing of the country's sectors and the largest 'employer.' There are nearly one million nonprofit organizations in the U.S. Well over ninety million people are involved in nonprofit activities, including both volunteers and employed staff."[37]

Grassroots financial institutions are springing up around the world. They are dedicated to developing their communities and to helping all the community members, including the poor, to participate in the local economy. Some development programs begun by these institutions include "incubators" that provide support, information, office space, and equipment for fledgling businesses.

Although a life without work may be beyond the dreams of most people, many often wish they could be their own bosses. "In the mid-twentieth century the trend was toward employment in large companies, and business start-ups were declining. But as the new century opens, self-employment is growing at a faster rate than wage- and salary-paying jobs."[38] Most new jobs in the United States are being created by small, service-oriented firms or suppliers of parts, and this trend is predicted to grow into the next century.[39] Jerry Pitts, a "downsized" health care manager, remodeled his garage and began a small sales operation for a telephone company. Some college students have begun businesses from their dorm rooms that bring in sales in the six-figure range. Absolute Screening and Printing turned out T-shirts with sales of $300,000 in the first quarter of 1993.[40] Millard Fuller, founder of Habitat for Humanity, started on his path to millionaire status while he was in college, providing a service that delivered birthday cakes to students from their parents.

Ten percent of Americans work for themselves and the trend is toward more women-owned businesses. In 1992, women owned 28 percent of the nation's businesses and were opening them at a rate of 300,000 per year, 50 percent faster than men. In 1994, over 6.5 million women business owners employed eleven million workers, more people than the combined Fortune 500 companies employ worldwide, providing jobs for over 10 percent of the U.S. workforce. By the year 2000, over half of all U.S. small businesses are predicted to be owned by women[41] and they are moving into traditionally male areas. Small businesses provided 80 percent of the net new jobs in the economy over the last decade and almost all the innovation; many of these companies are based on socially and environmentally responsible practices.[42] Some say the day of the "Mom and Pop" venture is long gone, but this may not be so. Even though the competition is fierce from large chains, if Mom and Pop are going high tech in a specialized market niche, they may well be developing highly efficient and successful companies.[43]

Here are some ways to become self-employed without starting out all alone all at once:

Employee stock option plans (ESOPs) are the way companies can share control while sharing some profits. ESOPs remain in effect until an employee leaves. Not all ESOP plans are designed to give workers autonomy; rather, they may give the company advantages, such as reducing worker turnover.

The *intrapreneur* holds an intermediate position between the cold, cruel corporation and the cold, cruel world of being on one's own. It is a term coined by Gifford Pinchot, III, a consultant to such companies as Exxon, to describe the *intracorporate entrepreneur*. Intrapreneurs remain company employees while contracting their services to their employer. Using company resources and support, they act as self-employed persons, often developing services or products that the company wants but to which it is unwilling to commit large-scale expenditures. For example, one artistically handy employee negotiated a contract with her electronics company to make a number of working engineering models at home. A clerical pool could set up its own systems in return for negotiated payment. An engineer could gather a team to do creative research. A teacher could be given a special assignment (with special pay) to develop a curriculum for his or her school district. A company benefits because it does not lose either a valued employee who might move to a competitor, or that person's good idea.[44] Intrapreneurship may require some capital, but it involves less risk than entrepreneurship. Look around your workplace for a possible intrapreneurial opportunity.

Contract work can be an offshoot of intrapreneuring or simply another way to begin a business of one's own. Some workplaces contract out to independent people certain jobs like data processing, accounting, preparation of income tax forms, and maintenance service. One woman began her own business by contracting to do newsletters for a number of companies that didn't wish to produce their own. Some individuals or groups provide services for members or clients, such as insurance coverage, discount purchasing, and warehouse storage.

Franchises are for people who would like to be independent business owners but would prefer less risk and more support than they would have if they were totally on their own. Franchises have moved beyond fast food into such growing areas as hairstyling, quick-stop shopping, weight-loss systems, computer sales, and a whole host of other types of business ventures. A new franchise opens every eight minutes of each business day; one out of twelve business establishments is a franchise. While Fortune 500 companies downsized by over a million jobs during the last ten years, franchises were adding nearly two million jobs to the economy. Franchises account for 40.9 percent of all retail sales, and total sales could reach $1 trillion by the year 2000,[45] with home health care one of the leaders.[46] Franchises fail far less often than other small businesses and generally need less start-up financing.

A person can buy into a franchise for as little as $35,000 to $50,000 in cash, borrowing the rest of the $70,000 to $130,000 total investment. Some people use the equity in their homes for the initial capital. A few states, Maryland for example, are encouraging women, minorities, and handicapped individuals to buy franchises by providing these fledgling investors with investment help. The parent company may provide training, equipment, marketing, name, themes, logos, uniforms, and other tools and support. The advantage of franchising to the parent firm is the opportunity to expand more rapidly than would be possible if it had to raise all the money necessary for moving into new markets.

Cooperatives and *collectives,* group-owned and democratically run enterprises, are a growing option for people to improve their work environments without having to venture out on their own. These joint undertakings

---

TIPS ON STARTING YOUR OWN BUSINESS

IS SMALL BUSINESS FOR YOU? YOUR QUALIFICATIONS SUMMARY

- Are you enterprising: confident, enthusiastic, optimistic, persistent, good with people?
- Are you trustworthy, energetic, healthy, hardworking, flexible, independent, balanced, organized, good at record-keeping?
- Are you a responsible leader, good decision maker, self-starter?
- Are you willing to learn, take advice, observe, and study other options?
- Can you face your mistakes, learn from them, and change your behaviors and attitudes?
- Do you have/can you develop a good support network: family, friends, associates?
- When you get an idea, can you get it off the ground?
- Do you know when to move on, not stay in one place forever?
- Do you have experience/education in the business you are considering?

INFORMATION GATHERING

- List ideas that you might turn into a business.
- Describe each one in a paragraph.
- Put each one through the decision-making process described in Chapter 8.
- Rank your ideas in order of desirability and likelihood of success.
- Evaluate each product or service: Is it innovative, of good quality, desirable, without heavy competition, something you would enjoy working with?
- Contact people listed in the telephone directory Yellow Pages and newspaper financial pages who run similar or related businesses or franchises. Use the information interviewing techniques discussed later in this chapter to talk with them.
- Explore the possibilities of working with a partner.
- Prepare a résumé, just as if you were job hunting, to clarify your qualifications to yourself and to your clients.

---

often result in increased motivation, sense of control, and productivity. In the 1960s, women in Japan began a milk-buying cooperative that gave them more say about price, quality, and environmental issues in food production. Now working directly with farmers, they have a membership of more than 218,000 households in over 100 branches, each member contributing about $9 a month. With its own line of sixty products they employ a full-time staff of over 700. As the fourth-largest co-op in Japan, they have $120 million in investments and in 1993 did $650 million in business.[47]

TIPS ON STARTING YOUR OWN BUSINESS *(continued)*

INFORMATION GATHERING *(continued)*

- Attend workshops for small businesses offered by local colleges, the Small Business Association, or other centers. Go to meetings of businesspeople in your areas of interest. Read related books.

- Do market research; sometimes just asking around can give you an idea of the market before you hire someone to do it professionally.

- Explore locations/types of spaces available/cost.

FINANCIAL/LEGAL PLANNING

- Begin with a clear statement of purpose.

- Develop a sample product or prototype, and find out whether people would buy it. Have people test it.

- Cost out possible expenditures: goods, services, equipment, insurance, real estate, advertising; develop a good accounting system.

- Find out about permits, licenses, and other documents you may need to get started.

- Work out a financial plan as carefully as you would a résumé or term paper. Do a complete description of the business, estimate of cash flow, one-, two-, and five-year projections, your own financial assets and liabilities, the amount of money you need to "tide you over" until the business gets going.

- Talk to a knowledgeable financial planner about various funding options.

- Get to know your banker. Getting credit is one of the largest hurdles, especially for women!

- Develop a credit rating by repaying a small personal loan promptly.

- Look into: loans from banks and private foundations; taxes, partnerships, stocks, qualifications of staff needed.

- Negotiate the terms of loans and other contracts and expenses; don't just accept the first suggestion.

- See a knowledgeable lawyer about various legal aspects of the business.

Your very own business may be the way you choose to go. Small businesses have grown from twelve million in the early 1980s to twenty million in 1993.[48] You will hear a great deal of advice about starting a small business. Some advisers encourage the budding entrepreneur to start with a flourish; others counsel going slowly and in small steps. Each case is unique, but the facts show that many small businesses fail in their first year through owners' lack of planning and experimenting as well as lack of capital. Most successful entrepreneurs have degrees and experience, but we still hear and read about people who begin small businesses on a shoestring and in no time are making a profit. "Find a need and fill it" says an old adage that still works.

Luke Elliott says that "even today, in the era of corporate cannibalism, it's possible to start a business on a shoestring." He and his wife, Cindy, started Photo Vision, a retail outlet for solar electric systems and other energy-related products with "$1,500 and a kitchen table."[49] Entrepreneurs must be sure to check local zoning, traffic, and licensing laws, before business starts booming, especially if they intend to use dangerous materials, take up parking spaces, or have other features that would invade the neighborhood. Learn about business in general and your field in particular before venturing into your own enterprise. Many local colleges and adult education centers provide workshops and counseling to help the prospective entrepreneur begin a business.

How can you find out what services your community needs that you might provide? Imagine how much archaeologists of the year A.D. 10,000 will learn about us if they get a look at some of our old telephone Yellow Pages. Scanning the Yellow Pages is one of the best ways to survey not only the businesses in an area but the lifestyles, too. These listings reveal surprising ideas for both employment and beginning businesses. Looking at Yellow Pages from other geographic areas can also tell you about businesses that might work in your community. You can determine whether a town is somewhat affluent by the number of upscale restaurant ads you find and the types of car dealers who advertise. Rural places will advertise a great deal of farm equipment; Silicon Valley will have pages of electronics firms. Comparing old phone books with new ones will tell you what businesses have failed. For example, solar energy companies took a beating when government subsidies were withdrawn in the 1980s and the message went out that energy conservation was not a priority. Talking to people who have similar businesses or who might order from you, and showing your product to people who might buy it are some ways to test your idea.

You can avoid investing a fortune; start small by having a simple, inexpensive business card made. Your first card does not have to be fancy. Some of the many ads that come in your mail may feature one for a small price. Or use a computer to print up your own and have it fast copied on card stock at your local copy store. For an extra fee the store will cut the copies professionally. Then begin handing your cards out to friends and relatives, perhaps offering to do your first work free or for a small fee. Media messages to the contrary, the best advertisement is word-of-mouth by satisfied customers. You can use evenings and weekends to test the waters while keeping your paying job as a backup. Because of the expense of setting up an office if you are a beginner, therapist Richard Patocchi advises you to rent office space part time; only after you have enough clients to justify expansion should you agree to rent the space for more time per week.

The person with a product or service to offer and the energy to do it all can find great satisfaction in being an entrepreneur. There is no question that beginning a business may be hazardous to your health on many levels, but you get to be your own boss—twenty-four hours a day! From the five-year-old selling lemonade to the weekend do-it-yourselfer remodeling the kitchen, self-interest is a powerful motivator for getting work done. Generally, business owners are happier with their work than employees.

There are many resources for those wishing to begin a small business. The U.S. Small Business Administration (P.O. Box 15434, Fort Worth, TX 76119) has local groups that give assistance to budding entrepreneurs, as do many local chambers of commerce. (Write to the U.S. Small Business Administration for a copy of "Checklist for Going Into Business.") The Department of Transportation, Office of Small and Disadvantaged Business Utilization (400 Seventh Street, S.W., Room 9410, Washington, DC 20590) will also send information. Your library can refer you to organizations and publications that can guide you. Community colleges, chambers of commerce, and other local groups often run workshops for prospective and current small business owners. As a business starts growing, an owner has to decide whether to brave the world of venture capital. Experience, competence at what you have already accomplished, and a good adviser are usually essential before you go into the deep water of big business. But we can count on small businesses to continue creating more jobs than large corporations into the next century, and much of that work is happening at home.

Worksteads

People who do work at home—word processing, translating, editing, cabinet making—are *worksteaders*. Whether you work for a company or on your own, it is now possible to do much of that work at home by computer. Telecommunications can bring people within sight and sound of each other even though they are hundreds of miles apart. One production plant is kept running on the weekends, even though the human in charge is generally ten miles away. Equipment thousands of miles in outer space can be operated and repaired from the earth by remote control. The Japanese have an experimental farm run by computerized robots. Who knows what goods and services will be produced from the electronic cottage of the future? Here's what two worksteaders say:[50]

> There are a whole bunch of soft industries that are information oriented or technologies that have no pollution whatsoever. . . . These kinds of industries could be right in our neighborhoods. . . . I've always lived where I work.

> —Peter Ziegler, Earth Lab Institute

> If a person is going to leave a job to work at home, [he or she] needs a very clear attitude about how [he or she] is going to live. I set up a rather modest goal of the kind of security I wanted to have before I left the law firm. I don't buy expensive clothes, for instance. I enjoy cooking so I don't go to restaurants much. If you have a place to live, where you can also work, you can get along on very little. The rest of life doesn't really take too much money if you have a place to be.
>
> —*George Hellyer, Attorney*

Productivity increases for those who work at home. Single parents, the elderly, and the disabled can find new opportunities worksteading. Lack of safety guides, however, and possible exploitation by an employing firm—meaning low wages, no vacations or benefits, and long hours—are causes for some concern. Isolation is another issue to consider. Career development is often put on hold while a person spends time developing the business. Combining child-raising with work at home can also prove to be a stressful alternative. In some cases workers may have to buy or lease equipment or office furniture. They may find their utility bills (for example, telephone link-up) and energy costs rising. Some companies, finding long distance work attractive, have moved their data processing work to Third World countries where worker wages as well as worker protection are minimal, thus subtracting from the available pool of jobs in the United States.[51]

Third-Wave Prosumers

When a truck driver with a college degree was asked what he intended to do with his education, he replied, "I will practice living, I will develop my intellect, which may incidentally contribute to the elevation of the esthetic and cultural levels of society. I will try to develop the noble and creative elements within me. I will contribute very little to the *grossness* of the national product."[52]

Some idealistic people prefer not to contribute to an economy they feel encourages mindless consumption of goods, wastes energy and resources, and contributes to a poor quality of life. These nonconformists, called *prosumers* by Alvin Toffler, are carving out unique lifestyles. Do-it-yourself and self-help tasks, bartering, and sharing are all parts of their diverse lifestyle.[53] The psychologist who helps people grow at the office may come home to a small farm and grow vegetables for self and sale. One veterinarian's varied schedule at one time included part-time spaying of dogs and cats at an animal shelter, along with research, writing, and private consulting. He and his artist wife grew many of their own vegetables and repaired their own car. Richard and Susan Pitcairn are third-wave prosumers in many aspects of their lives. Their book *Natural Health for Dogs and Cats* reflects their caring lifestyle.[54]

Prosumers Pat and Bill Cane live a largely self-sufficient lifestyle. In the past they have raised chickens, goats, bees, and raspberries, and have made goat cheese, jam, and honey. Their bountiful garden provides food for table and barter. Preparing seasonal nine-course gourmet meals for friends has paid their basic expenses. Pat has bartered computer consulting and beautiful stained glass for a variety of goods and services. They publish a quarterly journal called *Integrities* four times a year. And now they are facilitating projects in Latin American countries for women and men in need of support and development help. Bill wrote in his book, *Through Crisis to Freedom*, "In crisis, you are somehow enabled to get in touch with sources of life deep inside yourself—sources you never knew were there. And then mysteriously, like the blades of grass, you begin to know how to grow."[55] These new "old" lifestyles aren't for everyone, but they are options in a nine-to-five world for those willing to take the risk. Many people lived these simpler lifestyles years ago. In the technological future, we may be able to do less work and enjoy more of life's good things.

New Views

Most people, especially males, begin work after graduating from high school or college and keep at it until age sixty-five. But even the most exciting of career fields can pall after many years and workers must take steps to keep up their motivation. Going back to school, seeking promotion, changing positions or companies, looking for a unique approach to your job, finding enriching hobbies, fostering personal growth on all levels are all ways to keep up your work energy. Some industries such as Intel, Rolm, and Seagate have experimented with giving their employees leaves of absence for social action, educational projects, or for pure recreation.

An engineer working in Silicon Valley found that his boss expected him to live a very upscale personal life. He was urged to trade in his ten-year-old Honda for a new BMW and in general was criticized for many of his lifestyle choices. He decided to let his wife carry them financially for a few years while he went back to school to get a degree in spiritual theology. He is back with a new electronics company and a whole new perspective on life. By riding the train to work, he has time to read in his new field, and he does church work on weekends, to his great satisfaction.

As people explore alternatives, they create a variety of new workstyles. Many find they can make a living by working part time at several jobs. People who teach a course or two at community colleges may run their own businesses on the side, publish articles, or do graphics and some computer consulting. They may fish in the summer, teach skiing in the winter, and do a little farming and construction work in between.

Creative careers are other ways to work in a company or on your own. As you interview people and observe them on their jobs, look for those who have taken an ordinary job and brought it to life in a creative way, sometimes within a very structured bureaucracy. The position of "store manager" with its attendant duties may sound formidable or dull. But Monique Benoit of San Francisco gave it new life. Well known for her community involvement, she loved to shop in expensive antique stores and boutiques. She also cherished her independence and loved to travel, so she created her own job to satisfy these qualities. She sent a carefully composed letter to managers of her favorite stores, offering to "shop-sit" if they had to be away from the store for business or personal reasons. She received a good response and subsequent offers of part-time, temporary, and permanent full-time employment.

In Santa Monica, California, two women began a vehicle-repair referral service to put people in touch with affordable, honest, and reliable mechanics. They generated $750,000 in sales in 1992.[56] "Susie Skates" indulges in her favorite sport while delivering messages. "Flying Fur" delivers pampered pets around the country, while "Sherlock Bones" searches for missing pets. From Clutter Cutter, Rent-a-Yenta or Rent-a-Goat, Eco-Tourism or Eco-Weddings, to Mama's Llamas and Rent-a-Thief, people create careers with imagination instead of capital.

Here are a few ideas for small-scale, more traditional, although not always lucrative, careers: house-sitting, pet-sitting, matching housemates or travel companions; offering child care that includes instruction in a craft or hobby; providing shopping or transportation services or exercise classes for the elderly and disabled; doing photography at special events; making house calls for sick plants; acting as costumed servers or entertainers at parties, such as being Barney for children's birthdays; teaching do-it-yourself house or auto repair. Add producing and marketing very special gourmet home-grown/homemade food and herbs, perhaps by prearranged purchase, or a pick-your-own flowers opportunity; combining photography with a host of activities both recreational and professional; designing/evaluating children's toys for companies; designing play space, books, or furniture; making treasures from trash—for example, rag rugs, and quilts; conducting estate sales. The homeless in one community market their own home-grown vegetables, raised on a city lot, and sell used clothing and other treasures gleaned from donations. The possibilities are endless. One major mark of a fulfilling job is the invigorating and energy-giving feelings it provides.

Leisure Styles

All the above suggestions are aimed at helping you not only to find satisfying work but also to find time for satisfying leisure. Many people are opting for a less pressured, more serene life with less frantic activity. They start small home businesses that require only two or three days of work a week, retire early, and take time off to be with children instead of trying to juggle work and child care. Busy people are asserting their need for daily meditation, exercise, or other forms of relaxation to help them get in touch with deeper values.

We are just beginning to consider the possibility of integrating work and leisure. Some husbands are taking time off while their wives work; some people are easing into retirement with reduced schedules. Total involvement in work, then, may not be essential in an affluent, information society.

But not everyone could slow down and enjoy leisure, even if more were available. Some find leisure frightening. Some workers end up spending their vacations or retirements down at the workplace watching others work. For some people, work is life and they enjoy it. At the extreme, some highly successful people could be leading lives that are impoverished on many levels. Instead of getting in touch with other facets of their personalities, the total technologist avoids social gatherings and the confirmed clerk avoids art. But most of us need *some* structure in our lives, even though we might like to think of ourselves as free spirits. Work is the basic organizing principle for most people, so planning and learning how to use leisure in an enriching way becomes important. Too much work can consume us; too much free time can bore us. Too much materialism suffocates us; too little frightens us. Many people are continually trying to find the balance, but they are further ahead than those who don't even *know* their lives are out of balance.

When we look at basic needs and wants and compare them with the work that is being done, we might be tempted to say that *much of the work we do is not the work that needs to be done.* Aware people are evaluating their own work to see whether it not only meets their own needs, wants, and values but is socially responsible as well. After a certain point, they may wonder if the *money* is worth the *time.* They are often people with ideals, education, and skills who have some money behind them to aid in a unique transition. They find themselves working hard, often at jobs they themselves have designed and doing work they feel is of benefit to society. Leisure can enrich not only individuals but the planet as well.

Community

A workplace is not just an isolated entity existing in a vacuum. No matter how aloof it tries to stand, it is enmeshed in its local community in innumerable ways. From farm to city, from ocean to mountains, from prairies to wetlands, the geography of a locale affects a major part of a worker's life and workstyle. The predominant products and services provided by the area—logs or jam, silicon chips or potato chips—certainly influence a locale. The size of a workplace, whether it be a huge corporation in a small town or a small business in a big city, affects and in turn is affected by the place where it lives. The style of dress, housing, and transportation, the kind of leisure activities, schools, social life, and economic achievement will vary slightly or greatly from one place to another.

Many job seekers will choose a place that encourages the type of lifestyle they would like to lead. A person seeking a more sophisticated style may choose a Manhattan apartment and wear the latest fashions, while the Big Sur Coast of California is dotted with the tiny and isolated cabins of artists and writers in sweat shirts and jeans.

But beyond the physical level, people seek "community" that nourishes their emotional, intellectual, and spiritual levels. Just as in a company, a community has an unwritten psychological contract about how it treats its members and what it values. Many people would seek out a community for these qualities: a hospitable and human-scale place that does not force people to join in but provides opportunities for them to share experiences with like-minded people and to feel that each of them is valued and supported; it enables individuals to have a sense of belonging to a place and having a say in what goes on there. It is, in short, a place where they can feel at home! Sometimes just the design of a place can make it easy for people to meet— the local post office or friendly coffee shop. Sometimes an activity will draw people together: religion, community service, sports, recreation, politics, theater, and music are examples.

But some people value isolation whether they live in the forest or the busy streets of a large city. There is always a trade-off between privacy and community. Many new living styles are developing to give people the best of both worlds, shared housing and co-housing among them, where people have private spaces but may share some meals, child care, and recreational space with a community.

Former English professor and farmer-poet Wendell Barry sees the United States as Jefferson did—a collection of communities where people share more values than just the economic. They include hard work, devotion, memory, and association. He questions what we mean by "progress" if it means the loss of land and community.[57] Generally, the more a location is taken over by gigantic businesses and mammoth traffic systems, and the more people absorb themselves in technologies such as television, the more difficult it is to find human-scale community.

The Ins and Outs of Workplaces

So *now* is the time to collect information about workplaces you might consider. First, get a view from the outside by reading about workplaces and eliminating those that don't match your needs and wants. The next step is the information interview: getting the inside story about careers and companies by talking to people on site.

Information about companies is available from many sources, which may also help you find out whether the claims a business makes are true. Most libraries have a business reference section; most librarians love to help people and take pride in knowing where to find data. Look for books like *Everybody's Business: An Almanac, the Irreverent Guide to Corporate America* by Milton Moskowitz, Michael Katz, and Robert Levering, and *Rating America's Corporate Conscience* by Steven D. Lydenberg, Alice Tepper Marlin, and Sean Strub with the Council on Economic Priorities. *Who's Who in Commerce and Industry* will give you key names. Business references like the *Directory of Corporate Affiliations* (who owns whom) and Funk and Scott's *Index of Corporations and Industries* will be found in most large public libraries and universities. Standard & Poor and Dun & Bradstreet also offer business directories. Information on multinationals is found in the *Directory of Foreign Firms Operating in the U.S.*

Information about what donations a corporation has made is available from the IRS. The *Corporate Giving Directory* profiles more than five hundred major corporations and their foundations. Computer networks accessed with a modem can connect you with free databases such as the Rachel Database, created by the Environmental Research Foundation and RTK Net (Right to Know Network), created by OMB Watch. Free business directories are also available on some networks. The Department of Labor's Office of Safety and Health Administration (OSHA) has computerized records of workplaces that have been cited for worker safety violations, listed by industry. Environmental impact statements and records of environmental violations are available from the federal Environmental Protection Agency. Information on local companies such as deeds and licenses are kept by city or county governments.

Company unions, labor groups, environmental organizations, and consumer groups are other sources of information. Ask for an annual report and other company literature; notice who is on the board of directors and what their affiliations are; ask what legislation the company supports or has helped to get passed; attend a meeting of the company if these are open to the public.[58]

Business and professional journals in your field will provide a wealth of information. The *Journal of Small Business Management* can be obtained from the College of Business and Economics, West Virginia University (Morgantown, WV 26506). The *Encyclopedia of Associations* lists groups promoting their own wares and there is even a *Directory of Conventions*. *CO-OP America's Factsheet on Finding Green Jobs* is available free; the address is listed in Workplace-Take-Charge Groups in this chapter. For five dollars CO-OP America also will send you a *Guide to Environmental Education Programs at U.S. Colleges and Universities.*

Professional organizations, a source of job leads, also hire personnel—for example, in public relations and finance. Look at chambers of commerce,

Better Business Bureaus, real estate boards, and trade associations at the national, state, and local levels, not only for information but also for possible jobs.[59]

The U.S. Department of Labor has general and statistical information on all aspects of the labor market in the United States for those doing research for themselves or their businesses. This agency also has regional offices. The U.S. Bureau of Industrial Economics has information on trends in various fields. Your local chamber of commerce can inform you about the businesses in your town. College career center libraries, placement offices, and state employment offices are often stocked with material about companies. Some companies have public relations departments that send information if you write or call.

Don't forget to use the Yellow Pages of your phone book, a gold mine of ideas because just about every business in your area is listed there according to what it does. If you read the business section of your local newspaper regularly, you will know who is doing what and where in the work world in your area. Don't be afraid to call or write to people who sound interesting. Ask them to tell you more about what they do or congratulate them on some accomplishment or promotion. People appreciate positive feedback. Let them know if you are sincerely interested in some aspect of their work or workplace. The applicants best prepared for a job interview are those who not only know the company they want to work for, but also have a broad knowledge of the work world. Knowing some of the basics about a company, an industry, and its competition gives you confidence during the job hunt.

Information Interviewing

After doing this library research, people often feel that some pieces are still missing from the puzzle. Some are disappointed because many jobs described in occupational guides sound dull. But those descriptions are the bare bones of the job. You can put flesh on those skeletons by visiting workplaces and interviewing people about what they do. From here on, it's important to be *out*—talking to everyone about his or her job, out observing work environments.

How often have working friends given you a blow-by-blow description of life at Picky Products, Inc.? (Or about a class for that matter!) If *you've* worked for a company (or taken a course), you have information about it that's not easily available to an outsider. You know the people who are likely to help beginners; you know how tough or easy the supervisors/teachers are, how interesting or boring the work is—what it's *really* like!

Obtaining this inside story answers two questions: Is this a job you would really like? Is this a place you would really like to work? Unless you are an experienced and sophisticated job seeker with a broad knowledge of jobs, you need to gather as much firsthand information as you can before you choose a career and perhaps plan courses and get a degree. The job may require education or special training. Why not find out all you can before spending time, energy, and money on training for a job that turns out to be different from your expectations? You can also eliminate misconceptions about the preparation you need in order to be hired.

If you feel timid about approaching a stranger, practice by interviewing people in your family, then a friend or neighbor about his or her job. Talk to all the people you meet about what they do and how they like it, and who they can introduce you to in your career field. Ask people you know for names of willing interviewees. It's amazing how you can usually find someone who knows someone who knows someone. Your school alumni office is often in touch with graduates in different fields. An instructor in a field of interest may know a person who will talk to you. Seek someone close to the level at which you are applying. Don't ask to see the president of a company if you are searching out information about safety engineering. Rather, find a person who *is* a safety engineer or industrial technologist or technical supervisor.

If you want the interview to go smoothly, do not drop in unexpectedly on a busy person (unless you explain that you only wish to make an appointment for a later time when the person isn't busy). It's much better to make an appointment ahead of time at that person's convenience. Avoid calling during lunch hour, early mornings, especially Mondays, when everyone is getting organized, and late afternoons, especially Fridays, when people are getting ready to wrap up the day's or week's work. If you feel uncertain about going to an interview alone, ask a friend to introduce you, or ask someone with a mutual interest to go along. If it seems appropriate and *you are comfortable with the idea,* invite the person you will interview out for coffee or lunch after you visit the workplace.

Use the information interview sparingly, not casually. Wait until you have some idea of your direction. Then have carefully prepared questions to ask for which you have not been able to find answers through your research. You want to encourage people to talk easily about their work. Most people are sincerely interested in helping information seekers, but sometimes they cannot spare the time. Don't feel discouraged if you are refused an interview.

Following your skills and interests may lead you into work environments ranging from serene to frenetic. As a writer, for example, you could find yourself researching in a quiet library or risking your life gathering news in a war zone. There are many things you thoroughly enjoy but might hate if you had to do them under pressure—a thousand times a day—in a hot, crowded, noisy, and otherwise unpleasant place—for an irritable boss with ulcers! You may enjoy cooking but be fairly certain you would not enjoy serving some of a billion hamburgers every day. You might not like cooking

PEANUTS reprinted by permission of United Feature Syndicate, Inc.

regularly for any large group, even in the most elegant setting. You can find out by visiting various kitchens, talking to the cooks, and observing what they do. Barbara Rosenbloom and Victoria Krayer, who owned a charcuterie in Berkeley, California, showed one visitor the huge pots of heavy paté that had to be mixed, emptied, and cleaned, demonstrating that cooking can be very physically demanding.

Find out whether the company you are interested in (or one like it) gives tours. In some cases you can spend a whole day observing someone doing a job you might like. Remember, when you talk with people in your career field of interest, you are gathering all their biases. Each person likes and dislikes certain things about the job. Each one will give you a different view. Keep your antennae out to receive the emotional content of their messages. Then weigh all these messages against your good feelings and reasoned judgment.

There are other ways to meet people in your field of interest. Many professional groups welcome students at their meetings and have special rates for student/lay participation; the Society of Women Engineers, for example, is one of these. (The *Occupational Outlook Handbook,* which you used for your research in Chapter 3, lists names and addresses of such organizations.) Throughout the United States, the American Society for Training and Development has chapters that hold monthly meetings and annual conventions. At such times you can meet people who have access to local business information and contacts. Chambers of commerce and other community organizations hold regular luncheons with speakers. In social settings like these, it's possible to make contacts easily and explore possibilities for on-site visits. At workshops or classes in your career area of interest, speakers and participants can share information with you both formally and informally.

Much of your success will come from keeping your eyes and ears open. Begin to wonder what just about everyone you meet is doing. Almost every media news item is about people's doings. Which activities attract you? How can you learn more about these activities? Keep on looking, listening, asking questions—it's your best source of information. Eventually you will be talking to people who are doing work you would like to do. Something will click as you begin to share experiences and enthusiasms. You will make a network of friends who may later wish to hire you.

One caution. Most people are happy to answer most questions about their jobs until you come to salary, but there are ways to get an idea of what you might expect. Here are some possible approaches: "What is the approximate salary *range* for a position like yours?" "How much might an entry-level person expect to earn in this position?" A call to a local/state employment office can also provide approximate salary levels.

At first, many people hesitate to call a stranger in a large company—or even an acquaintance in a small one. One student, whose talents were apparent to everyone but herself, was terrified at the prospect. She grimly made the first phone call. To her amazement, the interview was delightful—that is, until she was advised to explore a graduate program at a nearby university. She forced herself to see the department head that same day. Another warm reception! Elated, she rushed out to call her career counselor from the nearest phone booth. She was chuckling, "Here I am, thirty-five years old, and as excited as any kid over talking to two human beings!"

Another student given the same class assignment simply didn't do it. She had been a psychology major with a love for art; she changed to business because it seemed more "practical," although it didn't seem to fit her creative "people" needs. Then she discovered organizational development and talked about her interests to someone who knew a management consultant who used graphic arts in his work. Her reluctance to interview vanished as possibilities began to open up.

Perhaps not everyone you meet will be helpful. You may meet a "Queen Bee" or a "King Pin"—someone who has made it and is unwilling to help others. Sometimes people are absorbed in a complex problem, are truly too busy, or have yet to learn what all self-actualizing people know: the more you help others, the more successful you'll be. Many successful people enjoy sharing their expertise. So if you don't give up, you will find warm-hearted people who understand your needs, your confusion, and you! Keep on searching for those who are sensitive to your concerns.

When people have spent time with you, follow up with thank-you notes. This courtesy will be appreciated and help employers to remember you when you begin the job hunt. The information interview process puts you in the hiring network. It can be an adventure—and it can be very profitable.

Work Experience

Work experience—even if you have to volunteer—is one of the best ways to get information. Try your school or state employment placement office for positions at different workplaces. Or sign up at a temporary employment agency with a good reputation to survey businesses, make contacts, and earn money on your own schedule. Once inside a company, you can get acquainted with people—the cafeteria can be a great meeting place—and watch the bulletin boards for job announcements.

Internships are sometimes available for students to do course research and cooperative work experience, sometimes with pay. These positions can last a day or two, a whole semester, or even a year. While these sorts of activities give you the opportunity to survey companies, they also give employers the opportunity to get to know you. Such contacts may be valuable resources for you in the future.

With some actual work experience, a young person who loves animals may find working at a veterinarian's office exciting or, with sick animals and worried owners, traumatic. On the other hand, every job will gradually (or quickly) demonstrate some unpleasant aspects. Basically, work is often hard work. You must function within the economic and time parameters of an organization or, if you are self-employed, meet clients' and society's demands. When both time and money are in short supply, deadlines and shortages create pressure.

As you become familiar with the workplace, your confidence will grow. By the time you are ready for an interview, you will understand the job and some of its problems. You will know some of the latest techniques in your trade or profession. You will know people in the field who may recommend or even hire you. Many people find out about job openings not yet listed simply by asking everyone they know for information about future possibilities. And with your newfound self-confidence, that first job interview will be duck soup—not sitting duck! You will be ready to hire an employer.

Self-Assessment Exercises

The following exercises will help you decide what kind of workplaces and workstyles you prefer and then help you locate those that match these preferences.

1. Where do you fit in?

a. Number the categories of workplace in order of importance to you:

____ Business	____ Education	____ Government
____ Industry	____ Health	____ Military
____ Entertainment/communication		

b. Check the workplace size that most appeals to you:

_____ Very small   _____ Moderate   _____ Very large

_____ Multinational

c. Check which you prefer:

_____ Indoor work   _____ Outdoor work

_____ Traveling/field   _____ A combination
          work

d. How far up the career ladder do you think you want to go? Explain:

_____

_____

_____

e. Check your work style/schedule preference(s):

_____ Traditional nine-to-five   _____ Intrapreneur

_____ Flexible schedule   _____ Contract work

_____ Part time   _____ Worksteader

_____ Temporary work   _____ Career creator

_____ Job sharing   _____ Third-wave prosumer

_____ Entrepreneur

f. Describe your ideal work schedule:

_____

_____

_____

_____

g. List three businesses in your field of interest from the phone book Yellow Pages:

_____

_____

_____

h. Identify possible contacts. Name three people you know who are in interesting careers in order of importance to you. Include the job title of each one.

_____   _____

_____   _____

_____   _____

Describe the characteristics you like of the most interesting of these careers:

_____

Describe the characteristics you dislike:

_____

2. Workplace Values

a. Rate this summary of corporate values H, M, or L (meaning high, medium, or low) in importance to you as a potential employee.

_____ Makes safe, quality, attractive, affordable products that fulfill legitimate needs and wants

_____ Is environmentally conscious

_____ Is an equal opportunity employer; follows fair and safe labor practices

_____ Supports workplace democracy and worker participation

_____ Is a good member of the community

_____ Is honest and fair in business dealings

_____ Respects people of all backgrounds

_____ Does not depend on repressive governments or military weapons contracts

b. Would you turn down a job because of violations of any of these issues?

Yes _____   No _____   Check which ones.

3. Researching Workplaces

Using library resources as much as possible, research one workplace in your career area. Use the information interview to ask for answers the library does not have.

Name of workplace _____ Phone number _____

Address _____ City/State/Zip _____

a. Organization

Divisions and locations _____

_____

Products/services _____

Number of employees _____ Job titles of interest to you _____

_____

b. Performance

Past and present market _____

_____

Company earnings as of past year _____

Future projections for growth and profit _____

Stability _____

Competitors _____

c. Other factors

Reputation/integrity _____

Environmental record _____

Social concern _____

4. Information Interview

Interview workers in a career field that interests you. Write the results of one such interview either here or on a separate sheet of paper.

_____   _____
Name of person   Company name

_____   _____
Job title   Address

_____   _____
Phone number   City/State/Zip

Here are some questions you might ask.

a. Why did you choose this field?

_____

_____

_____

b. How did you get your job?

_____

_____

_____

c. What do you really do all day?

_____

_____

_____

d. If you could redesign your job, which parts would you keep? Which would you get rid of?

_____

_____

_____

e. What were your most positive career decisions?

_____

_____

_____

f. If you had it to do all over again, what would you do differently in your career? What decisions do you regret?

_____

_____

_____

g. What are the major issues in your career field? The important books, journals, organizations?

_____

_____

h. What is the entry-level job title and its salary range?

_____

_____

i. What steps would a typical career ladder have, about how long would it take to move through each step, and what would each one involve—for example, job duties, salary?

_____

_____

_____

j. How available are jobs in this field expected to be in the future?

_____

_____

k. What are the requirements for the job: training, certificates, licenses, degrees, tools, union membership?

_____

_____

l. Will your company have openings in this field soon?   ____ Yes   ____ No

m. Could you recommend someone else I might interview?

_____
Name of person   Company name

_____
Job title   Address

_____
Phone number   City/State/Zip

5. *Workplace Checklist*

Using both the library and the information interview for information, rate one workplace of interest to you on the following checklist. Put a "+" in front of the ten qualities that are of most interest to you.

Company name _____Phone number_____

Address _____City/State/Zip _____

Management characteristics

	Good	Fair	Poor
_____ Honest/fair/ethical	_____	_____	_____
_____ Respectful	_____	_____	_____
_____ Open	_____	_____	_____
_____ Cooperative	_____	_____	_____
_____ Goal oriented	_____	_____	_____
_____ Flexible	_____	_____	_____
_____ Promote job security	_____	_____	_____
_____ Adequate preparation for layoffs	_____	_____	_____

Use of skills/interests

	Good	Fair	Poor
_____ Encourages growth/autonomy	_____	_____	_____
_____ Provides varied experience	_____	_____	_____
_____ Supports efforts	_____	_____	_____
_____ Acknowledges achievements	_____	_____	_____
_____ Is open to transfers/promotions	_____	_____	_____
_____ Offers educational opportunities	_____	_____	_____
_____ Provides training/development	_____	_____	_____
_____ Makes positive contribution to community	_____	_____	_____
_____ Is open to innovation	_____	_____	_____

Work environment

	Good	Fair	Poor
_____ Location/setting	_____	_____	_____
_____ Appearance of buildings	_____	_____	_____
_____ Work stations	_____	_____	_____
_____ Cafeteria	_____	_____	_____
_____ Restrooms	_____	_____	_____
_____ Colors	_____	_____	_____
_____ Light	_____	_____	_____
_____ Furnishings/equipment	_____	_____	_____
_____ Safe/environmentally conscious	_____	_____	_____
_____ Compatible coworkers	_____	_____	_____
_____ Friendliness	_____	_____	_____
_____ Orderliness	_____	_____	_____

Salary/benefits

	Good	Fair	Poor
_____ Salary	_____	_____	_____
_____ Medical/dental/vision care	_____	_____	_____
_____ Fitness facilities	_____	_____	_____
_____ Life/disability insurance	_____	_____	_____
_____ Vacations/holidays	_____	_____	_____
_____ "Business of living" personal time	_____	_____	_____
_____ Maternity/paternity leaves	_____	_____	_____
_____ Child care	_____	_____	_____
_____ Profit sharing	_____	_____	_____
_____ Moving/travel expenses	_____	_____	_____
_____ Flextime	_____	_____	_____
_____ Retirement benefits	_____	_____	_____
_____ Travel benefits	_____	_____	_____

Financial stability

	Good	Fair	Poor
_____ Sales prospering	_____	_____	_____
_____ No likely takeovers	_____	_____	_____
_____ Manageable debt	_____	_____	_____
_____ Positive cash flow	_____	_____	_____
_____ Special product or service	_____	_____	_____
_____ Little serious competition	_____	_____	_____

The community

	Good	Fair	Poor
_____ Recreational/cultural facilities	_____	_____	_____
_____ Medical/dental facilities	_____	_____	_____
_____ Acceptable schools	_____	_____	_____
_____ Transportation	_____	_____	_____
_____ Cost of living	_____	_____	_____
_____ Other amenities	_____	_____	_____

Complete this statement: I would (or would not) like to work there because

_____

_____

_____

What other questions might you like to ask a person you interview?

_____

_____

_____

6. Productivity Audit

How do you and the system in which you are working contribute to your productivity?[60] Identify a system (e.g., family, school, business) in which you work. Then put a check mark (✓) in the column that best describes your situation in the system. Total your responses and multiply by the value printed below it. Add all totals to get combined score.

	Always	Frequently	Occasionally	Seldom	Never
1. I have a good idea how my work contributes to the goals and life of my system.	_____	_____	_____	_____	_____
2. I know exactly when and how I will be evaluated for my work.	_____	_____	_____	_____	_____
3. I can go to my leader with a real problem and expect to be heard.	_____	_____	_____	_____	_____
4. If something goes wrong, I can communicate freely to the people who can do something about it.	_____	_____	_____	_____	_____
5. Our leadership does a good job of communicating decisions to everyone in the system.	_____	_____	_____	_____	_____
6. I have a sense that if I work hard I will be recognized and appreciated for it.	_____	_____	_____	_____	_____
7. There is a positive future for me in this system if I work hard.	_____	_____	_____	_____	_____
8. Our system does a good enough job of planning so that I can get my work done on time.	_____	_____	_____	_____	_____
9. Because priorities are clear in the system, I have no difficulty knowing what I need to do and when.	_____	_____	_____	_____	_____
10. I am free of headaches at work.	_____	_____	_____	_____	_____
11. When I experience personal stress, I have people to whom I can turn.	_____	_____	_____	_____	_____
12. I feel free to try out a better way of going my work.	_____	_____	_____	_____	_____
13. I have the resources I need to do a quality job.	_____	_____	_____	_____	_____
14. I know, and others know, that I and my work are important to the system.	_____	_____	_____	_____	_____

	Always	Frequently	Occasionally	Seldom	Never
15. When I point out problems and offer suggestions, I am seen as doing something good for the system.	_____	_____	_____	_____	_____
Total Responses	_____	_____	_____	_____	_____
Multiply by	6	4	2	1	0
	_____ +	_____ +	_____ +	_____ +	_____

Total Productivity Score [   ]

A score above 70 = Many factors are encouraging your productivity.

A score between 50 and 70 = Something is discouraging your productivity.

Below 50 = Your productivity is seriously inhibited. Answer the following:

What can you do to improve your productivity? What can the system do to foster productivity? How can you and the system best work together so that everybody wins?

 ## Group Discussion Questions

1. Write about or describe your ideal workplace and schedule to your group. Include your ideal community/geographical location.
2. Describe a business you might like to own.
3. In what ways is your household a workplace? Consider goods and services, management, finances, maintenance, communications, human resources, labor negotiations, your degree of commitment, emotional climate, skills you use, and functions you perform. Does your household respect the rights of its members? Care for the natural environment?
4. How "ad proof" are you? Go for a week without listening to or reading any ads or buying "nonessentials." How much money did you/could you save? Do you consider the ethics of a company before you buy its products? How?
5. What changes in the workplace (for example, in schedules) and in society could help solve the unemployment problem?
6. Do you believe most companies could live up to socially responsible guidelines? Name some that do. Could they improve? How?
7. What factors prevent workplace environments from improving?
8. Share any insights you gained from the information interviewing process.
9. Ask for career information from members of your study group. Trade resources and contacts for information interviewing.
10. Explain the following quote and give examples: "Much of the work we do is not the work that needs to be done."

7

The Job Hunt

Tools for Breaking and Entering

 FOCUS

- Learn about creative job hunting.

- Gather information about yourself into a good résumé.

- Prepare for an effective interview.

Y ou have thoroughly assessed your needs, wants, shoulds, values, and interests. You have envisioned your ideal lifestyle. You have researched your skills so thoroughly that you now have a marvelous list of what you can do. You have collected many words to describe yourself. You have looked over the whole job market and found jobs that would suit you well. You have reflected on the societal issues that will affect your life and your work. You have interviewed people, researched companies, explored workplaces. You have considered the job versus career issue, the career ladder, possibilities for future goals, creative careers, and owning your own business. You have zeroed in on a job title or two and some companies where you have contacts. In short, if you need no further training or education, you may be ready at last for the job hunt!

It is also highly possible that you have not yet completed some or many of the above steps, much less made a career decision. And if the job hunt is several years down the road, you may be tempted to wait to learn the process. However, putting it off might find you unprepared if a great job opportunity should arise or your current position disappears. Being prepared puts you steps ahead. And learning the process can sometimes facilitate decision making because it helps you focus on what a job requires of you. However you use this chapter, reviewing it just before you go out to job hunt can enhance your chances for success.

> I am rather
> like a mosquito in a nudist camp;
> I know what I ought to do,
> but I don't know where to begin.
> —*Stephen Bayne*

Job Hunting

Job hunting is often a full-time job. And like work, it is often hard work, whether you are hunting for full-time, part-time, or temporary work. All require the same care in preparation. Networking, résumés, letters, applications, phone calls, and interviews can make your head swim. The challenge and excitement of a career search may wear thin as you travel this long and sometimes weary road. A six-month search is not unusual. Keeping your wits about you and keeping up your courage are two essential skills.

A third business skill is good manners. You will be meeting many people, asking for their time, and depending on their assistance. *Please, thank you,* and *you're welcome* are good words to have in your vocabulary, whether you say them or write them. A businesslike, polite phone style is a definite plus, and be sure the message greeting callers on your answering machine reflects this same politeness. Shaking hands firmly, making friendly eye contact, climbing in and out of a car gracefully . . . all the things you've been doing forever can quickly come undone in a stress situation. And good table manners will definitely make the right impression if you find yourself invited to coffee or a meal. Waiting until others are seated before you sit down and seeing that they are served before you begin gobbling the first course will put you on the right track, along with handling your knife and fork with confidence. Some colleges are offering courses on manners. If you feel shaky and need some review, look around your area for such workshops or check your library for a basic book on etiquette.

Some people find it helpful to join a support group or start one at this time. Friends can be a source of ideas and emotional support if and when the going gets tough. Ask for assistance and understanding. It also helps to keep several options open—developing possibilities on your present job, taking a course or two, inching toward starting your own business—while you interview in several different areas.

There is no one way to job hunt, but use all the help you can get. Employers often use want ads and employment agencies, and many people find jobs through these sources. Be aware, however, that private employment agencies are like used car dealers. Some are reliable. Some will search for you, charging only the employer if you are hired. Some are there only to put bodies in place and collect a fee. Some are less than honest. They may put false ads in the newspaper to attract clients and use excessive flattery to get your signature on a contract. They may be able to collect their fee even if you find a job on your own without their help. Check with people who have used the services. Read the fine print before you sign over a big chunk of your paycheck for a job that may not be right for you. Even reputable companies may put a poorly written ad in the paper. If you think it is necessary, call for clarification about the job requirements.

People who follow all the steps in the career search process rarely have to pay someone to find a job for them. Job hunting is a natural next step in the process. But in general, the *least* effective strategy is sending out dozens of résumés to personnel departments, especially if you are looking for a job in a competitive field (or employment is tight). You may get a nibble or two, but not too many people are hired this way. Here is where your information interviewing will pay off to get you into the hiring network. Someone you've contacted in your information interviewing may even be waiting for your résumé and application.

Networking

Networking is a new "old" word. Whatever it's called—the buddy system, the old boys' network, or the new girls' network—the fact is that employers have always passed jobs along to people they know. People are networking when they shake hands and exchange business cards. People talk business everywhere—in the hallways, over coffee, on the golf course. These casual conversations may sound trivial, but they strengthen the links in the network.

Networking is *not* the same as information interviewing, although the two use similar techniques. When you do information interviewing you are simply asking for information about careers and companies. You are not asking for a job, although one might be offered and you might accept. But networking implies that you are using various contacts, including those acquired while information hunting, to find out about job openings. Career Consultant Martha Stoodley, author of *Interviewing: What It Is and How to Use It,* says that knowing when to use each technique is the key to success. Networking requires patience. Job openings are often only in the minds of the people who might be thinking of retiring, moving out or over. The company could be reorganizing. Managers could be feuding or be new on the job or both. She reminds us that "companies are run by human beings who are trying to juggle their professional challenges and personal lives." She asks, "Is it any wonder hiring doesn't always go like clockwork?"[1]

Where do you stand in the networking game? If you are new at creative job hunting, the inner circle may look like a closed circle that doesn't include you! But think again. How often have you or people you know heard about a job opening from a friend? And bring it close to home. Suppose you want to hire someone to take care of a child or ailing parent, fix your car, clean your house. No doubt you would feel safer asking for a referral from a friend. Employers feel better, too, when they hire someone they know or someone recommended by a trusted friend or colleague. If you have already done information interviewing, you have a good start on networking. Use the same process and the same contacts to find out about job openings and how to approach a given workplace. These insiders can offer you the inside story as well as moral support. Successful job hunter Mel Fuller says, "Believe the statistic that 70 percent of people are hired by word-of-mouth." He urges people to talk to their relatives, neighbors, friends, clergy, business contacts such as bankers, stockbrokers, insurance agents, doctors and dentists—in short, anyone who knows you. Go to association meetings, job fairs, and trade shows.

Even if you haven't developed a network of personal contacts, call on as many companies (or clients) as you can and apply for possible openings. Make contacts instead of staying at home alone reading the want ads all day.

Now is the time to keep your energy up. Plan a schedule: exercise, eat well, get plenty of rest, and talk to as many positive people as you can. In a tight job market, it's important to keep up your courage. Remember that rejections are part of the game; they do not mean you are unacceptable. Chances are you are just one of many good candidates. Later, the company you are interested in may offer you a different job from the one you had in mind. If the business is a good one, it may even be worth your time to take the alternate job, just to get inside the company, where changes in position are more easily arranged.

Although networking can help you access the job market, be aware that employers are required to follow affirmative action guidelines. They must advertise widely and screen an adequate number of applicants to give as many people as possible a fair chance at the job. Networking is not meant to give less-qualified people an unfair advantage over others, although it sometimes does. Asking for help is legitimate. Some companies and government agencies have helpful material available. But employers are not allowed to discriminate against better-qualified applicants. They will try to ensure that the help they give is available to all prospective employees. And some employers will simply be equally "unavailable" to all!

No one ever said the job hunt would be easy! Work on your résumé, schedule your time, set goals, and keep moving.

The Résumé

A résumé is a summary of personal information about you that is relevant to the job you seek. A good one marks you as a serious job seeker. Much has been written about the résumé. Some regard it as a sacred cow, *the* most important item to use in presenting yourself; others believe preparing a résumé is a worthless exercise. Still, many employers require them, so job hunters, an obliging lot, will continue to oblige, even though they realize that often they are one among hundreds of applicants. To cut down on the volume of résumés that come in every day, some companies have computers read them, check for specific skills and education, then figure out which categories of jobs the applicant fits, and send out an appropriate letter.[2]

There are two kinds of basic résumés: chronological and functional. If your work experience was fairly continuous and in related areas, use a *chronological* résumé, which lists your work experience in reverse order. A *functional* résumé, developed on the basis of three or four skill areas, can be used if you were in and out of the job market at various times or if your work experience does not appear directly related to the job for which you are applying. Writing both kinds of résumés may benefit you because this exercise gives you two different perspectives on yourself. It forces you to state clearly how your education and experience relate directly to the job you are seeking. Some people bypass both types and simply list achievements in skill areas that apply directly to the job being sought. Sample résumés are shown in Figures 7-1 through 7-8 and in the Appendix.

There is no one and only way to write a résumé, but some good basic guidelines to follow are these: (1) be brief, (2) be clear, (3) be neat, (4) be honest. The best résumé succinctly states *on one page* your education and work experience that specifically relate to the job for which you are applying. Employers want you to save all the exciting details for the interview. A résumé is easiest to read when it is in outline form with plenty of "white space," has good spelling, punctuation, and grammar, and is well reproduced.

Those who hire say they can spot phony résumés very quickly, especially those that are done commercially. Although it is important that you be truthful, a résumé isn't the place for true confessions. Emphasize your good points! Ask experienced friends to read and criticize your rough draft, but have confidence in your own judgment about what is right for you.

If you have access to a computer, use it to do your résumé or have it done. The advantages are many: you can tailor each version to a particular job and/or company; corrections and updating are a breeze; and you can use some subtle touches like **bold print** or *italics* that will add to its sharp look if you don't overdo them. If you must type your résumé, you can erase, use correction fluid, and even cut and paste sections in with tape; a copy shop can still produce a copy that will look perfect. Use a high-quality off-white, gray, or beige-tinted paper. If you plan to mail it, prepare a carefully typed, matching envelope addressed to the correct person. For a final touch, add a handsome commemorative stamp. You want your résumé to get a second look rather than the usual thirty-second glance.

Some people send a résumé with an individual letter addressed to a specific person in a company. Sometimes the résumé is attached to an application, or requested after an application has been received. The general idea is to give the employer a preview of you before an interview takes place. Always have your résumé handy and bring several copies to the interview because more than one person may want to talk with you.

Plan to spend at least twelve to fifteen hours writing a good résumé; then leave it and come back to it later for a fresh look. Because you can describe yourself in an infinite number of ways, doing a résumé means picking a winning combination that exactly fits the job you are seeking. The position objective you indicate must state that job title clearly and briefly and match the job for which you are applying. Employers do not have time to dig around in your résumé to find out what you want to do, nor do they have to. They want to know what you are bringing to a specific job. Such clarity is especially important if you have not made previous contact with the employer. And of course, because almost everyone wants an exciting, challenging job with opportunity for advancement (and a huge salary) in a dynamic and growing company with stimulating and forward-thinking managers and marvelous colleagues, that's understood—so don't mention the obvious. *You* decide if the workplace will work for you. And yes, you *do* need a separate résumé for each job title and sometimes even for each company!

As your career advances, you will not simply add new jobs to the list on your résumé; you will probably change the entire format. You may summarize early jobs, stress your newer high-level qualifications, and recast earlier entries to point toward your new job goal. The résumé will emphasize your achievements more, and each job entry will show increasingly greater connections to the next job goal. A top executive résumé may be more than one well-organized page, but it will include only those entries that are relevant to the new job goal.[3]

If you have been developing a list of file cards for each job, a résumé will not only be easier to do but also be easier to adapt. Start with the lists you made of all your favorite activities and skills in Chapters 1, 2, and 3. The ten basic skills empower you to *do* many different tasks in many different settings with data, people, and things because the skills are transferable. When you go job hunting, the key question a company wants you to answer is this: "What can you *do* for us?" The most important words to use on your résumé, then, are action verbs that tell what you've done, what you've accomplished, and therefore what you *can* do, and would *like* to do, and that relate to the job in question. Action verbs have an impact when they are relevant to the job you want. Collect businesslike nouns, adjectives, and adverbs to use with these verbs. Use words that clearly and specifically *express* what you can bring to the job; not words that only *impress*. A woman who worked for a sanitation district said she "gave messages to the guys in their trucks." On her résumé, this phrase was translated to "communicated by radio with personnel in the field."

Many-faceted skills such as management can be divided into a variety of functions and subfunctions, which in turn relate back to the ten basic skills. Management involves only three of the basic skills: medium to high intelligence, verbal ability, and sometimes (but not always) medium to high numerical ability. Yet many action verbs would apply: advise, arrange, budget, communicate, control . . . Here is an example of increasing clarity and impact.

1. Designed a marketing program . . .; 2. Designed an effective marketing program . . .; 3. Designed an effective marketing program that resulted in a 60 percent sales increase.

RÉSUMÉ FORMATS

Formats are useful as guidelines for those who have never or only occasionally prepared a résumé. After you become experienced with them you may wish to create your own format.

1. **Name, address, home phone, business (or message) phone:** List this information prominently at the top of the page. Give useful phone numbers and make sure that if you use an answering machine the message sounds professional; a prospective employer should know where to reach you, day or evening. If you do not wish your present employer to know you are job hunting, ask someone to take messages for you, when you are at work.

2. **Position objective:** State as specific and brief a job title as possible.

3. **Qualifications in brief:** Provide a short summary highlighting your education, experience, and skills to capture the attention of and assure the reader that you can do the job. Elaboration (but not repetition) is included in the body of the résumé.

4. **Experience summary:** Present experience in a form that is chronological, functional, or a combination of the two.

   Chronological: Begin with your most recent job and work backward.
   >   March, 1995 - Present: COMPANY, City, State, Job Title.
   >   Add a brief, concise description of what you did.

   In this type of résumé, you may wish to include a section on community service, military service, or whatever applies (see Figures 7-2, 7-7, and the Appendix: A-2, A-3, A-5, and A-7).
   >   As references are usually asked for on the application, it is not necessary to mention them on your résumé.

   Functional: Arrange the information by areas of competence, expertise, or effectiveness, such as public relations, management, organization, program development, sales.
   >   List several key functions that are related to your position objective.

   Follow each category with the businesslike action words you've collected, such as "planned" and "classified"; then summarize of the types of things you have accomplished. You may list employers and dates at the end or note them on the company's application form (see Figures 7-3 and 7-5).

   Combination of chronological and functional: If you use this format, highlight special skills relevant to your position (see Figure 7-4).

5. **Educational background:** (Place before work experience if it is closely related to the position objective.) List educational background to indicate general and specific training for a job. A person who has little or no educational training would omit this item.
   >   COLLEGE NAME, City, State, Degrees, majors, dates.

   If you received no degree or you are presently attending college, give the number of units completed (or say "degree candidate"), major, date, place.
   If you have not attended college,
   >   HIGH SCHOOL, City, State.

   >   Add any areas of specialty, if applicable, but the date of high school graduation is not necessary as this indicates your age. It is illegal for employers to ask a person's age.
   >   Include also relevant workshops, adult education, vocational training, either in summary form or in chronological order.

6. **Personal paragraph:** If you wish, include a statement describing your personal attitudes toward work that make you a valuable and unique employee (see Figures 7-4 and A-6).

KEVIN DONOVAN
643 Eagle Drive
Dubuque, Iowa 52001
(319) 555-6789

JOB OBJECTIVE: Customer Service Management Trainee

QUALIFICATIONS IN BRIEF

Learn job routine quickly. Possess ability to deal effectively with the public and flexible enough to work alone or in a team effort. Good driving record. Not afraid of hard routine work. Primarily interested in a swing shift to allow time to further my educational goals.

WORK EXPERIENCE

K-MART, Dubuque, IA   1996 to present
Customer Service/Bagger

Help customers with merchandise, stock shelves, maintain appearance of the store, bring carts from parking lot into building, and bag merchandise from checkstands.

DUBUQUE GYMNASTIC ASSOCIATION, Dubuque, IA   1994 – 1995
Gym Instructor

Sold memberships and equipment, outlined programs for participants, gave tours of the facilities to potential customers and guests, balanced monies and accounts daily, answered phones, and took responsibility for maintaining a smooth operation of the gym facilities, adding a professional tone.

S & S WROUGHT IRON, East Dubuque, IL   Summer 1994
VAN'S FURNITURE AND MATTRESS CO.,
Dubuque, IA   Summer 1993
Warehouse Worker

Moved furniture, paint, and equipment; helped with inventory control; assisted customers.

EDUCATION

LORAS COLLEGE, Dubuque, IA   1996 to present
Major: Business/Liberal Arts

Figure 7-1   Chronological résumé of a student attending a four-year college

JAMES N. RYAN
1801 Avenue Z
Sterling, IL 61081
(625) 555-1212

POSITION OBJECTIVE: Route Manager

QUALIFICATIONS IN BRIEF: AA in Electronics; three years' experience maintaining coin-operated amusement and music equipment; two years managing video arcade; course work in management; good human relations skills.

EDUCATION:

SAUK VALLEY COMMUNITY COLLEGE, Dixon, Illinois   June 1996
Electronics Technology AS Degree; Certificate in Business Management

Courses in electronics, including "troubleshooting" and electronic applications. Certificate courses in business management including employee recruitment and selection, performance standards and evaluations, supervisory skills, accounting and legal principles, materials management, business computers, marketing strategies.

EXPERIENCE SUMMARY

BLACKHAWK MUSIC CO., Sterling, IL   September 1996 to Present
Service Technician

Service on site, pick up, repair, deliver coin-operated music and game machines; maintain equipment; collect revenue on two multi-town routes; supervise several workers; developed a more efficient equipment rotation plan.

BLACKHAWK FAMILY ARCADE, Blackhawk Mall, Sterling, IL
Arcade/Attendant Manager   September 1992 to August 1996

Supervised video arcade, made minor repairs on equipment, developed inventory system for redemption center; hired, supervised, and scheduled all part-time employees; developed sales promotions; handled day-to-day problems.

THE DAILY GAZETTE, Sterling, IL.   October 1989 to August 1992
Delivery

Delivered papers, sold and collected subscriptions for 150 households. Increased route subscriptions by 20 percent.

COMMUNITY ORGANIZATIONS/SERVICE

SAUK VALLEY RECYCLING, Sterling, IL   August 1990 to Present

As center volunteer: sort materials, collect old newspapers, cans, and bottles from various locations. Manage yearly cleanup of river front.

Figure 7-2   Chronological résumé of a graduate of AS electronics program looking for position in video game distribution company

BETTY A. BUG
5403 W. Monroe Street
Chicago, Illinois 60644
(312) 555-9829

POSITION OBJECTIVE: Industrial Employee Trainer

QUALIFICATIONS IN BRIEF

BA in English, Mundelein College of Loyola, Chicago, 1988. Eight years' elementary teaching; four years' clerical experience in industry. Fluent in Spanish; demonstrated skills in instruction, supervision, communications, human relations.

EXPERIENCE SUMMARY

INSTRUCTION: Planned, organized, presented language and mathematics instructional material to elementary students; developed teaching modules to solve specific learning problems; developed computer programs for instruction and instructional material; used equipment such as Macintosh computer, overhead and movie projectors, audio and videocassettes, and a variety of educational software; did extensive research in various curricula; served on curriculum development committee; introduced new motivational techniques for students. Conducted staff in-service workshops, including installation of a teleconference downlink.

SUPERVISION: Supervised student groups, teacher interns, and a classroom aide; evaluated students, peers, and programs; moderated student activities. Interviewed, trained, and evaluated support personnel, volunteers, and teacher interns.

HUMAN RELATIONS: Did effective problem solving/conflict resolution between individual students and between student groups; initiated program of student self-governance; acted as a liaison between families of diverse cultural, ethnic, and economic backgounds and school personnel services; conducted individual and group conferences to establish rapport with parents and to discuss student progress. Represented school to the community.

COMMUNICATIONS: Presented new curriculum plans to parent groups; sent periodic progress reports to parents; developed class newsletter.

CURRENTLY EMPLOYED: Austin Elementary School, Chicago, Illinois

PREVIOUSLY EMPLOYED: Brach Candy Company, Chicago, Illinois

Figure 7-3   Functional résumé of a teacher in transition to industry

HELEN B. BELL
432 Spruce Street
Junction City, Kanas 66441
(913) 555-7035

POSITION OBJECTIVE: Office Manager with Accounting Responsibilities

EXPERIENCE:

Successful Accounting Work: Managed payroll, payroll taxes, accounts receivable, accounts payable, bank reconciliation, and executive credit card expense account; handled data entry. Acted as full-charge bookkeeper through monthly and annual profit and loss statements.

Supervision and Management: Directed office functions such as secretarial, accounting, customer relations, sales, employee performance, and schedules.

PRESENT EMPLOYER:

KINDERGARTEN SUPPLIER, USA, INC., Wichita, KS **Accountant**	10 years

PREVIOUS EMPLOYERS:

ELECTRA CORPORATION, Wichita, KS **Receptionist**	1 year
RIDGEWAY COMPANY, Topeka, KS **Accountant/Secretary**	1 year
ROD'S VAN AND STORAGE COMPANY, Topeka, KS **Accountant/Secretary**	2 years
HUMPHREY MOTOR COMPANY, Junction City, KS **Accountant/Secretary**	9 years
SCOTT STORES, Junction City, KS **Bookkeeper**	1 year

PERSONAL PARAGRAPH

The accounting field with its attendant and complex problems is fascinating and thoroughly involving for me. I am interested in ensuring smooth flow, efficiency, and accuracy of accounts in a moderately sized, growing company.

Figure 7-4   Functional/chronological résumé of a senior citizen/housewife returning to the job market

LAURIE REAUME
361 Calle de Florencia
Santa Fe, New Mexico 87501
(505) 970-9120

POSITION OBJECTIVE: Public Relations

ACHIEVEMENTS:

WRITING/PUBLICITY

- Compiled and published public service directory.
- Coordinated and edited corporate newsletter.
- Designed publicity brochure and employee handbook.
- Wrote and placed employment advertising.
- Gave presentations on company's innovative policies.
- Contacted media regarding personnel changes and events of interest to the community.

ADMINISTRATION AND ORGANIZATION

- Hired, supervised, and trained contract employees.
- Established and maintained resource/reference library.
- Planned, organized, and promoted company picnic.
- Developed and conducted new hire orientation program.
- Coordinated and presented work effectiveness seminar.

EDUCATION:

GOLDEN GATE UNIVERSITY, San Francisco, CA, MBA Candidate.

UNIVERSITY OF WISCONSIN, Whitewater, WI, BA Cum Laude.

QUALIFICATIONS SUMMARY:

Self-starter, excellent organizer, resourceful, team player.

Figure 7-5 Functional résumé targeted toward achievements of career woman moving into public relations from secretarial work

Cover Letters

A well-written cover letter is an excellent door opener for an interview (see Figures 7-6 and 7-9 and the Appendix). After you have made personal contact with someone in the company who seems interested in hiring you, targeting your résumé to that specific company and addressing a cover letter to that specific person, both geared to a specific job, may be an excellent strategy. Some employers, such as school districts and government agencies, have step-by-step procedures that make cover letters unnecessary. These employers may want only an application with your résumé attached. It's wise to learn and follow the expected procedures. In companies with less formal application procedures, employers often appreciate a short and clear cover letter stating what you are interested in. You can use it to amplify an important aspect of your résumé and to form a chain linking you directly to the employer.

- *Connecting:* State your reason for writing and your employment objective. Mention the person who referred you to this employer or the source of the reference, such as a classified ad.

- *Add more links:* Describe your experience in brief—one or two sentences should be ample.

- *Solder the links:* State what you can do for the company and tell how you will help this employer solve his or her problem.

- *Hold onto the chain:* Prepare the way for the next step by asking for an interview and indicating when you will call to set it up.

Sometimes you will get a negative response when you call for an interview. Be ready with a positive answer to reinforce your possible contribution to the company. For example, to "We don't hire people without experience," your reply might be, "I do learn very quickly," or "I have had a great deal of experience as a student doing such similar tasks as . . ."

5401 Monroe Street
Mobile, Alabama 36608
September 11, 1995

Ms. Jill Jones
Director of Marketing
PTT Corporation
Dogwood, AL 36309

Dear Ms. Jones:

As a word processor at Datatime Company last summer, I had occasion to meet with people from PTT. Your sales representative, Joan Carl, referred me to you. I was impressed with both your product and your personnel. I am a senior at Peachtree University. I would like to be considered for an internship position in marketing for the Spring Semester of 1996.

I am an energetic, enthusiastic person with a commitment to whatever I take on. My involvement in student affairs led me to plan and execute a successful campaign for student body vice-president. As vice-president I met and negotiated with faculty representatives and members of the board of trustees and hosted visiting guests of the college. My junior project in marketing won departmental recognition, while my 3.2 GPA put me on the dean's honor list.

With these qualifications, I feel that I can make a positive contribution to PTT. I look forward to meeting your campus recruiter, A. J. Lupin, next month to explore a marketing internship position.

Sincerely yours,

CHRIS CROSS

Figure 7-6 Cover letter of a college student applying for an internship

CHRIS CROSS
5401 Monroe Street, Mobile, Alabama 36608
(205) 555-1212

POSITION OBJECTIVE: Internship in Marketing

QUALIFICATIONS IN BRIEF:

BA Candidate in Marketing and Sales. Won departmental honors in Marketing. Word processor for two summers on PTT Systems. Good human relations skills, energetic, goal oriented.

EXPERIENCE SUMMARY:

DATATIME COMPANY, Mobile, Alabama   Summers: 1993–1995
Data Entry
Did data entry for marketing and sales department; logged product sales, sales personnel progress, and regional growth; interacted with service representatives.

McDOUGAL'S HAMBURGER'S, Mobile, Alabama   October 1991–May 1992
Part-time Waitress
Waited on customers, handled cash, oriented new employees. Suggested successful coupon marketing strategy that raised sales by 5 percent. Acted as hostess, manager.

COMMUNITY EXPERIENCE:

PEACHTREE UNIVERSITY STUDENT BODY, Peachtree, Georgia
1994–1995

Vice-President
Planned and executed my election campaign, worked extensively with faculty, administration, and board of trustees; hosted visiting college guests; spearheaded senior projects such as the Homecoming Dance and Career Day. Participated in student activities all four years.

BLOSSOM HIGH SCHOOL, Mobile, Alabama
Senior Class Secretary
Junior Vice-President
Participated throughout high school in student body activities, science club, and intramural basketball and soccer.

EDUCATION:

PEACHTREE UNIVERSITY, Peachtree, Georgia   June 1996
BA Candidate: Marketing and Sales

Figure 7-7   Résumé to accompany cover letter

JOANNE M. MALATIA
5405 Monroe Street, Aurora, IL 60504
(708) 555-1212

POSITION OBJECTIVE: Programmer/Analyst

EXPERIENCE SUMMARY

WATLOW ELECTRIC MANUFACTURING COMPANY, Batavia, IL
Computer Programmer/Analyst/Mapper Run Designer   October 1990 to present
Major Contributions:
- Developed a cross-checking system to improve on-time deliveries for major customers.
- Designed and implemented a computerized raw materials purchasing system.
- Coordinated implementation of corporate-side order processing and sales analysis system.
- Performed sales forecasting and analysis that contributed to company strategy.

Responsibilities:
- Define data processing problems and objectives.
- Formulate logical procedures for problem solution.
- Perform general maintenance on all hardware at Batavia Plant.
- Instruct and train all positions on computer applications.
- Hardware: Unisys 220 Mainframe, IBM-compatible PC/DOS.
- Software: Mapper Database Language, BASIC, Microsoft Word.

LOVEJOY REHABILITATION CENTER, West Chicago, IL
Data Collector for Research/Education Department   January 1987 to October 1990
Major Contributions:
- Internship: Directed a system investigation of the Materials Management Department.
- Documented existing manual system; recommended purchase of computer system.

Responsibilities:
- Performed patient telephone interviews and evaluated data received.
- Implemented follow-up evaluation system and assisting with patient tracking system.
- Completed daily tallies of calls completed and maintained card file system.
- Entered follow-up collection of data, Hewlett Packard PC/DOS.
- Assisted wth Statistical Analysis using SAS, SPSS, and BASIC.

MCDONALD'S OF STRATFORD, Bloomingdale, IL
Administrative Assistant to General Manager   June 1985 to February 1987
Responsibilities:
- Managed and balanced daily books and cash sheets while maintaining cash flow.
- Assisted managers with schedules and planning.
- Oriented and trained new employees.

EDUCATION

DeVry Institute of Technology, Lombard, IL: Bachelor of Science Degree, October 1990
Major: Computer Information Systems
COMPUTER EXPERIENCE: COBOL, BASIC, RPGII, Assembler, Pascal, JCL, IBM
3033, IBM PC/DOS.

Figure 7-8   Résumé of a technical person with a BS Degree in Computer Science

5405 Monroe Street
Aurora, IL 60504
January 24, 1996

Dierk Van Symms, Manager of Technical Services
Effective Micro Systems, Inc.
130 Meridian Drive, Suite 411
Aurora, IL 60504

Dear Mr. Van Symms:

EMS Marketing Respresentative, Kevin Skahan, acquainted me with your company. Your services to your manufacturing companies are impressive. There is a great need for improvement of technical applications in manufacturing. Considering my almost five years of hands-on experience, both manual and computerized, in a manufacturing environment, I feel that I can offer special attention to detail that a manufacturing company or distributor deserves.

I have been with Watlow Electric Manufacturing Company since graduating from DEVRY with a BS in Computer Information Systems for Business in 1990. My effective problem solving, communication, and planning experience with their office and factory applications has resulted in higher customer satisfaction and fewer complaints about scheduling and delivery.

I am now seeking a technical business position working approximately thirty hours per week. I would like to meet with you to further discuss the possibility of a work opportunity with Effective Micro Systems, Inc. I will call you in one week to set up a time convenient for both of us.

Sincerely yours,

Joanne M. Malatia

Figure 7-9   Cover letter to accompany résumé

Letters of Reference

Be prepared to supply the names of people who have written or will write letters of reference for you or who will answer questions about you by phone. *Do not* name someone until you have asked that person's permission to be listed as a reference and he or she has agreed. The people you ask should generally be professional people such as teachers or school advisers, or former employers. The most valuable references come from individuals who can speak from personal experience about your work abilities.

Ask the person writing the letter to mention your specific job and personal responsibility skills that relate to the position you are seeking. Some people who write many letters of reference may ask you to write the letter for them to revise and sign. And some may decline your request entirely. Because of possible legal implications, many people may be reluctant to write reference letters even though they would like to.

When you apply for a job, the usual procedure with references is to provide names, if they are requested, or to bring copies of letters to the interview. Some college placement offices keep a file for each of their graduates with copies of letters of reference, a current résumé, and transcripts; the placement office will send these out to prospective employers for a nominal fee. If you have letters of reference on file at your college, have them sent to the prospective employer either right before or soon after your interview. If the competition is fierce and you are almost certain this is a job you want, it may be appropriate to ask a couple of key people to write letters or even make phone calls to the person who may hire you. Ask a teacher or counselor who knows your skills, an acquaintance in the company to which you are applying, or some other professional acquaintance known to the interviewer or to the person you will be working for to speak on your behalf. Understand, however, that this is not the usual procedure and should be used with discrimination.

The Application Form

The application form provided by the company may determine the employer's first impression of you. It must look sharp. *A form that is prepared carelessly or sloppily may cause you to be eliminated from consideration for the position. Be sure to fill out an application as clearly, completely, and neatly as possible.* Try to obtain two copies ahead of time. (Sometimes companies will mail them to you by phone request.) Use one copy for practice and keep it for your files.

Applications vary from one company to another, but each form requires an accurate record of your past work experience and education. To help you in preparing every application you will make, create your own file containing all the information you may need to include. Use the format in the Data File exercise in Chapter 1. Check your records carefully for accuracy. You will need names, addresses, and dates for both your education and work experience. Obtain this information now if you do not have it. Employers often verify these facts, and the information on your application must match what they learn from your former employers or educational institutions. The more careful you are, the better you look. Be clear if you are asked what you did in previous employment. Know exact job titles, the types of equipment you've used, and the salary range you are interested in. Here are some helpful hints to remember.

- Read the *whole* application form *before* you begin to fill it in. Follow all directions, and note the fine print.
- Print with a blue or black pen, or better still, type answers carefully and completely, but succinctly.
- Fill in all blanks. Write in N/A (not applicable) if a question does not apply to you.
- Have your Social Security number available. Some companies ask to see a driver's license. (Revocation or denial of a driver's license can indicate a problem.)
- Your reason for interest in the position should state an advantage to the employer. Research the company and know what you can do for it.
- An arrest is not a conviction. Arrests need not be mentioned.
- Provide accurate names and addresses of those who have given you permission to use their names as references. Have original reference letters available, plus copies to leave if requested.
- Reread the application carefully. Typos or other errors give a bad impression
- Sign the application.

The Interview

Usually an employer interviews individuals whose applications, letters, or résumés have proven interesting, those who have made a personal contact, or those who have been referred. Many managers feel uncomfortable with the interview and are not skilled at it, so be prepared to take control tactfully while letting the manager guide it. Some school districts and government

HERMAN

"Night work! You mean when it's dark?"

agencies have a very formal interview procedure. Try to learn whether the employer uses a structured or an informal interview so as to be better prepared.

An interview is a purposeful conversation between an employer or delegated interviewer and a prospective employee. Its purpose is to exchange information. The interviewer needs to learn whether the interviewee has the qualifications necessary to do the job. The applicant needs to make sure that he or she understands the job, the company, and what is expected. Here we cover the key points in the interview and review a set of practice questions and answers.

The interviewer may be a department head, project director, or even a series of people familiar with various aspects of the job. A group of staff members may act together as an interviewing committee. In a small business,

INTERVIEW OVERVIEW

GET READY

Check: The company (from reference section
of library, public relations department of firm, contacts, friends)

    Location
    Products/services
    Potential market
    Earnings
    Policies

Check: Important items you wish to cover:

    How you fit in
    Your strengths
    Your experiences
    Your interests

GET SET

Check: Items for your application:

    Social Security number
    References
    Person to notify in case of accident
    Details of past experience:
     Name of company
     Full address and phone number
     of company
     Dates worked
     Salary
     Job titles
     Supervisors
     Duties, projects, skills
    Education (dates, majors, degrees)
    Copies of résumé
    Examples of work if relevant

Check: Exact time, date, location
(building and room)
    Availability of parking
    Name of interviewer (and
    pronunciation)

GO

Check: Your appearance

    Neat, clean, conservative outfit
    No gum, no smoking, no
    fidgeting
    No sunglasses or outdoor
    clothing
    Comfortable sitting posture,
    straight but at ease

Check: Your attitude

    A serious job seeker
    Definite goals
    Willing to work and work up
    Reasonable approach to salary,
    hours, benefits, or other aspects
    of the job
    Uncritical of past employers,
    teachers, coworkers
    Evidence of good human
    relations
    Sense of humor
    High personal values
    Wide interests, openness,
    flexibility

Check: Your manner

    Confident, not overbearing
    Firm handshake
    Enthusiastic but not desperate or
    gushy
    Courteous, attentive
    Good voice, expression
    On target answering questions
    Leave promptly after the
    interview

Go alone

you may be interviewed quite casually and briefly by the owner. Large corporations often employ professional interviewers. Reputable companies want their interviewers to present a positive image. Interviewers want to do a good job, too, by hiring the best people. Their jobs depend on it!

An interview is not a time for game playing or for one person to try to trap the other. It will be counterproductive for both parties if they deceive each other. *The interviewer will recommend an employee who doesn't fit. The worker will be dissatisfied.*

Like a good composition, the interview usually has a beginning, a middle, and an ending. Introductions and casual conversation are designed to help you feel at ease.

After a few minutes, most interviewers will guide you to the purpose of the meeting, which is to find out what you can *do* for the company and what your qualifications are for the job. A good interviewer will also give you information along the way to help you make your decision. The interviewer may discuss job duties, hours and overtime, salary and benefits, vacation and sick leave, opportunities for advancement, and company policies and procedures.

Some interviewers will give you a tour of the workplace. Depending on the level for which you are being considered, an interview might be over in fifteen minutes or last several hours or even extend over some days. Most information can be exchanged in thirty to forty-five minutes. Interviewers bring these meetings to an end and usually tell you when you will be notified about their selection of an applicant. They are generally seeing other people interested in the job, sometimes many others.

A successful interview might be one in which you *don't* get the job. In some cases, the interview reveals that hiring you would not be good for either you or the company, which only means that the interview has accomplished its purpose. *In any event, you want to appear at your best.*

Getting Prepared

When you are meeting someone you wish to impress, common sense and courtesy are your most reliable guides. If you are in doubt about dress and manner, it's best to lean slightly toward the conservative. Prepare what you will wear ahead of time. Be sure that your outfit is clean, pressed, polished, and *comfortable*. When purchasing your "dress for success" suit, try sitting in it, moving in it. Then wear it a time or two, perhaps to an information interview. *And of course, be on time.* Since many workplaces are banning smoking, employers will tend to look with disfavor on someone who smokes. Seattle University professor of business William L. Weiss says that "in a race for a job between two equally qualified people, a nonsmoker will win 94 percent of the time."[4]

The very best preparation for an interview is practice—practice talking to people about their jobs; practice calling for appointments to see people in order to ask for career information. If you have done information interviewing and networking, you will be accustomed to sharing enthusiasm about the career of your choice, and this enthusiasm will come across naturally at the interview. Go to interviews even if you think you might not get a job, and then honestly assess your performance.

More immediately, do homework on the company you are approaching. Many have brochures; many are listed in standard library references. A call to the public relations department can sometimes result in a wealth of material. Talk to people who may know the company. Ask questions at the interview about the job as well as the company's process and organization instead of self-serving questions that indicate you are interested only in what the company can give you. Try to see how you best fit in. Know the important facts about the job, including the salary range. Prepare to bring relevant examples of your work, such as sketches, designs, or writings.

In some career areas, salaries are nonnegotiable and not an issue—government, teaching, and union jobs are examples. In others, salaries are negotiable. In such cases, the interviewer may ask what salary you expect. If you have no idea of the range and were not able to find out ahead of time, ask. Unless you are a superstar, don't ask for the top of the range, but don't undervalue yourself, either. Know the minimum you'll accept—and know your worth. Place yourself somewhere in the middle and leave it open to negotiation. Also, you might ask for a salary review in six months or so.

It's better not to ask about salary and benefits at the initial interview, especially with a manager because sometimes he or she doesn't know the answers. It may sound as if that is your only interest in the company. A better way is to check out all this information beforehand. Ask the personnel office for brochures on company benefit plans. And definitely check them out before accepting a job offer.

Interview Behavior

As a job seeker, you should approach each interview by being yourself, being true to yourself, and trusting your own judgment about the style that suits you best. You can build self-confidence by practicing ways of talking and listening effectively and by learning to answer an interviewer's questions. Here are some key points to practice.

- *Good eye contact:* Get comfortable with and use this form of personal contact. If you like your interviewers, your eyes will communicate warmth and interest.

- *Appropriate body language:* Be relaxed and open, interested and attentive. Notice how bodies speak! Become aware of ways in which your body sends messages of boredom, fear, enthusiasm, cockiness, nervousness, confidence. And become aware of others' body language. For example, your interviewer's body language may indicate that you need to paraphrase or restate a response or give a concrete example.

- *Appropriate voice melody:* Try to come across with vitality, enthusiasm, and confidence. Remember that low, relaxed tones convey confidence and competence; high, squeaky tones convey insecurity. Tape record your practice to expected questions so that you can hear yourself; at least practice them out loud, alone, or with someone who will give you honest feedback.

- *Active listening:* Indicate that you have heard and understood what the interviewer has said. For example, if the interviewer mentions tardiness as a problem, say, "It must be difficult to have employees who are constantly late. I can assure you I'll make every effort to be on time."

- *Good choice of words:* Use language that is respectful but not overly formal. If you do your interview homework and practice, the right words should come easily. Much of what you "say" will of course be conveyed by your manner, not your words.[5]

Practice Questions

You will be asked questions about your previous work experience and education, your values, and your goals. You may possibly be asked questions about your family life and leisure activities, but very personal questions are not appropriate in an interview.

Questions dealing with factual information should not be a problem if you have prepared well. Have on hand your own card file of all education, previous jobs, and other experience, with correct dates, place names and addresses, job titles and duties, names of supervisors, and other relevant information in case these might slip your mind. Usually this information is on the application. The interview centers on clarification of points on the application and résumé.

If you have been working regularly and successfully in your field for a period of years, the interview will be mainly a chance for you to tell what you have done. If you are a recent graduate, the discussion may focus on your education and casual jobs.

If you have been in and out of the job market or have had problems in the past, the interviewer will want to explore the reasons. Be relaxed and not defensive. Look on the interview as a chance to make a fresh start. Assure the interviewer that you will not be a problem but a solution. All the questions in the interview are different ways of asking "Can you do the job?" It's not fair to expect to be hired if you can't do the job well. If you keep that clearly in mind, you will be·able to support your answer, "Yes, I can do the job," with all sorts of relevant data.

Practice answering interview questions until you feel comfortable. Prepare concise answers so you won't ramble. Omit personal information and especially any negative information about your past jobs and employers. Some people get carried away and start talking about their childhood, personal problems, and all sorts of irrelevant data that wear interviewers out and hardly charm them.

Here are some typical, commonly asked questions, along with answers for you to consider.

Tell me something about yourself. This request, one of the most frequently asked by interviewers, could be followed by a dismayed silence as you race your mental motor trying to find something to talk about. If you are prepared, you will jump in happily with the reasons you feel your skills, background, and personal attitudes are good for the job and how you see your future with the company. You will seldom have a better opportunity than this to talk about yourself.

Why are you leaving your present job? (Or Why did you leave your last job?) If the circumstances of your leaving were unpleasant or your present conditions are unbearable, these personal problems will be the first answers to pop into your mind—but they should be the last answers you give. Everyone leaves a job for more than one reason, and negative reasons can be made positive. If your boss was oppressive, coworkers disagreeable, or the job was too difficult, a move can provide opportunity for growth in a variety of ways. It's difficult for anyone to improve on a job when feelings are all negative. Here are some possible replies:

- "I seemed to have reached a point where there was little potential for growth."
- "I have learned my job well and would like to try new dimensions in a growing [or larger, or innovative] company."
- "I decided to change careers, and I just got my degree."
- "I left to raise a family, and now I am ready to return to work permanently."
- "I moved [or the company reorganized or merged or cut back or slowed down]."

Your application indicated that you have been in and out of the work force quite often (or haven't worked in some years). What were you involved with in those periods of unemployment? Here the interviewer has several concerns. Your skills might be rusty or you may have had some problems keeping a job. Another is that you might be likely to leave after being trained for this job, a cost to the company. Be prepared to give assurance that your qualifications are such that you can handle the job and that you plan to stay with the company. Knowing your abilities and what the job demands can clarify this subject for you.

What are your weaknesses and what are your strengths? Smile when they ask this one. Have a list you have memorized about what you do best, such as, "I work well with other people on a team basis." If the job you are applying for matches your personality type, your weaknesses will be in areas not important for the job. On a conventional job (C), for example, artistic strengths (A) would get in the way. So you might say, "I'm not very creative. I prefer to follow a set routine." Or if the job calls for machine work (R), you might say your communication skills (S) aren't the best. Investigative applicants (I) may say that they get absorbed in their research, whereas enterprising (E) ones may say that rather than developing a product they prefer making contact with people to influence them to buy the product. Whatever personality type the job calls for, weaknesses of the type opposite yours on the hexagon can be turned into pluses!

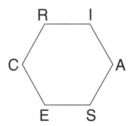

Do you have any reason to feel that you cannot perform the described job duties well? In some cases, physical or mental limitations can interfere with job performance, but it is illegal for an employer to discriminate against anyone only on the basis of a disability. The Americans with Disabilities Act says it has to be clear that disabled applicants cannot do the job even if reasonable accommodations are made for them.

Made-up situations that test a person's knowledge of the job may begin with questions like "What would you do if . . .?" The quality of your solution is not nearly as important as your attitude. A calm approach is the best bet. It's better to cushion your statements with answers like, "One of the things I might consider would be . . ." If you commit yourself to a process of what you *would* do, and it isn't the solution the *interviewer* would like or consider, you are in an awkward position. Give your answer a cushion of several possible choices, and indicate that you would carefully assess the situation.

How did you get along with . . .? This question can be asked about supervisors, coworkers, subordinates, even teachers. Few people get along with everyone. If you generally do, say so. If you had a problem with someone, there is usually no need to tell the whole tale here. The ability to work out problems is a plus. Be positive, not blaming or complaining.

Would you accept part-time or temporary work? Employers are more inclined to hire for full-time work from a part-time or temporary employment pool than to take a person from the outside. If you plan to stay with the company, ask if a temporary or part-time job may result in a permanent hire before you say yes. If you want a temporary job and are offered a permanent position, however, consider their cost and time of training you. It takes most employees at least several months to begin to earn their pay. "No" is a better answer if you really want temporary or part-time work when you are offered a permanent, full-time position.

Why do you want to work for our company? Most people looking for a job are more interested in getting a good job than in being particular about where they work, and this attitude can make them appear not to care about the company. One of the most important things you should do before you go to an interview—or ask for one—is find out all you can about the company. Identify some positive aspects of policies, procedures, or products you can discuss with interest. Do your homework—so you will have work to come home from.

How long do you expect to work for us? The truth is that a company will not keep employees past its ability to use their skills. And you are not going to work for a company past the time that it is good for you. The best answer might be, "As long as it is good for both of us."

Do you have any questions about the company or the job? An interview doesn't have to be one-sided. Be ready for this question by preparing some questions of your own ahead of time to show your interest. Employers, down at the bottom of their company hearts, believe the myth that good people are hard to find. If they are asked to define a good person, that person is always someone who is really interested in the company and in the job that he or she does. So this is an ideal time to relate your interest, enthusiasm, and commitment to the company and the job.[6]

There are some questions you must resolve honestly ahead of time:

- Are you willing to or can you move or travel, work overtime, take a temporary or part-time job?
- Do you have plans for your next job, your next few years, starting your own business, changing fields, going back to school?

In every case the real questions are these: *Can you do the job? Will you stay with the company?*

Sometimes you may be asked questions that startle you. If you feel unprepared, it's wise to say, "I need a few moments to think about that."

Then take a few deep breaths, relax, and begin confidently. If you still draw a blank, be prepared to deal with the situation, perhaps by saving, "Maybe we could come back to that later," or "I really should be prepared to answer that but I'm not." It's a learning experience and you learn that you can keep cool.

Be prepared for some difficult ("whew!") questions if you have a poor work record, have ever been fired for serious problems, or have been convicted of a crime. Take a deep breath, relax a minute, look at the interviewer, and say in your own words something like this: "Yes, I made a mistake [or have done poorly in the past], but I learned my lesson, and I'm determined that it won't happen again." Then stop. Do not keep on explaining. If you sound confident and not defensive, the interviewer will be more likely to accept your answer. Perhaps you can include some recent experience as evidence that you've made some changes in your life. Again, you need to reassure the interviewer that you are capable of doing the job.

You might be startled by inappropriate questions that appear to have nothing to do with job qualifications, or even illegal questions that indicate discrimination. The interviewer should not ask for any personal information. Questions about age, race, religion, nationality, political views, or disabilities are improper unless the answers are job related. Also inappropriate are questions that discriminate between males and females—for example, questions about family planning, child care, or pregnancy.

Decide in advance how you will answer such questions if they are asked. If the issue is not really important, you might prefer to answer the question rather than risk alienating the interviewer with a refusal. If you'd prefer not to answer, you might say, "I wasn't aware this was a requirement for the job," or "Can you explain how this question relates to the job?" You can appeal to the law in obvious cases of prejudice; in less serious instances, a good sense of humor and respect for others can be enormously helpful. Don't win the battle and lose the war!

Nelva Shore, a California employment specialist and coworker with the author at Mission College, says, "It really doesn't matter what questions are asked as long as you can talk!" Be ready to talk positively about yourself, your goals, and your reason for applying. Practice talking. There is no other way. One woman who stood out in an interview later told about how she had practiced sitting down in front of a mirror; she practiced talking out loud, answering questions, making eye contact, controlling voice melody—every phase of the interview—until she felt totally at ease. Her enthusiasm came through unspoiled by anxiety. You can learn these skills, too.

Follow-up

If you aren't told the results at the end of the interview, feel free to ask when you will hear them. In the private sector (nongovernment) it is appropriate to send a thank-you letter right after the interview that encourages a reply (see Figure 7-10), perhaps asks for more information, or accepts an offer (see Figure 7-11). Then call after a week or so if you haven't heard. It is also important to write promptly if you decide to decline an offer.

Sometimes there is a delay in hiring someone after an interview. Several months may go by because of changes inside the company. A key employee may decide to quit or retire, for example; or an employer may decide to fill another position first; or a complex reorganization may take more time than planned. Tactfully keep in touch with your contact in the company or with the personnel department until you are certain there is no opening for you or you are hired. Job Shop participant Hal Thomas suggests returning after one to two weeks to see if the position has been filled; returning in one to two months, perhaps with work samples, to show continued interest, and then sending a letter and work samples (if applicable) in six months.

After you are hired, you may be asked to supply such items as a birth certificate, proof of citizenship, a green card if you are an immigrant, a photograph, and proof of age. Have these items ready if you feel they might be required.

Job Offers: Too Many or Too Few?

You probably will not get a job offer during your first interview. But suppose you do get a job offer—or two or three—in this early phase of your career search. Maybe you had planned to do personnel work, but the welding shop would welcome you! Beware quick decisions. You can easily get carried away with excitement and leap into the first job that comes along.

Some jobs sound rewarding in terms of personal growth opportunities, but the salary is so low you could not live on it without making sacrifices. Another job pays very well, but the work sounds dull and disagreeable. You might even be offered a temporary job; it would fulfill your immediate needs, but you'd be back on the job market in six months or so. Should you accept one of these less desirable jobs just to get hired or to get experience? Some companies and even employment offices have been know to advertise one job but place you in another, far less desirable position or increase your beginning work load to unmanageable proportions just to see if they can avoid hiring a second person. Called *bait and switch, corporate-style,* this unsavory practice can stall a career but make the victim much wiser in checking out a job ahead of time and also knowing when to quit an unreasonable situation.[7] When either employer or employee is less than honest in the hiring game, they both lose.

Now is the time to review your needs, wants, and values to become very clear about what you want the job to do. Perhaps your goal is just to

5405 Monroe Street
Aurora, IL 60504
February 26, 1996

Dierk Van Symms, Manager of Technical Services
Effective Micro Systems, Inc.
130 Meridian Drive, Suite 411
Aurora, IL 60504

Dear Mr. Van Symms:

Thank you for the chance to discuss a work opportunity with
Effective Micro Systems, Inc. I have completed the EMS Interview
Survey, and it is attached for your review.

I am pleased about the possibility of working for EMS. After meeting you, Leah, and Cindy, and Pam by phone, I feel that I would fit
in quite well on your team. Each of you has confirmed what I
already suspected—that EMS is a quality organization.

I look forward to meeting with you again. Please feel free to call
me at home or at work.

Sincerely yours,

Joanne M. Malatia

Enclosures

Figure 7-10   Thank-you letter following an interview

get into a special company that you've chosen. Taking a job you don't particularly like could give you this chance. If you do your best in that job, you
may be able to obtain the position of your choice—or one like it—should an
opening occur. Some companies will hire on a temporary basis and then
transfer and promote from within before they open jobs to outsiders.

When you do decide on a job offer, work out details such as schedule
or benefits, before final acceptance. Then your acceptance letter can "con-
firm our conversation."

If you aren't hired for the job you really want right away, you may be
only one of many well-qualified applicants. In a competitive field, you may
spend six months or more of continuous job hunting to find a job. Whether
you should take a less desirable job depends on how long you can afford to
wait and continue the search. If you job hunt for many months without a
nibble, you may need to consider alternatives: other careers, new training,
other opportunities in your present position, additional paid or volunteer
experience that might be useful in a different kind of job.

Choosing may be difficult because you have in mind a portrait of the
perfect workplace. But when you actually go job hunting, you will find that
perfection doesn't exist. You need a job because the rent is due and you have
car payments to make.

You may have to start at the bottom and work up to the job you want.
Suppose you, a business major with a fresh degree from a good university,
are offered a job as a mail clerk. Or you have a master's degree in computer
programming, but you are offered a job as a computer operator. You may
feel such offers are beneath your dignity. But before you ride away on your
high horse, consider these facts: one major oil company makes a practice of
hiring as mail clerks new graduates who are candidates for all management
and public relations jobs. In so doing, they have a chance to look you over
before entrusting a more important job to you. And you have a chance to
network inside and explore possibilities before getting too entrenched. Be
wary of turning down a job that fails to meet your expectations. Ask some
company employees what the offer means. Ask the interviewer what the
growth potential of the job is and whether you might be given a performance
review in three to six months for a possible promotion.

Job hunting requires that you keep involved at all times in some part of
the process. The more exacting your requirements, the longer you will job
hunt and the more often you will be turned down. But if you can accept
some frustration as a normal part of the job-hunting process, you will not be
discouraged. Keep in mind a clear picture of the place you would like to
work so you will recognize it when you find it. Focus on the changes you can
make to begin to experience more satisfaction in the workplace.

540l Monroe Street
Mobile, Alabama 36608
October 30, l995

Ms. Jill Jones
Director of Marketing
PTT Corporation
Dogwood, AL 36309

Dear Ms. Jones:

I am very pleased to accept an internship in marketing with PTT Corporation. It will be a pleasure to associate with the people I have met at PTT. The work you outlined in your letter sounds very challenging. I appreciate the chance to further my education in this way.

I look forward to starting on February 1. Please call if you wish to discuss any aspect of my internship further.

Sincerely yours,

Chris Cross

Figure 7-11   Acceptance letter

Self-Assessment Exercises

1. The Job Hunt Begins

a. Begin your résumé. Write a rough draft of some items you will use. Then polish and type a good copy.

Name _____

Address _____

Home Phone _____ Work Phone _____

Position Objective _____

Qualifications in Brief _____

_____

_____

Experience Summary (Optional: Try *both* Chronological and Functional) ____

_____

_____

_____

_____

_____

Education _____

_____

_____

Personal Paragraph _____

_____

_____

_____

Special notes (honors, works published, organizations, etc.) _____

_____

_____

b. Write a cover letter to accompany your résumé.

2. Practicing an Interview

Some interviewers use a rating scale to grade your performance on various points of importance to them. Figure 7-12 shows a scale used by recruiters who come from various workplaces to interview students on campus. Role-play an interview. Then, using the interview rating chart, rate yourself or ask someone to rate you on your interview skills. Here are some what/how/why practice questions.

Work experience

What have you done to get where you are?

What were your major responsibilities on your last job? (or last military experience)

What did you like most about that job?

What did you like least about that job?

What problems did you face? How did you overcome these problems?

What did you learn on your last job?

How do you feel your last job used your ability?

Why did you leave your last job?

What impressions did you leave behind on your last job?

Why do you want to work for us?

What do you feel you can contribute?

Education

What were your favorite courses (workshops, seminars)?

Why did you choose your major?

How would you rate your instructors?

What activities and clubs were you in? How did you participate?

How did you finance your education?

What further education are you planning?

Skills and value

How do you get along with people (supervisors, coworkers, instructors)?

What are your transferable (general) skills?

INTERVIEWING RATING CHART—CONFIDENTIAL

Santa Clara University
Career Planning and Placement Office

Firm _____

Recruiter _____   Date _____

I. CHARACTERISTICS OF CANDIDATE

A = Interview preparation
B = Clarity of career objectives
C = Realistic career objectives
D = Appropriate academic preparation
E = Personal appearance
F = Communicative ability
G = Emotional maturity
H = Self-confidence
I = Motivation
J = Overall rating

II. EMPLOYER INTEREST

1 = Particularly high interest
2 = Interest with further consideration necessary
3 = Prefer not to make offer
4 = Need placement counseling

III. ADDITIONAL COMMENTS

RATING SCALE   1) Outstanding   2) Above average   3) Average   4) Below average   5) Poor

NAME	I. CHARACTERISTICS OF CANDIDATE										II.	III. COMMENTS
	A	B	C	D	E	F	G	H	I	J		

Figure 7-12   Interview Rating Chart

What are your work-specific skills?

What are your personality-responsibility skills?

What are your strengths?

What are your weaknesses?

How important is money to you?

How well do you work on your own?

How many days did you take off last year for sickness and personal business?

How do you feel about overtime? Flexible hours? Part-time or temporary work? Travel? Moving to a new location?

What do you do when a coworker is behind schedule?

What kind of decision maker are you?

Goals

What do you see yourself doing in five years?

How do you plan to get there?

What areas of growth and development do you plan to work on?

What salary would you like to earn?

Tell me about yourself!

3. More Interview Questions

Make up some questions that you would like an interviewer to ask you.

4. The Application Form

Carefully fill out the application form in Figure 7-13 and sign it.

5. The Job Hunt Checklist

If you are job hunting now, establish a goal: for example, you will contact fifty people by information interviewing, networking, applying for jobs, writing letters, making telephone calls, and sending résumés on request. To check your progress, answer the following questions *yes* or *no.*

_____ Have you interviewed twenty-five people to obtain information about jobs and companies?

_____ Have you applied for work directly to twenty-five companies?

_____ Have you written an effective résumé for each job title?

_____ Have you contacted a network of at least twenty-five people who could help you?

_____ After each interview, do you critique yourself honestly?

_____ Have you written letters to thank the people who interviewed you?

EMPLOYMENT APPLICATION

Personal Data

Position Applied For | Application Date   /   /

Name (last, first, middle)

Social Security Number | Driver's License Number (if required by job)

Address

City | State | Zip Code

Home phone (   ) | Message Phone (   )

Date available for work ____ / ____ / ____ | Have you been employed here before? ❑ Yes ❑ No

Are you legally eligible for employment in this country? ❑ Yes ❑ No

(Proof of U.S. citizenship or immigration status will be required upon employment.)

If you are under 18, can you furnish a work permit? ❑ Yes ❑ No

Type of employment desired: ❑ Full Time ❑ Part Time ❑ Temporary ❑ Seasonal

Have you ever been convicted of a felony in the last 7 years? ❑ Yes ❑ No

(Such conviction may be relevant if job-related, but does not bar you from employment.) If yes, please explain

Employment History

List your last four employers, assignments or volunteer activities, starting with most recent employer, including military experience.

From   To | Employer | Phone (   )

Job Title | Address

Immediate Supervisor & Title | Summarize the nature of work performed and job responsibilities.

Reason for leaving. | Beginning rate/salary $ per | Ending rate/salary $ per

From   To | Employer | Phone (   )

Job Title | Address

Immediate Supervisor & Title | Summarize the nature of work performed and job responsibilities.

Reason for leaving. | Beginning rate/salary $ per | Ending rate/salary $ per

Figure 7-13   Sample Application Form

From To	Employer	Phone ( )
Job Title	Address	
Immediate Supervisor & Title	Summarize the nature of work performed and job responsibilities.	

Reason for leaving.	Beginning rate/salary $ per	Ending rate/salary $ per

From To	Employer	Phone ( )
Job Title	Address	
Immediate Supervisor & Title	Summarize the nature of work performed and job responsibilities.	

Reason for leaving.	Beginning rate/salary $ per	Ending rate/salary $ per

Skills and Qualifications

Summarize special skills and qualifications acquired from employment or other experience that may qualify you for work with our Company.

Education Record

High school	Dates attended *(optional)*
Degrees or Diplomas	Course of Study
College/University	Dates attended
Degrees or Diplomas	Course of Study
Other	Dates attended
Degrees or Diplomas	Course of Study

References

Name	Phone Number ( )	Years Known
Name	Phone Number ( )	Years Known
Name	Phone Number ( )	Years Known

It is understood and agreed that any misrepresentation by me in this application will be sufficient cause for cancellation of this application and/or separation from the employer's service if I have been employed. Furthermore, I understand that just as I am free to resign at any time, the Employer reserves the right to terminate my employment at any time, with or without cause and without prior notice. I understand that no representative of the Employer has the authority to make any assurances to the contrary.

I give the Employer the right to investigate all references and to secure additional information about me, if job related. I hereby release from liability the Employer and its representatives for seeking such information and all other persons, corporations or organizations for furnishing such information.

Signature of Applicant   Date   /   /

Figure 7-13   *(continued)*

8/

Decisions, Decisions

What's Your Next Move?

 FOCUS

- Survey the options.
- Learn a decision-making process.
- Set realistic goals.

*T*hroughout the career-search process you have been making many small decisions, often without even realizing it. And because of them, you have likely zeroed in on a general career area if not a job title and the educational background or college major that you would need to make a satisfying career move.

Author and educator H. B. Gelatt reminds us that most people make most decisions easily most of the time without thinking too much. Each personality type has its own decision-making style, ranging from the dynamic, energetic, and enterprising risk takers who are alway ready to meet ever new and greater challenges, to the conventional, slower moving, and more careful individuals who are willing to undertake only those challenges that look most manageable.

Although few people can be fully defined according to personality types, one may say that in general the following behavior patterns among different personality types commonly occur. The social person often acts out of caring for others but is not always practical about making the best decisions. Both the realistic and the conventional types tend to stay within secure societal norms. The conventional type follows the lead of others; realistic types will decide independently, often disregarding people's feelings but generally staying on the conservative side. The creative/artistic person, on the other hand, will see so many possibilities—including some that follow no known guidelines—that it's hard to make choices. And whereas the enterprising person leaps first and gets the facts later, the investigative type keeps researching, hoping that working on a decision long enough will make the results absolutely certain. What kind of decision maker are you?

> I try to take one day at a time,
> but sometimes several days
> attack me at once.
> —*Ashleigh Brilliant*

We can fantasize a perfectly self-actualized person bringing all these factors into balance: caring for others with just enough hardheaded realism to be practical; creating new systems while following guidelines when appropriate; searching out just enough facts before risking the decision.

In *Please Understand Me,* authors Keirsey and Bates note that people whom they call *judgers* want things in their lives settled, so they make decisions promptly and with satisfaction. The opposite personality type called perceivers like to keep all their options open, so they tend to delay decisions until the last possible minute.[1]

For anyone faced with tough decisions, for the person who tends to agonize over every decision, for those who delay decisions, an organized decision-making process can provide perspective. In this chapter we will consider a *decision-making dozen:* four attitudes, four options, and a four-phase, decision-making process.

Attitudes

Four attitudes can help you make a good decision: stay calm; be persistent; keep your perspective; be confident.

Stay Calm

Although a certain amount of anxiety can motivate a person to make a decision, too much can interfere with it. If you are under severe pressure, you may try to escape through any of a million fantasies: quit work or school altogether and drop out; join the Marines; end your marriage; run off with your secretary; sell everything, hitch up the wagon, and head west! The uncertainties are as numerous as the fantasies: Am I OK? Is there anything at all in life for me, or is this all there is? Will my health hold up? Will my kids ever get settled? Will I? Will I ever have kids? Will I look like a fool if I go back to school? Can I keep on succeeding? Do I even want to? Sometimes turbulent thoughts can seem like part of the decision-making process. You can practice letting them go, however, just like leaves in the wind, by affirming that you have made good decisions in the past and you can do so now.

Be Persistent

Take one step at a time. You rarely have to put a life decision into action in one immediate, straight-line leap! It often takes thought and some zigzag testing to sort out all the possibilities. If a decision to get a four-year degree seems overwhelming, a small decision to look at college catalogs in the library or talk to an educational counselor or teacher may be a manageable first step. But make up your mind to keep moving toward the decision you seek.

Keep Your Perspective

Stop and occasionally review your direction. If it is helpful, use the exercises in Chapter 9 to assemble information that is relevant to a career decision. Identify your strong and weak spots. Keep focusing on what you want your life to be like.

Be Confident

If you are honest, you know that you have made some good decisions in the past—from what to wear to where to work! A lack of confidence can be a giant block on the road to good decision making. As Ken Keyes, Jr., says, "Beware what you tell yourself!"[2] Compare the person who says,"I don't deserve success, I'm just not good at much of anything," with the person who might say, "Everyone—including me—deserves success." Sometimes our bad feelings can send us in search of a problem: "Don't cheer me up because it will ruin my misery program." Affirmations, those positive and negative thoughts we think over and over again, are so powerful that the authors of the children's book *Make It So!* ask children to speculate, "So—I've been wondering—could most of my problems be caused by me?"[3]

You can't know the future. Some decisions will work out; some will not. In order to improve your life, you change what can be changed, accept what can't be changed and work with it, and hope you have the wisdom to know the difference.

> When you don't know which way to turn, son,
> try something. Don't jest do nothin'!
> —*Grandpa to grandson*
> *in* Cold Sassy Tree[4]

Four Options

At this time you have four options. Go back to or remain in school, seek a new job, keep the same job with a new approach, or keep the status quo by deciding not to decide.

Back to School

If you are already in school, committed to staying there, and clear on your program of studies, then you have already made a decision and do not need to look at this section.

More and more people are returning to school more often and staying there longer. Learning to learn, to be a generalist, to have a broad view of the world, to continue learning and developing abilities—these are essential skills for the future. The majority of jobs now require some postsecondary education and training; many unskilled jobs are either being automated or moving offshore. Industry is slowly realizing that trained people are more important than new hardware, but upgrading workers is more difficult than they realized.[5]

Fast fading are the days when a high school graduate could expect to get a long-lasting and decent-paying job that would support the American Dream of a family, house, car, and a yearly vacation. A high school dropout is eight times more likely than a college graduate and three times more likely than a high school graduate to be unemployed.[6]

The Department of Labor tells us that in 1989 more than 42.4 percent of women and 36.7 percent of men twenty-five years and older had graduated from high school, and 23.8 percent of women and 28 percent of men had completed four years or more of college. Although college degrees have been declining in value lately because increased numbers of people are obtaining them, a degree will still have greater earning power than a high school diploma. Every year, a class of dropouts who leave school earn about $237 billion less than an equivalent class of high school graduates and thus pay $70 billion less in taxes. Female high-school graduates (with no college) working year round, full time, earn about the same as fully employed men who had completed fewer than eight years of elementary school.[7]

About 82 percent of all Americans in prison are high school dropouts, representing an average yearly cost each of $20,000 to taxpayers.[8] "People with professional degrees earn $5 for every $1 in lifetime income of folks who don't finish high school," according to the Census Bureau. In 1992, people with advanced degrees had average annual earnings of $48,653; those with bachelor's degrees, $32,629; high school graduates, $18,737.[9] Degrees will continue to make employment, upgrading, promotions, and raises more attainable. And yet many degree holders will find it frustrating to be "underemployed"—that is, to work in jobs that don't fully use their education. And of course, there are always the notable exceptions: people with little education who make a dramatic contribution to their work. Commitment, opportunity, and sometimes hard times can bring people to achieve what their circumstances would not predict. But generally, without knowledge and training, survival into the 2000s will be difficult.

Do not let your age or your previous school record discourage you. The average age of all adults going to school is over thirty, and there's no maximum in sight. One newspaper article described a man of ninety-two receiving an AA degree.

Many women who have not worked much outside the home, as well as returning men, are fearful: "Am I too old to learn, too old to compete with younger college students?" Some people feel that they are incompetent because of difficulties with subjects in their early school years. The surprise comes (and this happens with few exceptions) when reentry students report a great growth in confidence along with newfound goals, even though they may have previous school records that qualify as disasters. Because they are mature and motivated (although they don't always *feel* that way), they can reach their goals. So can you.

A Mini-orientation to College You may wonder what courses you would take if you returned to school. If your high school education was incomplete or deficient, or if you began college and picked up some poor grades, consider basic skills courses in language and math at adult education centers or community colleges. You also may find courses for personal growth and enrichment in these schools. Many are noncredit courses that provide an

HERMAN

3/26   ©1977 Universal Press Syndicate

"If I have to keep going to school, all the best
jobs are gonna be snapped up."

easy way to start back to school. Assertiveness training, for example, can be a good way to gain confidence to face difficult situations both in the workplace and at home.

At the community college you can also sample various majors (areas of specialty), explore and prepare for a career, or take courses to transfer to a four-year college. Pick up a catalog at the college bookstore and look for introductory courses. The titles of these courses frequently include words such as "beginning," "orientation to," "introduction to," or "principles of." The catalog will tell you the required courses and general degree requirements for each major. Usually advisers or counselors will be available to help you through the maze of choices. Search for someone who understands exactly where you are now and how you feel.

If you want a four-year degree, you can do your first two years at a community college and transfer, or you can go directly to a four-year college. In either case, your course of studies will be something like this:

First year: General education courses (GE), introduction to a major, and electives (free-choice courses)

Second year: Exploration of a major, GE, and electives

Third year: Major requirements, electives, and remaining GE

Fourth year: Major requirements and electives

You will probably need more math if you are interested in either science, health, four-year business or technical fields, architecture, or engineering. Adult education programs offer math courses at the high school level and sometimes beyond. Community colleges offer not only high school level courses but also most of the college courses at the freshman and sophomore level. Both offer remedial arithmetic. The usual sequence is this:

High school: Arithmetic, introductory algebra, plane geometry, intermediate algebra, trigonometry, college (pre-calculus) algebra or "senior math"

College: College algebra, analytic geometry, calculus (two to three semesters or five quarters), and other advanced courses as needed and required

First, check to see how much math you need for various programs. (You may not need any at all.) Then try to start where you left off or where you feel most comfortable. Before you try to enroll in any course, however, find out whether you must complete any prerequisites first. (A *prerequisite* is a course that you need to take before enrolling in a more advanced course. Sometimes experience will take the place of a prerequisite.)

Because most people will be working in the global economy or at least in areas of the United States with a diverse population, they will have contact with people of other cultures and languages. Consider enrolling in a language, history, or anthropology course as part of your general education to give you some understanding of other cultures.

If returning to school seems impossible—because of distance, for example—investigate tutoring services, correspondence courses, and courses by TV. Some colleges and universities administer tests such as those in the College Level Examination Program (CLEP), which enable you to earn credit by examination. Some schools give credit for work experience. You may be required to go to the campus to sit for exams or to take certain courses, but overall such programs decrease the time you need to spend on campus. Some colleges offer courses in weekend sessions that can lead to a degree.

If finances are a problem, apply for financial aid. Students of all ages can get grants and low-interest loans for education. But some graduates have found that paying back a loan is a struggle, especially if their first jobs do not pay well. Some students change their lifestyles; mortgage, sell, or rent their houses; sell their cars and ride their bikes; work part time and go to school part time.

You may be *in* school wondering if you should be *out*. Most everyone will tell you that returning is difficult once you leave, as you know already if you have ever stayed out even a short time. And if you begin working, perhaps start a family or buy a house, returning to school can become a very remote possibility very fast.

On the other hand, many people have found that being out of school for a time was a good experience for them. They have worked, traveled, joined the military, and found new energy to return to school. Talk to people who have gone either way: those who have managed to survive the struggles of college learning and those who have stopped out for a time. Talk to a counselor, get some help with your studies in the meantime, and then make your decision following the steps discussed later in this chapter.

Remember, too, that not all learning takes place in school. You can teach yourself many things, and you can find other people who will help you learn. You can enroll in work experience courses or seek internships where you will work off campus. Much depends on having a goal and working toward it—and being flexible enough to see alternatives.

As you know, most jobs by definition require only average to somewhat-above-average skills. Talking to people in the field can help you to assess your motivation to go on with your education, especially if your desired profession will require years of training. Remember, however, when you meet competent professionals who are all trained, experienced, and "way up there," they didn't get there in one step. The most valuable asset you can have in acquiring a high-level ability is the patience to persevere until you learn it. But hard work is fun if you are doing what you enjoy. As you go along, new horizons will open up. You can also float to your level; that is, before the end of your training, you may choose to stop out at a point where you feel comfortable. Instead of going straight on to become a certified public accountant, you might try working as an accounting clerk, which might lead you in a direction that you hadn't seen before. Or you may find along the way that you'd like to float sideways to a different area with similar satisfiers. The more homework you've done on your interests, the more quickly you'll be able to make such changes.

If you want to get more detailed information about your skills, your aptitudes to develop skills, or areas in which your skills need sharpening, you can contact a counselor at a local college, in your state employment office, or

ALTERNATIVE ROUTES TO EDUCATIONAL CREDIT

HIGH SCHOOL CREDIT

Adults can earn high school equivalency certificates through the General Education Development (GED) program. Contact your local school district or:

GED Testing Service
One Dupont Circle N.W., Suite 20
Washington, DC 20036-1163

COLLEGE CREDIT

At various colleges, look for flexible alternatives, such as TV courses, weekend programs, credit by examination, and credit for work experience.

Credit by Examination: You can take examinations to earn college credit. Contact the College Level Examination Program (CLEP) for information:

CLEP
CN 6601
Princeton, NJ 08541-6601
(215) 750-8420

Or contact the Proficiency Examination Program (PEP):

ACT: PEP
American College Testing Program
P.O. Box 4014
Iowa City, IA 52243

Credit for Noncollege Learning: The Center for Adult Learning and Educational Credentials at the American Council on Education evaluates courses given by private employers, community organizations, labor unions, government agencies, and military education programs. Contact

American Council on Education
The Center for Adult Learning and
Educational Credentials
One Dupont Circle N.W., Suite 1B-20
Washington, DC 20036

Credit for Experience: You can apply for college credit for your work experience. Contact

Council for Adult and
Experiential Learning
(CAEL) National
Headquarters
243 W. Jackson Blvd.
Chicago, IL 60604

Educational Testing Service publishes *How to Get Credit for What You Have Learned as a Homemaker or Volunteer.* It may be purchased for $5. Contact

Educational Testing Service
(ETS)
Publication Order Services
(TO-1)
CN 6736
Princeton, NJ 08541-6736

Credit for Correspondence and Independent Study: The Division of Independent Study of the National University Continuing Education Association (NUCEA) sponsors a wide variety of correspondence and independent study courses that are available through its membership institutions. The Association publishes *The Independent Study Catalog, the NUCEA Guide to Independent Study through Correspondence Instruction.*

NUCEA
Suite 615
One Dupont Circle, N.W.
Washington, DC 20036
(202)659-3130

ALTERNATIVE ROUTES TO EDUCATIONAL CREDIT *(continued)*

To order the publication, contact

Peterson's Guides
Department 1308
P.O. Box 2123
Princeton, NJ 08543

Home Study Schools
A book entitled *Bear's Guide to Earning College Degrees Nontraditionally* (1990, $23.95 plus shipping) is available from

C & B Publishing
P.O. Box 826
Benicia, CA 94510

Another relevant publication is *We Succeeded through Home Study,* by Dr. G. Howard Poteet, available for $6 from

DETC Publications
1601 18th Street N.W.
Washington, DC 20009

For additional information on accredited home study schools, contact the following organizations:

Charter Oak State College
66 Cedar Street
Newington, CT 06111

The Ohio State University
    Clearinghouse on Adult, Career,
    and Vocational Education (ERIC)
1900 Kenny Road
Columbus, Ohio 43210-1090

Regents College Degrees
7 Columbia Circle
Albany, NY 12230

Thomas A. Edison College
101 West State Street
Trenton, NJ 08608

International University Consortium
Univ. of Maryland University College
University Blvd. at Adelphi Road
College Park, MD 20742-1612

Specialized Programs: Degree, Nondegree, Apprenticeships
Conservation Directory (Lists environmentally-related college degree programs)

National Wildlife Federation
8925 Leesburg Pike
Vienna, VA 22184

Ecology Action/Bountiful Gardens
19550 Walker Road
Willits, CA 95490

Food First/Institute for Food and
    Development Policy
Ask for Alternatives to the
Peace Corps and Education for
Action
398 60th Street
Oakland, CA 94618

The Green Center
237 Hatchville Road
East Falmouth, MA 02536

International Honors Program
    in Global Ecology
19 Braddock Park
Boston, MA 02116

Institute for Social Ecology
P.O. Box 89
Plainfield, VT 05667

For the free publication *A Woman's Guide to Apprenticeship,* send a self-addressed label to

Women's Bureau
U.S. Department of Labor
Washington, DC 20210

For special training programs, contact your local state employment office.

in private practice. You can arrange to take such tests as the Career Ability Placement Survey (CAPS) or the General Aptitude Test Battery (GAT-B).

Back to the Job Market

If you are not going directly into the job market or if you do not plan to change jobs at this time, you may wish to skip this section. For some people, seeking a job after some time out of the labor pool can seem difficult. One woman who from choice had not worked for years had this to say:

> Last fall, quaking and shaking, I had made up my mind I must not put off the job-hunting ordeal any longer. I told friends that I was going back to work and one responded that her husband needed an assistant. An interview was set up and I found myself two weeks later working with a fine man who has been very understanding of my initial lack of self-assurance. My 60-day performance report was a very satisfactory one (was delighted to have "initiative" get the best grading); and at six months received a 12 percent raise, but, best of all, the following remarks: "in recognition of outstanding contribution to the department." I love the work, and most of all, I love the self-assurance it's given me. Tell others as scared as I that it's not all that hard. Take that first plunge, and you've got it made. And on a second note, my family is delighted with the new and confident me!
>
> —Carol Shawhan

Same Job/New Approach

If you are not employed, you may wish to skip this section for now. Those who are already working and have looked over the job market may find that their present job isn't so bad after all. "Then why," they wonder, "do I feel dissatisfied?" One common explanation is, "I'm not comfortable with my coworkers." Would some fine-tuning in human relations/communications improve your work life?

Human relations can absorb much of your energy as you seek to accommodate the various personalities from many backgrounds that you meet at work. Sometimes a change in yourself can make a vast difference. You can learn to communicate more effectively, assert yourself in a tactful way, grow in self-confidence, and become more considerate and understanding of the problems of others. Usually, you will find it necessary to strike a balance: not make a federal case out of every annoyance, yet be able to make changes in a situation that clashes sharply with your sensibilities. Review your personal responsibility skills from Chapter 3.

If your job is beginning to call for new duties, such as public presentations or writing, some of your basic skills may need improving. Put energy into your job and learn as much as you can in order to grow and develop. Your self-confidence will improve along with your skills.

Some people create a job within a job by assessing the tasks they like or dislike. Sometimes it's possible to trade tasks with others, ask for a reorganization, even hire someone to work along with you if your workload warrants it. Tackling a new project, changing departments, doing the same function in a new locale—each of these can be a creative way to get a fresh start.

Amazingly, some people are so successful they are promoted beyond the level of their own self-confidence, which has to catch up with their new position. Sometimes a step down—a career direction we rarely consider— can be a welcome change and may come closer to actualizing your values if the job pressures become really unbearable. One executive, laid off and then rehired into a lower position, says, "The money doesn't add up, but for the first time in my life I don't give a damn. I haven't felt this good in years!"[10] If you are dissatisfied with yourself, consider enrolling in some personal-growth classes—or at least do some reading in the area of personal growth. If a problem is weighing on you, discuss it with a trusted friend or a counselor. Many problems have obvious solutions that we may miss when searching alone.

Even if one workplace doesn't work for you, the career itself may still be a good choice. Try to separate the job from the place and people. There may be problems in the workplace, such as discrimination, sexual harassment, and poor management, that you have not caused. You may blame yourself or believe that you can solve them alone. You may press charges where there are violations of the law, but often it's wise to get some advice first from relevant government agencies or groups such as the National Labor Relations Board or, if you are a woman, the Commission on the Status of Women. Try to find a trusted guide who can help you if you decide to go that route. There will be times that you simply decide to move on to a different workplace while keeping the same career.

Deciding Not to Decide

If you have already made a decision about your direction, you may decide to skip this section; others may not feel ready to make a commitment to a career/life decision. When you keep the status quo, you are deciding not to decide—which can be a good decision. Sometimes important decisions need time to percolate for insights to come. You might stay in the same job, take more classes, or continue to be at home with your children. But if you feel that your life needs change, try to set a time limit for your next move—say, six months to a year. If your present situation is uncomfortable for you, take some sort of action to work toward improvement—even if it is just reading helpful books or writing out a plan.

Decision Making: A Four-Phase Process

Those who find decision making difficult or who have not zeroed in on a career/life decision may find this four-phase process helpful: gather information, weigh alternatives and outcomes, check values, and design strategies. This is a way of using all the small decisions you have been making throughout this book to focus on a career.

Every decision calls for accurate information. In working through this volume you have been gathering all the information you need to make a career decision. You have learned how to pull information from a variety of sources and resources. You have already made many decisions about who you are and what you like. You may need to review this material now.

Alternatives and Outcomes

There are alternatives to every career decision—that is, there are many things that you *could* do; for example, you would like to change careers and you could become either a nurse or an engineer. Whichever alternative you act on will have several outcomes. Some outcomes may seem desirable, others undesirable. Before you make an important decision, try to imagine what the result will be in both the immediate future and some years down the line. Without a workable crystal ball, it's hard to predict exactly how a decision is going to turn out. You make the best one you can and then see what adventures it leads to!

People are often able to picture only one type of outcome. Some, burdened by fears, see only disasters—major and minor. Other overly optimistic folks see nothing but grandiose positive effects. Most major decisions, however, produce a mixture of outcomes. You can take a job with a good salary, for example, but find that you will need extra training or have to work overtime. Even a dark outcome can have a light side. The extra training you get may feel like a waste of time, but later it turns out to be just the background you need for another situation. Working overtime may result in your making new friends. Hardly any decision has perfect results.

Even the most carefully reasoned, good decisions can bring disappointing results. And everyone at times makes a poor decision. In such cases, try to avoid blaming yourself; instead, give yourself credit for having taken the risk. Many alternatives seem risky only because they involve the risk of others' disapproval: What will people think? In fact, you may find yourself preserving the status quo solely out of fear of others' opinions, giving them power over your life. There is no way to change and grow without some risk.

Every change, however, even if it's only rearranging the garage, has an impact on others. Caring for those around you involves bringing them along with your decision making; that is, communicating your own needs honestly while listening to theirs, keeping them informed as you make changes. Hardly any change is perfect. There will be advantages and disadvantages to most moves. The idea is to *maximize the advantages.*

> It would be easier to play my part in life
> if I had a copy of the script.
> —*Ashleigh Brilliant*[11]

Brainstorming Alternatives

When you brainstorm, you write down every possibility without censoring it. Don't worry about whether an idea will work or what others will think. The important part is getting down as many alternatives as possible and then sorting them out. If you omit any, you may miss one that, on second look, might be possible and desirable for you.

You may have decided on a career for which there seem to be few opportunities. To find related alternatives, list all the functions of a person in that career. Then check the functions you think you'd enjoy most. If "history teacher" is on your list, do you like history, or appearing before an audience, or both? What can you do with history besides teach?

You could develop a unique lecture series on a topic of current interest—such as the architectural history of Victorian homes in Dubuque—to present to community groups. You could tutor, learn to be a docent (a person who conducts groups through museums), work as a tour guide or as a historian for a state park department or get involved in history-in-the-making in politics.

If you can get along without teaching, you could develop a tour series on tape or by map—for example, a walking tour of Atlanta or other historical places; you could write news articles about historical subjects, such as the Indians of the Upper Michigan Peninsula; you might work in a library, publishing company, heritage or historical center, or a bookstore where you might specialize in historical books.

Perhaps, after thinking it over again, you will decide that teaching is more important to you than history. Consider teaching other subjects (check school districts for local trends); volunteer in schools, recreation centers, and senior citizen centers; work as a teacher aide; teach small classes at home in areas such as woodworking, cooking, vegetable gardening, or auto repair; try teaching or giving lectures on these or other subjects to community groups such as the Parent-Teacher Association or Girl Scout and Boy Scout troups. Consider teaching recreation skills such as dancing, yoga, riding, swimming, tennis, music, bridge, exercise, skiing, golf, massage, boating. Some fitness "trainers" now visit people in their homes to show them how to use and plan a program for their exercise equipment and to monitor their progress.

With a little work, some of those activities can be parlayed into a lucrative business, but others cannot. A job must fulfill the needs and wants of other people to such an extent that they will part with something, usually money, in exchange for goods or services produced in that job. For people who would like to teach and earn a more secure living, an often-overlooked area is industry. Larger industries have training programs and orientations for new employees and inservice training for continuing employees. Someone must be the teacher in these industrial settings.

Working in marketing and sales, public relations, or human resources, including such areas as job development or affirmative action, can involve you in many situations similar to teaching: giving site tours, helping people find employment, and working with other people problems that arise. Again, know what functions you would like to perform, and many more options may become visible.

Go back to the Key Qualities Indicator in Chapter 2, and the Job Group Chart in Chapter 3 and consider the factors that are important to you. Consider related jobs again and *brainstorm, brainstorm* with friends, relatives, neighbors, acquaintances, strangers, or anyone who will give you five minutes of time and a dip into his or her experience pool. For just about any career you choose there are alternative jobs that can offer you most of what you would enjoy.

If you still want more than anything to follow a career that is highly competitive, don't be afraid to face that competition.

Here are some other ideas to give you a start:

- Don't overlook entry-level or support-service job skills, such as word processing and cashiering, to gain access to businesses of interest to you. Often you can then work into jobs closer to your interest field, in places from art galleries to auto shops, by beginning at the bottom.

- Use your main career interest as a hobby while you work at something else to support yourself. Who knows where it will lead? Walter Chandoha pursued a business degree while maintaining his interest in photographing cats. He has been a professional animal photographer for many years now and is doing better than he ever dreamed.[12] Maybe his business background has been a help! He also writes occasional articles for organic gardening magazines, another use of his creative talent.

- Investigate training programs in various industries and government agencies.

- Consider earning extra money, perhaps at home, in one of these areas: catering; cake decorating; woodworking; picture framing; custom design of clothing or toys; recycling or redoing clothing, furniture, or household appliances, or other tools or gadgets; auto repair; house painting; yard cleanup; pet care; growing vegetables on consignment; translating; making telephone wake-up calls or operating an answering service; providing income tax service; computer work, perhaps in a medical, technical, scientific, or legal specialty, doing bookkeeping, newsletter layout and editing, or other graphics such as designing stationery or business cards. Your telephone Yellow Pages will give you additional ideas. More people than ever are finding work at home to their liking.

- Consider direct selling for companies of good reputation, for whom you can virtually be your own boss. Write for member list and information by enclosing a long, stamped, self-addressed envelope to Direct Selling Association, Suite 600, 1776 K St. NW, Washington, DC 20006. Write for a publications list from the Council of Better Business Bureaus, Inc., 4200 Wilson Boulevard, Arlington, VA 22203. Request a *Directory of Business Development Publications* and a list of videos (including *The Business Plan* and *Marketing: Winning Customers with a Workable Plan*) from U.S. Small Business Publications, P.O. Box 30, Denver, CO 80201 or P.O. Box 15434, Fort Worth, TX 76119, or pick up copies at any local field office. Ask advice from friends who have sold such items as cosmetics or cleaning products. Consider franchises. They exist in a wide variety of fields from construction to specialty foods.

- Consider temporary employment, a growing area that provides flexible time, a sense of independence, and in some cases many employee benefits. One of your local agencies can provide a way to survey businesses, make contacts, and make money on your own schedule in a wide array of jobs. Advertise your skills and classes through friends, supermarket bulletin boards, local community groups. Donate samples and do demonstrations. Be aware that finding a job in an area of your favorite hobbies may not be as satisfying as you might think. Mark Twain fulfilled his dream of becoming a full-fledged riverboat pilot, but said, "Now, the romance and the beauty were all gone out of the river. All the value any feature of it had for me now was the amount of usefulness it could furnish toward compassing the safe piloting of a steamboat." Author Lyle Crist concludes, "He [Twain] had gained the mastery . . . and lost the beauty."[13] Keep your options open. The wider your "satisfaction band," the more likely you are to achieve satisfaction. When you have done everything you can but end up with a job you don't care for, you still have some choices.

- Volunteer experience can be extremely valuable in skill development. Some groups even pay volunteers a small stipend and provide them a place to live. Pinpoint the skills you would like to develop and ask for experience doing these things—for example, public relations, fund-raising, supervising people, organizing materials or activities. Be specific. Ask to be paired with a pro who will teach you some tricks of the trade. Be aware, however, that volunteer organizations are usually just as accountable for time and money as any business and cannot always accommodate your needs. To get started, send for a list of over two hundred independent organizations seeking change in the conditions of hunger, homelessness, injustice, and environmental destruction: *Invest Yourself, the Catalog of Global Volunteer Opportunities,* available from the Commission on Voluntary Service and Action Inc., P.O. Box 117, New York, NY 10009, (800) 356-9315.

Weigh Alternatives

There are many ways to weigh alternatives, all of them basically similar. We will use an exercise called Decision Point to organize and clarify these alternatives.

For example, if you were trying to decide whether to take a job in New York or one in Chicago, you would put the New York job in the balance first and write in such projected negative or undesirable results as longer work hours and hectic commuting conditions. On the positive side, you might list high pay, exciting work, status, closeness to family, and cultural opportunities. You then check whether the result is likely or unlikely to occur. On the positive side, you may find out high pay is not very likely. On the negative side, hectic commuting may also be unlikely if the company allows telecommuting and flextime, or if affordable living space is reasonably close to the job site. Unlikely means that that result should not influence your decision very much if at all. Going further, you might want to rank your likely positives and negatives to see which are the most important.

Next, of course, you would weigh Chicago in the balance, for who knows what possible positives might turn up that would make the Windy City irresistible—a fabulous job and luxurious, affordable housing close to old college friends? Then compare the results to see which looks better to you, New York or Chicago. Overall, the positive results of one alternative may quite outweigh all the negatives. And you may choose to ignore the negatives. It's up to you! What decisions have you made in the past? How have they turned out for you? Review one of these decisions as if you were just about to make it now.

Decision-making exercises can help to organize and clarify your possibilities, but they cannot make the decison for you. They involve using your rational, logical self. After such a process, give your intuition time to voice your sense of appropriateness and certainty about the decision. At some deeper level, you will usually know that your choice will work for you. You will feel finished and at peace after the struggle. You will be ready to let go the alternatives, perhaps with a twinge of regret, for there are good sides to everything. You will be ready to move on and take the steps you need to reach your goals.

Check Values

As you make choices, you express your value system—because values are revealed in what you do, not in what you say. Every step of this career search process has been related to your values. As a final check, consider your decision in terms of these values. If you want to live very simply, why seek a high-powered, energy-consuming job, the only reward for which is money? On the other hand, if money seems important to you, look at the bottom line. If you want both a family and a career, plan for it. You might wish to review Rating Values from Chapter 1 and any other values that might possibly be affected so that your choice reflects these priorities.

Design Strategies

This book outlines a great many steps you can use in making a good career decision. To carry out your next career/life decision, develop a good set of strategies—that is, a step-by-step procedure to make it a reality. Think of each step as a goal. Your goals need to be clearly stated. It won't do to say vaguely that you will "do better in school," or "start job hunting." Rather, set a specific goal: "I will read and outline history notes for two hours each evening and review them for half an hour every morning until the midterm," or "I will call five people tomorrow to ask for an information interview." Set time limits for reaching one successive step after the other. The time limit helps to discourage procrastination. And when you successfully accomplish your goals, you will find that your zest for continuing will increase.

If time is a problem for you, learn to manage it. Some people pack their lives with so many activities that they experience failure, frustration, or frenzy instead of accomplishment. Others take on too little and end up feeling bored and uninvolved. Here are some techniques for managing time:

- List all the tasks on your agenda and rank them in order of importance.

- Keep a "very important" list, a "so-so" list, and a "nice if I can get around to it" list of tasks that need doing.

- For one week, keep track of all your activities on the time chart in the exercises at the end of the chapter to discover where you are spending your time.

For further help with time management, read Alan Lakein's *How to Get Control of Your Time and Your Life.*[14]

Some people want to rush ahead to that satisfying job. They may leave school without finishing a degree, leave a job where they were getting valuable experience, or miss the job they really want by grabbing anything that comes along. As difficult as it seems at the time, waiting and finishing one phase of life before starting another is sometimes the best decision.

Goals are dreams that are measurable.
—*Anonymous*

Job Hunting . . . Again? Again!

Many people are rushed into a career decision these days without being the least bit prepared. The reason? They find themselves laid off. Whole towns are shocked to realize that they have depended for almost all the employment in a community on one company that now decides to leave. Even a whole country can face hard times when it depends on one industry. The collapse of the Philippines' sugar industry due to falling prices worldwide in the 1980s put the whole country into a severe economic decline. A war, a political decision to fund or not to fund certain projects and programs, any number of happenings can lead to downsizing or restructuring as well as expansion in your workplace. The challenges and options that seem so far away move right into Main Street. The farming community of Watsonville, California—during a year that included earthquake, drought, unexpected freezing weather, and the lure of cheaper labor—saw farms fail, food processing plants move to Mexico, and businesses close, affecting the whole community. As we approach the twenty-first century we will see more and more workers being dislocated, relocated, and retrained as the global economy shakes out into new forms. Many people will be repeating the career search process.

You may have earned a degree and learned new skills in preparation for your career. You may have found that dream job that embodies your most important values and interests and in which you are encouraged to develop your skills. You may have put a great deal of energy into your job and plan to stay with it. You may have a growing family and a hefty mortgage. But even if you planned to stay at the same place in the same job for a long time, some day, burnout or boredom may prompt you to wonder, "Is this all there is?"

Even with a job that seems secure and satisfying, it is always wise to have your résumé ready and a game plan in mind in case you (or your employer) decide to call it quits. Job hunting in a tight job market with your benefits running out, the mortgage payment due, and applications that generate only rejections can undermine the strongest ego. Here is what some

people do all the time: they keep up the contacts they have made by net-working; they continue the self- and career-assessment process; and they keep learning new skills. Preparing for change is an important part of career development.

It helps to be money-wise and to have a plan for lean times. Consider what you really *need* to survive and look for sources to fund your needs. Some people try to have money saved to pay a few months' worth of expenses. They keep bills paid, and pay cash instead of using credit cards. In a time of under- or unemployment, some reduce expenses, move to a less expensive location, use cheaper transportation, have a garage sale and sell off excess baggage, plant a garden of basics to save on food bills, join or start a small co-op to buy food wholesale, find people who could share resources. Your expanded activity lists from Chapters 1 and 2 may indicate what you might do to earn needed cash. Psychological as well as financial preparation will greatly enhance your confidence when the time comes for a move.

Bartering creatively can bring surprising results. One young man with no money or place to stay bartered lawn care at a veterinary clinic to get shots for his dog, while a neighborhood soup kitchen and some friends saw him through his rough times. Connie Stapleton of Middletown, Maryland, asked a service station manager if he had any work she could do in exchange for repairs on her car. When that brought a negative response, she asked what he liked least about his job. He said, "Collecting bills!"[15] She began making collections in exchange for free car care. An artist bartered stained-glass windows for expensive dental work.

If you have been fired or laid off, evaluate the causes so that you can avoid them in the future. Despite the very real trauma involved in being job-less, you can use the experience to advantage by preparing for your next job. Ask for help with job hunting from friends, relatives, and neighbors without hiding your job loss. As everyone knows, it can happen to anyone.

If you are unemployed and haven't had a chance to prepare for it, now is the time to work out a plan of action to avoid sitting at home reading the want ads and feeling terrible. Being a couch potato will rarely bring success! First, review both the data collected in this book and the job market information in the Job Group Chart and related resources. Second, follow good job-hunting techniques: update your résumé, renew your contacts, and collect letters of recommendation. Third, join or start a support group. Fourth, work out a daily schedule of things to do that include not only job hunting but other important business-of-living activities, like exercising and visiting friends. In the meantime, consider temporary work, part-time work, "just any job," negotiating to share a job, going back to school. Try to keep your life in balance on not only the physical but also the emotional, intellectual, and altruistic levels. Enjoy the "unemployment benefits" such as sleeping late some mornings, catching up on errands, or enjoying an occasional walk. The more you can relax with your new leisure, the better you'll be able to plan your next step.

Basic physical needs may seem so imperative at such times that concerns about emotional, intellectual, and altruistic needs and wants can fly out the window as you begin to believe that any job will do! But perhaps this is the time to gather some emotional support, to use every bit of your intelligence and knowledge to carve out more than a survival path. The insights you gather may be just what you need to boost your confidence and morale and open up unsuspected possibilities. Survey the skills you developed on your last job. Did that job put you in touch with new interests? What did you dislike about that job?

A layoff can be a liberating experience—if you don't get too hungry—and a good time to reevaluate a career and make changes. Unemployed people have started businesses, often on a shoestring, found rewarding partnerships, and created satisfying new careers. Many people have moved from the corporate complex to small-business ownership. They have gone from designing microchips to designing sandwiches in their own delis, from making hardware to making beds in their guest cottages by the sea. Numbers of individuals who were forced to make a change as a result of unemployment have been delighted with the results.

Even if a risky venture isn't for you right now, get together with others to share such resources as physical necessities, ideas, job leads, and support. Call your local school career center for help. If you are unemployed, keep busy with courage.

In any case, you will find a more balanced and satisfying life by developing your potential as far as possible in all areas. There are those who have found that volunteering to help people more needy than themselves gave them new insights into all the resources they *do* have. A number of them have even met individuals who offered them a job.

The Great Gap

Some people complete the entire career search process without making the big decision. If you are still unable to choose a career, you may need more time to gain confidence and clarify your values. You may need to give your creativity time to work. There is a point—we could call it the Great Gap—where you must cross over from process to action. No matter how much support you've had, how many inventories you do, and how many people you talk to, the decision is yours alone to make.

Perhaps you need to take a "dynamic rest" along the road to success. Read some books about the problem that's holding you back. Discuss it with a friend or counselor. Paradoxically, sometimes we need to accept the status quo before we can change it.

And reassessment time will probably come around again and again because people change careers and jobs often in their lives. Some people take some time each year to evaluate their situation. They review the balance in their lives among its physical, emotional, intellectual, and altruistic/spiritual components. Which of these need levels motivates *you* most? The more you grow, the more your lower needs will be fulfilled, and the more you will become a self-actualizing person who acts out of concern not only for yourself but for other people and the planet. Everything you do will express what is finest in human nature. All your motivation will flow from the altruistic.

In *Elegant Choices, Healing Choices,* psychologist Marsha Sinetar, Ph.D., says that elegant choices are those options in life "tending toward truth, beauty, honor, courage." They are choices that are life supporting, whereas choices that take one away from truth, morality, and self-respect are life-defeating.[16]

> Until one is committed, there is hesitancy, the chance to draw
> back, always ineffectiveness. . . . There is one elemental truth,
> the ignorance of which kills countless ideas and splendid plans:
> that the moment one definitely commits oneself, then Providence
> moves too. . . . A whole stream of events issues from the
> decision, raising in one's favor all manner of unforeseen incidents
> and meetings and material assistance which no man could
> have dreamed would have come his way. Whatever you can
> do or dream you can, begin it. Boldness has genius, power, and
> magic in it. Begin it now.
>
> —*Goethe*

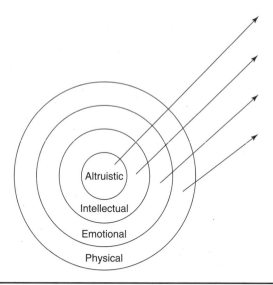

Sources of Motivation SOURCE: *Courtesy of Mission College/IDS*

Change Is Here to Stay

H. B. Gelatt says, "For those of you who are worried that I might change my mind again, let me assure you, I will. Fortunately, this is a trait whose time has come. Changing one's mind will be an essential decision-making skill in the future. Keeping the mind open will be another. Learning to be good at being uncertain is becoming a modern-day asset in decision-making. The hard part to learn is to be positive about the uncertainty."[17] Thus does decision-making expert Gelatt laud a trait he calls "positive uncertainty." Some people might like to avoid it, but in this age change is inevitable. Some understanding of your past, confidence in your future, flexibility, and the willingness to accept "ambiguity, inconsistency, and uncertainty" will make the process of decision making more manageable.

What causes people to make life changes, sometimes very far-reaching and dramatic ones? Often, consciously or unconsciously, people may be searching for something new, working out the details without expressing the process to anyone. And when they reach a decision, it may seem sudden to the observer.

Sometimes people have such a powerful experience that they begin to see their lives in a totally different way. They or someone close to them may have a serious accident or become quite ill; someone they care about may die; their marriage may break apart; they may travel to and live in a very different culture. Often experiencing a war or the extreme poverty of a developing country can cause people to question their lives. A retired military man and vice-president of a bank made such a change after working in Third World development, traveling to Guatemala, and seeing the activities of an older couple involved in helping the rural poor in that country. He felt so alive and energized by these experiences that he went back to Yale to get a master's degree in forestry to use to help the environment in re-developing countries.

People are more than squares on a page or checks in a box. They are pain and purpose, hopes and dreams, woundedness and wholeness. They are a compendium of cultural constraints and conditioning with the ever-present possibility of breaking loose into wondrous patterns with surprises at every turn.

Success: New Directions

We began this book by looking at success, and since then, you have been learning good things about yourself: your interests, values, and skills. You've learned how to find or make a place for yourself in the job market. You've learned to assess jobs and workplaces and how to network effectively. You've learned to change attitudes and feelings and "own" all the good things about yourself by positive affirmations. When you believe in yourself as a capable person, you are on your way to further growth, to self-actualization, to fulfillment. When you are true to yourself and all that is best in you, you will be a success!

You are unique. The person you are and could become, the success and happiness that you can achieve, can be done only when you listen to your own voice. Mythologist Joseph Campbell says, "If you follow your bliss, you put yourself on a kind of track that has been there all the while, waiting for you."[18] Some people just won't give up until they have found their bliss in satisfying work and a lifestyle that is uniquely their own.

"A mark of the adult is the willingness to recognize material limitations, to recognize that no single life can embrace the multitude of experiences available to humankind: climb all the mountains, chart all the seas, master all the arts," wrote Ted Berkman. "Freed from the tyranny of 'want it all,' I find that I have all I need: books and friends, the beach at sunrise, the towering silhouette of the Santa Ynez mountains. . . . There is time to savor and to serve."[19]

Success has been popularly defined as achieving your goals. But in this day and age of the global village, with only a few years to 2001, success is much more than that, much more than media and corporate images. Success must be seen in a larger context with a deeper vision. Success must ultimately include a balanced life, a life in which we have taken care of ourselves and those dependent on us, but in the context of global concerns. Success, then, means achieving realistic goals, using effective strategies based on our interests, skills, and true values, accounting for the basic needs and the legitimate, enriching wants of ourselves and others. The most far-reaching successes are those that transform us into better people and creators of a better world. Some people create so much joy within themselves—despite facts, trends, and predictions—that they are happy anywhere. Perhaps that joy, after all, is the key to success. The steps you take will create your life. May your career choice make you a "true person." May your dreams be actualized.

> The richest person in the world is not the one who has the most friends, nor the one who knows the most, but the one who is wise enough to distinguish between the essentials of life and the nonessentials and go forth like an adventurer, with the wind and the rain and the sun in his face.
>
> —*R. L. Duffus*
> The Tower of Jewels:
> Memories of San Francisco

Self-Assessment Exercises

1. Decision-Making Style

How do you make decisions? Check (✓) the appropriate columns. Then mark plus (+) before items you'd like to improve.

	Usually	Sometimes	Rarely
■ I make decisions after considering alternatives.	_____	_____	_____
■ I make decisions easily, on time, without undue agonizing.	_____	_____	_____
■ I base decisions on reasoned judgment of the information available.	_____	_____	_____
■ I base my decisions on feelings and intuition.	_____	_____	_____
■ I tend to think my decisions will turn out to be disasters.	_____	_____	_____
■ I tend to imagine my decisions will have spectacular results.	_____	_____	_____
■ I consult with others, but my decisions are my own.	_____	_____	_____
■ I finalize my own decisions without shifting responsibility to others.	_____	_____	_____
■ I compromise when the needs of others are involved.	_____	_____	_____
■ I make some decisions to fulfill my own needs.	_____	_____	_____
■ I "test out" major decisions ahead of time if possible.	_____	_____	_____
■ I take responsibility for the results of my decisions.	_____	_____	_____
■ If a decision doesn't work, I try another plan, without great regret.	_____	_____	_____

2. Decision Point: Selecting Alternatives

If you are on the verge of a decision but are having trouble choosing the alternative that would work best for you, list those alternatives here (for example, if you are trying to decide which geographical location would suit you, list all the possibilities; if you are deciding on a career, list those possibilities):

Alternative a. _____

Alternative b. _____

Alternative c. _____

Alternative d. _____

3. Decision Point: Weighing Alternatives

a. Write one of the alternatives you are considering: _____

b. In the blanks below list as many negative and positive results as you can that might occur if you followed that alternative. Check whether they are likely or unlikely.

c. If you have many more likely negative results than positive results, you may wish to choose another alternative.

d. Rank the positive and then negative results in order of their importance to you.

Negatives (Undesirable outcomes)	Likely	Unlikely	Positives (Desirable outcomes)	Likely	Unlikely
_____	_____	_____	_____	_____	_____
_____	_____	_____	_____	_____	_____
_____	_____	_____	_____	_____	_____
_____	_____	_____	_____	_____	_____

e. Compare results:

- Do the positives outweigh the negatives?   Yes _____   No _____

- Overall, do the positives seem more likely and desirable than the negatives? Yes _____   No _____

f. Repeat this procedure for each of your alternatives. Then write a paragraph comparing your results for each alternative. Discuss how these results will affect your final decision.

g. Ten years down the path, which decision would you like to have made? What results might occur only later? Add your insights to the paragraph in f.

h. Spend time choosing your decision; spend some of it alone. Cross the Great Gap!

4. Goals and Strategies

Write down the decision you've chosen to carry out. This becomes your goal. State four or more steps or strategies you will take to accomplish this goal. How soon would you like to accomplish this change and its related strategies?

Decision or goal _____

Is this goal realistic? _____   Does it agree with your values? _____

Steps I will take   *Date to be accomplished*

a. _____   _____

b. _____   _____

c. _____   _____

d. _____   _____

e. _____   _____

5. Time Management

How will you manage your time in order to reach your goals?

a. State the number of college credits you
   plan to carry in your next term.   _____

b. Allow at least two hours of study for each
   credit or unit (units times 2).   _____

c. State the number of hours you will work per
   week (include family care).   _____

d. Total the number of hours each week you
   have committed so far.   d. ⬚

e. Estimate the number of hours per week you devote to
   sleeping   _____
   eating   _____
   commuting   _____
   household chores   _____
   business (bank, dentist, shopping, etc.)   _____
   communicating with family and friends   _____
   exercise   _____
   recreation/leisure   _____
   miscellaneous/unexpected   _____
   Add the total   e. ⬚

f. Add the total in boxes d and e to see how many hours
   per week you spend in all activities—the big total!   TOTAL (d + e). _____

g. Remember, there are only 168 hours in a week. Do you have too much scheduled? _____   Too little? _____   Just enough? _____

6. Your Weekly Schedule

Fill in a reasonable schedule for yourself. Try to follow it for one week, then revise it.

WEEKLY SCHEDULE

Time	Monday	Tuesday	Wednesday	Thursday	Friday	Saturday	Sunday
6:00							
7:00							
8:00							
9:00							
10:00							
11:00							
12:00							
1:00							
2:00							
3:00							
4:00							
5:00							
6:00							
7:00							
8:00							
9:00							
10:00							
11:00							
12:00							
1:00							
2:00							
3:00							
4:00							
5:00							

7. Back to School

If going to college is on your list of possibilities, check (✓) the answers that explain why. If college isn't for you, check any other training alternatives that appeal to you.

Why college?

_____ Not sure, but wish to explore and find out about it

_____ Personal enrichment

_____ Hope to improve basic skills

_____ Would like to obtain a high school equivalency diploma (G.E.D., or General Education Development diploma).

_____ Would like to finish high school work and earn a diploma

_____ Wish to earn a career program certificate

_____ Plan to earn a two-year degree at a community college

_____ Want to earn a BA or BS degree from a four-year college or university

_____ Want to do graduate work

_____ My mother/father/boss/spouse made me come to college!

Other training alternatives?

_____ Apprenticeship programs with unions in various crafts

_____ Adult education in local school district

_____ Proprietary schools (private schools that teach a special job skill)

_____ On-the-job training programs or management training programs

_____ Off-campus or extension college work by TV, job experience, week-end college, and other options for the busy person

8. School Subjects

a. Check (✓) the columns that describe your feelings about school subjects.

	Like	Dislike	Did well	Did not do well	Avoided
Reading	_____	_____	_____	_____	_____

	Like	Dislike	Did well	Did not do well	Avoided
Writing	____	____	____	____	____
Speech/drama	____	____	____	____	____
Math	____	____	____	____	____
Science	____	____	____	____	____
Social studies	____	____	____	____	____
Arts/crafts	____	____	____	____	____
Music	____	____	____	____	____
Industrial/technical	____	____	____	____	____
Business	____	____	____	____	____
Health	____	____	____	____	____
Agriculture	____	____	____	____	____
Physical education	____	____	____	____	____
_____	____	____	____	____	____
_____	____	____	____	____	____
_____	____	____	____	____	____

b. Circle the subjects you'd like to study further.

c. Now look at your "worst" subjects. Are there any you'd like to try again? Not try again?

Try again_____Not try again_____

9. Some College Majors Arranged by Personality Type and Job Group

On p. 279 is a checklist of over two hundred college majors, check (✓) those of interest to you.

10. Blocks and Barriers: Finding the Keystone

To find out what is holding you back, ask yourself whether you are dealing with barriers within yourself. Place a check (✓) before any that apply:

R REALISTIC

Mechanical

___ Aero Maintenance/ Operations
___ Air Conditioning/ Refrigeration Technology
___ Solar Technology
___ Air Traffic Control
___ Anaplastology
___ Automotive Technology
___ Biomedical Technology
___ Construction Technology
___ Electronics Technology
___ Food Service Technology
___ Hazardous Materials
___ Industrial Administration
___ Engineering/Technology
___ Laser/Microwave/Digital Technology
___ Machine/Tool Technology
___ Quality Control
___ Radiologic Technology
___ Robotics/Computer- Assisted Manufacturing (CAM)
___ Semiconductor Management
___ Telecommunications
___ Transportation
___ Watch Repair
___ Welding Technology

Industrial: No majors

Nature

___ Agriculture
___ Animal Health Technology
___ Nursery Management
___ Park Management Technology
___ Wildlife Management Technology

Protective

___ Administration of Justice/Private Security
___ Fire Science
___ Safety Engineering

Physical Performing

___ Physical Education/ Kinesiology

I INVESTIGATIVE

Scientific

___ Biological science
___ Agriculture
___ Animal/Avian
___ Bacteriology
___ Biology
___ Botany
___ Conservation

I *(continued)*

___ Enology
___ Entomology/Pest Science
___ Environmental Science
___ Food Science
___ Forest Science
___ Genetics
___ Kinesiology
___ Marine Biology
___ Microbiology
___ Nutrition
___ Soil/Water/Wood Science
___ Toxicology
___ Zoology
___ Cybernetics
___ Engineering
___ Aeronautical/ Aerospace
___ Agricultural
___ Bioengineering
___ Civil
___ Computer Science
___ Electrical/Electronic
___ Environmental/Earth Resources
___ Material Science
___ Naval Architecture
___ Nuclear
___ Robotics
___ Science
___ Systems
___ Transportation
___ Linguistics
___ Mathematics/Statistics/ Applied
___ Medical
___ Dentistry
___ Medical Technology
___ Medicine/Surgery
___ Optometry
___ Pharmacy/Pharmacy Technology
___ Veterinary Medicine
___ Physical Sciences
___ Chemistry
___ Geology/Earth Science
___ Meteorology/ Atmosphere
___ Oceanography
___ Physics/Astronomy
___ Social Sciences
___ Anthropology
___ Consumer Economics/ Science
___ Ethnic Studies

I *(continued)*

___ Geography
___ History
___ Peace and Conflict Studies
___ Psychology
___ Sociology
___ Urban/Rural Studies
___ Women's Studies

A ARTISTIC

Applied Arts

___ Architecture
___ Commercial Art
___ Computer-Assisted Design (CAD)
___ Film/Photography
___ Fashion Design
___ Interior Design
___ Industrial Design
___ Graphics
___ Journalism
___ Landscape Design/ Ornamental Horticulture
___ Media Specialty
___ Technical Drafting/ Modelbuilding/Illustrating
___ Printing/Lithography/ Desk-Top Publishing
___ Radio/TV
___ Technical Illustrating/ Writing

Fine Arts

___ Art/Art History
___ Dance/Drama
___ English
___ Foreign Language
___ Humanities
___ Literature
___ Music
___ Philosophy
___ Speech

S SOCIAL

Human Services

___ Community Health Worker
___ Counseling
___ Dental Assistant/Hygiene
___ Dietician
___ Health Science
___ Respiratory Therapy
___ Nursing RN, LVN, Assistant
___ Ophthalmic Dispensing
___ Pediatric Assistant
___ Physical/Occupational Therapy/Assistant
___ Primary Care Associate
___ Psychiatric Technology
___ Psychology–Clinical

S *(continued)*

___ Public Health
___ Radiology/EKG/ Phlebotomy
___ Social Service
___ Speech Pathology and Audiology

Accommodating

___ Cosmetology
___ Food Service
___ Gerontology
___ Leisure/Travel

S/E SOCIAL/ENTERPRISING

Leading/Influencing

___ Advertising
___ Business Admininstration
___ Convalescent Hospital Admininstration
___ Education
___ Financial Services
___ Health Care Management
___ Insurance
___ Labor Studies
___ Law
___ Library Science
___ Management/Supervision
___ Manpower Administration
___ Office Administration
___ Public Relations
___ Recreation
___ Volunteer Administration

E ENTERPRISING

Persuading/Selling

___ Fashion/Retail Merchandising
___ International Trade
___ Law
___ Marketing/Sales
___ Political Science
___ Purchasing
___ Real Estate
___ Speech/Communications

C CONVENTIONAL

Business Detail

___ Accounting
___ Paralegal
___ Banking/Finance
___ Court Reporting
___ Data Processing
___ Insurance
___ Secretarial
___ Administrative
___ Clerical
___ Medical Assistant/Records
___ Legal
___ Unit Clerk
___ Word Processing

Blocks within you

- Locked into your stereotypes
- Too complacent to change the status quo
- Lacking confidence/awash in fear
- Weak skills
- Negative attitudes
- Caught in health or emotional problems
- Bogged down in transitions like divorce, death of spouse, immigration adjustment
- Longing for improved personal relationships
- Afraid to make a commitment
- In the habit of procrastinating
- Over-researching—losing yourself in the library
- Experiencing conflicts about values
- Too many "shoulds"

Barriers outside you

- A really poor job market/economy
- Societal expectations
- Imperative roles such as parenting
- Physical realities such as illness

What steps can you take to overcome these blocks and barriers?

_____

_____

_____

_____

_____

_____

_____

_____

_____

_____

11. *Positive Affirmations*

Everyone is a mixture of faults, foibles, and failings along with skills, successes, and strengths. Check (✓) the statements that match your thought patterns. Select one *positive* statement and say it many times a day over a week's time. Know that attitudes and feelings can be changed.

Negatives	Positives
____ I don't think I'll ever figure out what I want to do.	____ I can take steps to figure out what to do.
____ I'm not interested in anything.	____ I'm interested in many things.
____ Nothing is much fun.	____ I enjoy many of my activities.
____ I'm dumb.	____ I can learn.
____ If my first choice doesn't work out, I'm stuck.	____ I can plan alternatives.
____ I'm tired of trying because nothing works.	____ I have the energy to make things happen.
____ I'm afraid.	____ I can be courageous.
____ I never have fun.	____ I can create a good time.
	____ I can make a good decision!

Group Discussion Questions

1. Describe your decision-making style. What factors might cause someone to "decide not to decide"?
2. Share your educational plans. Define lifelong learning and the form it can take in your own life.
3. What new approaches can you take to improve your work/educational/life situation?
4. How do values relate to decisions?
5. What values might prompt a manager to step down to a lower job status?
6. What values might take the place of work in your life?
7. How can a person prepare for unemployment?
8. Share an important decision you would like to make.
9. What is the most important decision you have ever made in your life?
10. Discuss with a group or write your feelings about important decisions you have made and those you would like to make.

9

Work Affects the Soul

The Final Analysis

FOCUS

- Review the career decision-making process.

- Gather personal information into one place.

- Review and update your goals.

*T*he Final Analysis is a place to summarize the information you have gathered from the self-assessment exercises in this book. It will give you an overview of the important areas of your life that are affected by work. It will help you assess your career search process and determine how effectively this process has helped you choose the career that will lead to growth and self-fulfillment on all levels. It may help you make some final decisions, and it provides a handy future reference.

To complete the Final Analysis, review the self-assessment exercises and summarize the data here. Feel free to add additional information about yourself and the career/life decisions you are considering.

Chapter 1   Needs, Wants, and Values: Spotlighting You

1. Review the Life Problems Checklist (p. 27) and Tapping into Feelings (pp. 27–28). Then list those areas you would like to expand and those you would like to change or eliminate.

   I want to develop   *I want to change*

   _____   _____

   _____   _____

   _____   _____

   _____   _____

2. Review Needs and Wants. Check the balance in your life. Do you have enough? What do you need or want on these four levels?

   I have enough   *I would like*

   Physical level

   _____   _____

   Emotional level

   _____   _____

   Intellectual level

   _____   _____

   Altruistic level

   _____   _____

   Is your life in balance on these four levels?   Yes _____   No _____

FENWICK Courtesy of Mal Hancock
Reprinted from *The Saturday Evening Post* © 1987.

If not, how can you improve the balance? _____

_____

_____

_____

3. Review Rating Values (pp. 28–30) and write six of your most important values here:

   a._____   c. _____   e. _____

   b. _____   d. _____   f._____

4. Review your autobiographical data. Summarize what you learned about yourself in the two exercises in Drawing a Self-Portrait (pp. 31–33) and Creating an Autobiography (pp. 35–37).

   _____

   _____

   _____

5. Review Candid Camera—3D (pp. 33–34). List the four activities you enjoy most.

   a. _____   c. _____

   b. _____   d. _____

6. Describe success for yourself _____

_____

_____

_____

Chapters 2 and 3   Job Satisfiers

1. Review the Personality Mosaic in Chapter 2. Then list your types and the scores for each type in order from highest to lowest.

   First _____   Fourth_____

   Second_____   Fifth _____

   Third _____   Sixth _____

2. Which level of involvement with Data, People, and Things do you enjoy? See page 00.

   Data   High level _____   Modest level _____   Little or none _____

   People High level _____   Modest level _____   Little or none _____

   Things High level _____   Modest level _____   Little or none _____

3. Circle the numbers of the ten key qualities that represent important skill areas for you. On the line before each skill, write M if you prefer a modest level, H for high level of ability. Then circle the numbers of the key work qualities you prefer.

   Key Qualities of Data/People/Things

   _____ 1. Logical intelligence   _____ 6. Facility with multidimensional forms

   _____ 2. Intuitive intelligence   _____ 7. Businesslike contact with people

   _____ 3. Verbal ability   _____ 8. Ability to influence people

   _____ 4. Numerical ability   _____ 9. Finger/hand agility

   _____ 5. Exactness with detail   _____ 10. Whole body agility

   Key Qualities of Work

   _____ 11. Repetition   _____ 12. Variety

   _____ 13. Physical risk   _____ 14. Status

4. From the Personal Responsibility Skills Checklist (pp. 65–66), list your best personal skills and the ones you could improve.

Best Skills   *Could Improve*

_____   _____

_____   _____

_____   _____

_____   _____

_____   _____

_____   _____

5. List your work-specific skills.

_____

_____

_____

List the work-specific skills you wish to acquire.

_____

_____

_____

6. List three jobs groups by decimal code and title from the Job Group Chart in Chapter 3 in the order of your own interests.

a. Decimal code _____   Title _____

b. Decimal code _____   Title _____

c. Decimal code _____   Title _____

7. Tell how your top job group matches your personality, skills, interests, and work qualities. Use a separate sheet of paper if necessary.

_____

_____

_____

_____

_____

_____

8. List the job title you would like most. _____

9. Do you want a career or "just a job"? Explain your answer.

_____

_____

_____

10. How does your career choice match your values?

_____

_____

_____

Chapter 4   Roles and Realities: Sinking the Stereotypes

Review the roles you play from Thinking about Your Roles (p. 116). Then complete the following:

1. I enjoy being a _____

   because _____

2. I would like to improve my role as a

   _____

3. I'd like to be more accepting of people who are

   _____

4. Review Identifying Major Components of Your Life (p. 117). List those you would like to improve.

   _____   _____   _____

   _____   _____   _____

   _____   _____   _____

Chapter 5   Work: Challenges, Options, Opportunities

1. List one major challenge of importance to you, and tell why it interests you.

   _____

   _____

2. List two options you would like to be involved with to meet your most important challenge and tell what you would like to do.

_____

_____

_____

3. Does your career choice enable you to be involved with either of these options? How?

_____

_____

_____

4. What does the *Occupational Outlook Handbook* (or similar references) say about the employment outlook for the career of your choice?

_____

_____

_____

5. What is the salary range for the career of your choice? _____

   Would this career support your lifestyle?   Yes _____   No _____

6. List three alternate careers that you would consider. List one positive and one negative feature of each.

   Career   *Positive feature*   *Negative feature*

   a. _____   _____   _____

   b. _____   _____   _____

   c. _____   _____   _____

Chapter 6   Workplaces and Workstyles: Scanning the Subtleties

1. Use findings from your research to describe the ideal workplace. Consider size and complexity, type of environment, emotional rewards, and work routine you would like.

_____

_____

_____

_____

_____

_____

2. Review the Career Ladder (p. 166). How far up the ladder do you want to go? Explain your answer.

_____

_____

_____

3. Review Researching Workplaces (pp. 200–201) and Workplace Checklist (pp. 204–206). Then list the four corporate values that are most important to you (see Workplace Values, p. 200).

a. _____

b. _____

c. _____

c. _____

4. Describe your ideal job.

_____

_____

_____

_____

_____

_____

5. Describe your ideal boss.

_____

_____

_____

_____

_____

_____

6. Describe your ideal work day.

   _____

   _____

   _____

7. Describe your ideal balance of work and leisure.

   _____

   _____

   _____

8. If you were to decide to open your own business, what steps would you take first?

   a. _____

   b. _____

   c. _____

9. Where would you like to work? How do the workplaces you are interested in present challenges of interest to you? Present options you would enjoy? Match your values?

   _____

   _____

   _____

10. What does work mean to you? Describe your personal work ethic.

   _____

   _____

   _____

   _____

   _____

   _____

Chapter 7   The Job Hunt: Tools for Breaking and Entering

To prepare for the job hunt:

1. Name the title of a job you might apply for _____

2. List five of your characteristics that relate to that job and tell how:

_____

_____

_____

_____

_____

Chapter 8   Decisions, Decisions: What's Your Next Move?

1. What is your next move in the career search?

_____

_____

_____

2. Educational planning sheet

   a. Do you now have the skills and training you need to obtain a job in the field of your choice?   Yes _____   No _____
   If you need more preparation, which of the following do you need (see p. 277)?

   _____ Apprenticeship   _____ Workshops or seminars

   _____ On-the-job training   _____ Other _____

   b. If you need more education, which of these alternatives are you considering (see p. 277)?

   _____ A few courses   _____ A BA or BS degree

   _____ A certificate   _____ Graduate school

   _____ An AA or AS degree   _____ Other _____

   c. List an appropriate major (or majors) for your career choice (see p. 279).

   _____   _____

   d. What kind of college do you plan to attend?

   _____ Two-year   _____ Four year

   _____ Public   _____ Private

   _____ Out-of-state   _____ In-state   _____ Local

e. List colleges or universities that offer the major you have chosen. (Use educational references in your library or a college counseling center.)

_____   _____

_____   _____

f. Obtain catalogs from colleges of interest to you. To gather as much information as possible, visit the campuses and talk with people who are familiar with each school. For example, will you need

_____ Financial aid   _____ Housing

_____ Special entrance tests   _____ A specific grade point average

_____ Other _____

g. Begin course planning here:

Major requirements	*Graduation requirements*	*Electives*
_____	_____	_____
_____	_____	_____
_____	_____	_____

3. Complete the bottom line: I plan to be employed in the job of my choice by (date) _____

4. Review the inventories and your autobiography. Check each item in the Final Analysis. Does it all fit together?   Yes _____   No _____

Hang Loose
I'm
just
going
to
hang
loose
,
that's
the
best
way
to
go

—*Michele F. Bakarich*
© *1978 Reprinted with permission.*

Appendix

Sample Résumés and Letters

The sample résumés and letters in this Appendix are those of real job seekers ranging from college student to senior citizen, from engineer to houseperson returning to work. Each résumé is unique to one person as your résumé will be unique to you. But you can use these sample résumés in a number of ways. Notice the variety of forms and styles. Select the ones that seem to fit your situation best. Use them as models to create your own unique résumé.

The sample résumés can be used for role playing also. As you read them, pay attention to the person behind the résumé as an interviewer would. Think of questions you might ask the person represented by each résumé, and use these questions in mock interviews.

The letters that accompany résumés are called "cover letters." In addition to "covering" your résumé, letters may be used to thank people who have interviewed you and to keep in touch with them until you are actually employed.

5096 W. Monroe Street
South Bend, Indiana 46637
May 22, 1995

Mr. William A. Cline
U.S. Department of Forestry
115 E. Birch Bark Lane
Sault Ste. Marie, Michigan 49783

Dear Mr. Cline:

This is to let you know that I am still interested in working with the Forest Service in the Michigan area. I expect to be in touch with you around November regarding the jobs of recreation assistant and resource assistant that you mentioned to me for next year.

By the way, I applied for (and got) the spotted owl project job at Gifford Pinchot National Forest last summer. Thanks for notifying me about it. (It was never listed with Civil Service.)

If you know of any promising late-opening summer jobs in your area this year, I would appreciate it if you would let me know.

Thanks again.

> *Yours truly,*
>
> *Daniel P. Magee*
>
> *(219) 555-1212*

Figure A-1   Letter maintaining contact with a prospective employer

KATHLEEN M. NEVILLE
791 Peony Lane
Mountain View, CA 95040
(408) 555-1696

POSITION OBJECTIVE: Supervisor/Inventory Control

QUALIFICATIONS IN BRIEF:

AS in Restaurant Management
BA candidate in Business Management
Supervisory experience
Good human relations skills
Reliable, responsible, creative worker

EDUCATION:

SAN JOSE STATE UNIVERSITY, San Jose, CA   Present
Major: Business Management

FOOTHILL COMMUNITY COLLEGE   1985
AA Degree in Restaurant Management
(Core Courses at Mission College)

WORK EXPERIENCE:

LINDA'S DRIVE-IN, Mountain View, CA   August 1982 to Present
Supervisor/Cook
Inventory, order, prepare, and stock food supplies. Settle employee and
customer problems and complaints. Orient/train new employees; evaluate
employee performance. Do minor repairs/maintenance. As occasional acting manager, open and close shop, handle cash/cash register.

Babysitting and housekeeping throughout junior   Prior to 1982
high and high school.

ACTIVITIES:

GIRL SCOUTS   1977–81
Supervised day camp; planned activities, taught games, arts and crafts,
sports, camping skills, and first aid. Solved conflicts. Received art award.

MUSIC/DRAMA   1977–1985
As Assistant Director supervised costumes, sets, props. Performed in
Summer Theatre Workshop. Foothill Youth Symphony, Jazz, Symphony,
Marching/Pep Bands from elementary school through community college.
Toured Expo 1982.

Figure A-2   Chronological résumé of a young person applying for a first full-time job. It is the résumé of the college student whose work skills provided the example of the "Candid Camera—3-D" exercise in Chapter 1. Her brief statement of qualifications emphasizes education and transferable and personal responsibility skills.

KATHLEEN M. NEVILLE
541 Austria Drive, Sunnyvale, CA 95087
(408) 555-9829

POSITION OBJECTIVE: Food Service Coordinator

QUALIFICATIONS IN BRIEF:

AS in Restaurant Management
BA in Business Management
Computor capability for production and inventory control
Supervisory experience
Good human relations skills
Organized, reliable, responsible, creative worker

EDUCATION:

SAN JOSE STATE UNIVERSITY, San Jose, CA BA Degree
Major: Business Management

FOOTHILL COMMUNITY COLLEGE   1985
AS Degree in Restaurant Management/Core Courses at Mission College

WORK EXPERIENCE:

GARDNER FOODS, San Jose, CA   June 1990 to Present
Administrative Assistant/Supervisor

Provide administrative support to Executive Chef. Supervise kitchen
staff in daily operations. Meals on Wheels Food Coordinator for the
Santa Clara County program. Control complete data base; maintain current operating inventory, initiate all product changes; and purchase supplies from approved vendor catalog. Data entry for all operations areas.

PIZZA TIME THEATERS, Milpitas, CA   June 1985 to May 1990
Order Entry Supervisor/Inventory Control

Supervised complete order entry operations for 260 locations. Buyer for
all inventory, and supplies. Maintained three million dollar inventory.
Researched discrepancies in report files, and corrected any errors.

LINDA'S DRIVE IN, Mountain View, CA August 1982 to June 1985
Supervisor/Cook

COMMUNITY ACTIVITIES: Community music and theatre groups

**Figure A-3   Résumé of same individual as on previous page, more experienced,
some years later**

541 Austria Drive
Sunnyvale, CA 95087
September 17, 1996

Mr. Archibald Manx
Gato Food Corporation
1000 Back Street
Los Gatos, CA 95030

Dear Sir:

Recently your accountant, Bruce McDougall, said that you are beginning the search for a food service coordinator.

I have worked fourteen years in the food service industry and most recently as administrative assistance/supervisor in food services at Gardner Foods. I feel that I could bring my experience and good skills to the management of your well-known and very fine food service operation.

Enclosed is a copy of my résumé. I will call you next week for an appointment to discuss this with you further.

Sincerely yours,

Kathleen M. Neville

Figure A-4   Cover letter to accompany preceding résumé

AMALIA LENA
1643 W. Davis Drive
Fort Lauderdale, FL 33325
(305) 555-3669

JOB OBJECTIVE: Medical Office Manager

QUALIFICATIONS IN BRIEF: Five years' experience as medical secretary/
receptionist; six years as bank teller, four years as bank manager, preceded by
four years of clerical work. Extensive community service activities. Special skills:
especially good at business contact with people; fluency in Italian; limited fluency in Spanish; excellent memory for names, current computer fluency.

WORK EXPERIENCE:

CYPRESS MEDICAL CLINIC, Fort Lauderdale, FL   1988–Present
Medical Secretary/Receptionist   Answer phone, make appointments in a
high traffic office; greet patients and show them to examining rooms;
interact with three doctors; evaluate patient problems; prepare examining
rooms; prepare and update charts.

MANATEE NEON SIGN COMPANY, Manatee, FL   1984–1988
Bookkeeper, Computer Operator, Clerk

CIVIC FEDERAL SAVINGS, Fort Lauderdale, FL   1974–1984
Head Teller, Manager Typed, cashiered, dealt with public at teller window, paid bank bills. Worked with computer. Handled transactions and
answered banking questions by phone. As manager, did general supervision of personnel and procedures, including management of vault cash.

DADE COUNTY SANITATION DISTRICT, Miami, FL   1961–1964
Office Clerk   Filed, typed, radio communication with personnel in the
field, general telephone work, paid department bills, occasional payroll
management.

MIAMI MEDICAL CLINIC, Miami, FL   1960–1961
Medical Records Clerk   Checked and delivered medical records to doctors'
offices.

EDUCATION:
ST. VINCENT'S HIGH SCHOOL, Ft. Lauderdale, FL
Concentration in business education courses.
Subsequent workshops dealing with human relations and crisis counseling.

COMMUNITY SERVICE ACTIVITIES:
Girl Scout/Cub Scout Leader, seven years
Elementary School Teacher Aide
Hospitality Chairperson for PTA Group
Crisis counseling, individually and in small groups

**Figure A-5   Chronological résumé showing career path of a woman who returned
to work after raising a family**

REINALDA GUZMANN
146 Perdido Avenue
Watsonville, CA 95076
(408) 555-1212

POSITION OBJECTIVE: Community Outreach Director

EDUCATION:

CABRILLO COLLEGE, Aptos, California: AA Degree   June 1995
Sociology Major
Took additional courses in psychology and Latin American History.

EXPERIENCE SUMMARY:

PAJARO VALLEY SHELTER SERVICES, Watsonville, CA February 1994 to Present
Facilities Manager
Interviewed prospective families for transitional housing; set up and ran orientation programs for residents that included budgeting, home maintenance, and conflict resolution; supervised maintenance of buildings; collected rental fees. Did community liaison work by contacting various agencies for client services; worked with churches and other agencies to meet needs of homeless families.

Office Manager
Answered phone, set up appointments, wrote letters, kept mailing list up to date, set up newsletter content, did mailouts to over 1000 supporters.

PERSONAL PARAGRAPH

As a child of migrant farmworkers and a former homeless parent with three children, I understand the needs of poor families in this area. Working with families in need and community agencies has given me good experience in finding ways for families to improve their situations.

FIGURE A-6   Chronological résumé of a formerly homeless mother with three children who lived and worked at a shelter and returned to school. Because she worked at only one place, her résumé looks almost functional

JERRY MARTIN-PITTS, M.H.C., R.C.P
3320 Saddleback Way, Tucson, AZ 85733
(602) 555-1213

OBJECTIVE
To develop and manage health care services

QUALIFICATIONS
- Cardiopulmonary Department Manager for nineteen years
- Master's degree in Health Counseling
- Arizona State License, Respiratory Care Practitioner
- Excellent human relations, organizational, teaching, and facilitation skills

EXPERIENCE SUMMARY
Pilar Hospital:
- Coached and developed a staff of 53 people
- Interviewed, hired, oriented, and evaluated staff
- Resolved personnel issues
- Scheduled staff
- Developed and managed multiple budgets
- Planned, designed, and developed department facilities
- Participated in and chaired multiple-service meetings
- Taught and implemented continuous process improvement skills
- Managed equipment and supplies for seven departments
- Developed and implemented policies and procedures
- Handled patient, visitor, physician complaints and relations
- Developed and coordinated employee recognition programs
- Developed, coordinated, and facilitated employee/volunteer mission/values retreats; developed mission/values statements
- Developed ethical guidelines for health care decision making
- Prepared department for outside regulatory agency surveys/licensing
- Developed and expanded respiratory services in skilled nursing facilities
- Developed and coordinated patient-focused care models
- Developed Therapist Driven Protocols and Clinical Pathways

Community Experience:
- Thunderbird Medical Clinic: Facilitate Smoking Cessation Program   1987–Present
- American Cancer Society: President of Tucson Board of Directors   1987–1989
- American Lung Association: President-Elect of Board of Directors   1984–1987
  Chairperson of Human Resources Committee
- Arizona Society of Respiratory Care: President   1989–1991
- Samaritan Counseling Center: Founding Board of Directors   1985
- Hospice Caring Project of Tucson: Founding Board of Directors   1978
- Pilar Hospital Speakers Bureau Lecturer on Stress Management,   1980–1994
  Living with Chronic Illness, Smoking Cessation, Working with the Dying

EDUCATION
University of Connecticut	B. A., B. D.	1964
Arizona State University	Teacher's Certification	1965
Samaritan Respiratory School	CRTT	1972
Xavier University	M. H. C.	1984

Figure A-7   Health care manager in transition because of hospital downsizing and restructuring

Bowling Green, KY 42101
March 17, 1995

Dr. Gladys C. Penner, Chancellor
University of the Trees
369 Dogwood Blvd.
Bowling Green, KY 42l0l

Dear Dr. Penner:

After considerable thought, it has become clear that a career change is appropriate for me at this time. As of June 1, 1995, I will be resigning from the University of the Trees as Career Center Coordinator and Counselor.

I have enjoyed and greatly profited from my years of teaching and counseling at UOT. Your considerable expertise, openness to innovation, and general professionalism have been a significant factor in my job satisfaction.

Perhaps on occasion I might return to teach a short course or a night class for I plan to stay in the field of Career Development. I will be expanding my private practice and my consulting in that area.

I wish to express my appreciation to the college community for the many years of support it has given me, for its commitment to excellence, and its dedication to students.

Sincerely yours,

Allison E. Stevenson

Figure A-8 Letter of resignation

NOTES

CHAPTER 1

Needs, Wants, and Values: Spotlighting You

1. *Inc,* February 1995, p. 6.
2. Bill Cane, *Through Crisis to Freedom* (Chicago: Acta Books, 1980), p. 2l.
3. Clarissa Pinkola Estés, *Women Who Run with the Wolves* (New York: Ballantine, 1992), p. 221.
4. Page Smith, *Redeeming the Time: A People's History of the 1920s and the New Deal,* Vol. 8 (New York: McGraw-Hill, 1986), p. 953.
5. "Potpourri," Financial Resource Center, Santa Cruz, CA, May 1992.
6. Victor Frankl, *Man's Search for Meaning* (New York: Washington Square Press, 1963).
7. Lewis Vaughn, "The 10 Happiest Things You Can Do," *Regeneration of Health and the Human Spirit* (Emmaus, PA: Rodale Press, 1986), p. 40.
8. Eileen R. Growald and Allan Luks, "A Reason to Be Nice: It's Healthy," *American Health Magazine;* reprinted in the *San Francisco Chronicle,* March 4, 1988, p. B-4.
9. Helena Norberg-Hodge, "The Cost of Development," *In Context,* 25, 1990, p. 28.
10. See Gary Carnum, "Everybody Talks about Values," *Learning* (December 1972), pp. 30, 113–115; S. B. Simon, S. W. Howe, and H. Kirschenbaum, *Values Clarification* (New York: Hart, 1972).
11. Edward Goss "Patterns of Organizational and Occupational Socialization," *The Vocational Guidance Quarterly,* December 1975, p. l40.
12. Ken Keyes, Jr., *Handbook to Higher Consciousness* (St. Mary's, KY: Cornucopia Institute, 1975), p. 52.
13. Abraham Maslow, *Motivation and Personality* (New York: Harper & Row, 1954), p. 91; see also Marilyn M. Bates and Clarence Johnson, *A Manual for Group Leaders* (Denver: Love Publishing, 1972), and Keyes, *Handbook to Higher Consciousness.*
14. *Sojourners,* Feburary 1987, p. 13.
15. Pat Mathes Cane, "The Call to Be Brothers and Sisters," *Integrities,* Spring 1989, p. 8.
16. David Suzuki, "Towards a New Ecological Future, The Importance of Grass Roots," *Talking Leaves,* Winter 1992, p. 3.
17. *Catalyst,* Summer, 1991, p. 16.
18. U.S. Department of Health, Education, and Welfare, *Work in America* (Cambridge, MA: M.I.T. Press, 1973), pp. l86–187.
19. Lance Morrow, *Time,* May 11, 1981, p. 94.
20 S. Norman Feingold, "Career Education: A Philosophy," B'Nai B'rith Career and Counseling Service, 1640 Rhode Island Avenue, NW, Washington, DC, September 1973, p. 11.
21. Virginia Y. Trotter, "Women in Leadership and Decision Making: A Shift in Balance," *Vital Speeches,* April l, 1975, pp. 373–375.
22. Hans Selye, *Stress without Distress* (Philadelphia: J. B. Lippincott, 1974), p. 96.
23. Fernando Bartolomé and Paul A. Lee Evans, "Must Success Cost So Much?" *Harvard Business Review,* March–April 1980, p. 142.

CHAPTER 2

Personality and Performances: Pieces of the Puzzle

1. John Holland, *Making Vocational Choices: A Theory of Careers* (Englewood Cliffs, N.J: Prentice-Hall, 1973).
2. Rose Marie Dunphy, *The Christian Science Monitor,* May 20, 1985, p. 34.
3. Wynne Busby, "Chips Off the Old Block," *Creation Spirituality,* Winter 1994, p. 47.
4. *This Time,* from H.O.M.E., Orland, ME, Fall 1988, p. 7.
5. Compiled from the following sources: U.S. Department of Labor: *Dictionary of Occupational Titles,* vol. 2, 1965; *Guide for Occupational Exploration,* New Forum Foundation, Distributed by The American Guidance Service, Publications Building, Circle Pines, MN 55014, 1984; *U.S. Army, Career and Educational Guide,* Counselor Edition, 1978.
6. *Regeneration,* September–October 1989, p. 10.
7. Jean Houston, "The Church in Future Society." Taped address to the Lutheran Brotherhood Colloquium, University of Texas, Austin, January 1979. See also Jean Houston, *The Possible Human* (Los Angelas: J. P. Jarcher, 1982).
8. Virginia Y. Trotter, "Women In Leadership and Decision Making: A Shift in Balance," *Vital Speeches,* April 1, 1975, pp. 373–375.
9. See Sydney A. Fine, "Counseling Skills: Target for Tomorrow," *Vocational Guidance Quarterly,* June 1974; also Sydney A. Fine, "Nature of Skills: Implications for Education and Training," *Proceedings,* 75th Annual Convention of the American Personnel Association, 1967.

CHAPTER 3

The Career Connection: Finding Your Job Satisfiers

1. U.S. Department of Labor and National Forum Foundation, *Guide for Occupational Exploration,* 1979 and 1984 (Washington, DC: U.S. Department of Labor).
2. Compiled from the following sources: U.S. Department of Labor, *Dictionary of Occupational Titles,* vol. 2, 1965; U.S. Department of Labor and National Forum Foundation, *Guide for Occupational Exploration,* 1979 and 1984 (Washington, DC: U.S. Department of Labor); U.S. Army, *Career and Education Guide,* Counselor Edition, 1978; U.S. Department of Labor, *Handbook for Analyzing Jobs,* 1972 (Washington, DC: U.S. Department of Labor).
3. U.S. Department of Labor, *Dictionary of Occupational Titles,* 1978.
4. *The Enhanced Guide for Occupational Exploration,* 1991 (formerly by U.S. Department of Labor, 1979), JIST Works, Inc., 720 N. Park Avenue, Indianapolis, IN 46202; (317) 264-3720.
5. *The Enhanced Guide for Occupational Exploration,* p. 459.
6. *The Enhanced Guide for Occupational Exploration.*

CHAPTER 4

Roles and Realities: Sinking the Stereotypes

1. Diane Cole, "Motherhood: Child Care in Days Gone By," *Register-Pajaronian,* March 6, 1995, p. 6.
2. Elie Wiesel, "The Foreigner in Each of Us," *The Christian Science Monitor,* August 7, 1991, p. 23.
3. Conference Notes, "Putting Diversity to Work," *Santa Clara Magazine,* Spring 1994, p. 20.

4. Sabrina Brown, "The Diversity Advantage," *Santa Clara Magazine,* Spring 1994, p. 22.

5. "Every Country Treats Women Worse Than Men," *Register-Pajaronian,* May 25, 1993, p. 16.

6. "Vivienne Walt, "Population Meeting Deciding Future of the World's Women," *Register-Pajaronian,* September 14, 1994, p. 15.

7. Peggy McIntosh, "Unpacking the Invisible Knapsack," *Creation Spirituality*, January–February 1992, p. 33.

8. "Sex, Race Bias Hurt Economy, Reich Says," *San Francisco Chronicle,* September 27, 1994, p. A-3.

9. Lisa Genasci, "Women's Work, More Take on Non-traditional Jobs," *Register-Pajaronian*, March 11, 1995, p. 11.

10. "Women in Management," *Facts on Working Women* (Washington, DC: U.S. Department of Labor, Women's Bureau, December 1989), p. 1; "Big Firms' Glass Ceiling Intact, Labor Chief Says," *Register-Pajaronian*, August 12, 1992, p. 8.

11. Maggie Mahar, "Trendicators," *Working Women*, June 1994, p. 18.

12. Janet L. Norwood, *Working Women: Where Have We Been? Where Are We Going?* (Washington, DC: U.S. Department of Labor, Bureau of Labor Statistics, April 1990), p. 2.

13. "Women Pay More Than Men Do for Many Services, Book Says," *Register-Pajaronian*, May 18, 1993, p. 14.

14. "Facts on Working Women," U.S. Department of Labor, Women's Bureau, December 1993, pp. 4, 8.

15. CBS Evening News, September 25, 1994.

16. *Women and Nontraditional Work*, National Commission on Working Women of Wider Opportunities for Women (1325 G. St. N.W. Lower Level, Washington, DC 20005, November 1989), p. 1.

17. Levinson, *The Seasons of a Man's Life* (New York: Ballantine, 1978), pp. 20, 43–46.

18. Charles S. Clark, "'Second Shift' Including More Men," *Register-Pajaronian*, September 17, 1992, p. 4.

19. Rob Hiaasen, "Changing Times Mean Changing Diapers," *Register-Pajaronian,* February 18, 1995, p. 11.

20. "Absent Fathers a Global Phenomenon, Study Says," *Register-Pajaronian,* January 17, 1995, p. 1.

21. Bess Myerson, "Someday I'd Like to Walk Slowly," *Redbook* , September 1975, p. 176.

22. Daniel Levinson, *The Seasons of a Man's Life* (New York: Ballantine Books, 1978), p. 158.

23. Mark Lloyd, "Affirmative Action: Solution or Problem?" *The Christian Science Monitor*, January 18, 1991, p. 19; "Final Hearings Held on the Glass Ceiling," *Register-Pajaronian*, September 27, 1994, p. 14.

24. Mitch Finley, "My Three Sons," *Santa Clara Magazine*, Fall 1990, p. 47.

25. Julie Barton and Virginia Daugherty, lecture discussion, Santa Clara University, February 8, 1991.

26. Lisa Genasci, "Activist Becomes Part of Clinton Administration," *Register-Pajaronian*, August 20, 1994, p. 20.

27. "Gap Between Rich and Poor Isn't Narrowing," *Register-Pajaronian*, October 18, 1993, p. 18.

28. Donna K. H. Walters, "Gender Pay Gap Narrows Because Men Lose Ground," *Register-Pajaronian*, September 14, 1992, p. 10.

29. "Americans Marrying Less and Later, Divorcing Less, Census Report Says," *Register-Pajaronian*, December 9, 1992, p. 5.

30. "Millions of Youngsters Live in 'Blended' Families, Census Bureau Analysis Shows," *Register-Pajaronian*, August 30, 1994, p. 15.

31. "Baby Death Rate Falls; Still Higher Than 21 Nations," *Register-Pajaronian*, December 10, 1994, p. 16.

32. Marvin J. Cetron and Margaret Evans Gayle, "The Family Connection," *The Futurist*, September–October 1990, p. 39.

33. James R. Wetzel, "American Families: 75 Years of Change," *Monthly Labor Review* (Washington, DC: U.S. Department of Labor, Bureau of Labor Statistics, March 1990), p. 51; Constance Sorrentino, "The Changing Family in International Perspective" (Washington, DC: U.S. Department of Labor, Bureau of Labor Statistics, March 1990), p. 11.

34. Suzanne Gordon, *Prisoners of Men's Dreams* (Boston: Little, Brown, 1991), p. 43.

35. Anne-Marie Foisy-Grusonik, "The Superwoman Fallacy," *Santa Clara Magazine*, Winter 1992, p. 44; cf. Pamela Kruger, "All Twentysomething Women Want Is to Change the Way America Works," *Working Women*, May 1994, p. 61.

36. Hilary Cosell, "Wrong Dreams," *Ladies Home Journal*, April 1985, p. 171.

37. Caryl Rivers, "Odyssey toward a Freer Marriage," *San Francisco Chronicle*, January 1, 1975, p. 17.

38. Lester R. Brown, "The New World Order," *State of the World, 1991* (New York: W. W. Norton, 1991), p. 10.

39. "Family-leave Law Goes into Effect," *Register-Pajaronian*, August 3, 1993, p. 3.

40. Richard Whitmire, "Moms with a Dad Attitude," *USA Weekend*, November 16–18, 1990, p. 18.

41. "Population Data," *The Futurist*, January-February 1992.

42. *The Christian Science Monitor*, August 29, 1990, p. 21.

43. Mary Ellen Barrett, "Scared Serious," *USA Weekend*, August 17–19, 1990, p. 4.

44. *Historical Statistics of the U.S. Colonial Times to 1970 Part I* (Washington, DC: U.S. Department of Commerce, Bureau of the Census, 1975), p. 15.

45. *Statistical Abstracts of the United States* (Washington, DC: U.S. Department of Commerce, Bureau of the Census, 1986), p. 25.

46. "Life Expectancy in Nation Rises, but Gaps Remain in Gender, Race," *Register-Pajaronian*, September 1, 1993, p. 5.

47. Lillian Hellman, *An Unfinished Woman: A Memoir* (Boston: Atlantic Monthly Press, 1969).

48. "Social Security Works against Working Women, Study Says," *Register-Pajaronian*, July 22, 1994, p. 15.

49. Monroe W. Karmin, "The 'Other' Generation Gap," *U.S. News and World Report*, October 31, 1988, p. 55.

50. "Better Days for Older Americans," *The Christian Science Monitor*, June 7, 1982, p. 28.

51. Political letter, 1988.

52. "Population Data," *The Futurist*, January–February 1990.

53. Kathryn Lawlor, "Always an Alien," *Salt*, Spring 1991, p. 7.

54. Lucia Mouat, "Despite Minority Gains, Gap between Races Still Looms Large," *The Christian Science Monitor*, November 21, 1990, p. 8.

55. William A. Sundstrom, "The Poverty Challenge," *Santa Clara Magazine*, Spring 1994, p. 24.

56. San Juan American Indian Council, California Indian Market, May 7, 1995, and "One Earth One People Peace Vision; World Cultures Arts Festival," June 25, 1995.

57. Terence Wright, "Liberation, My Nation, Migration," *Diaspora*, Fall, 1980, p. 1.

58. Nancy Nussbaum, "Number of U.S. Poor Goes Up 1.2 Million," *Register-Pajaronian*, October 5, 1993, p. 1.

59. "Growth of Hispanic-owned Businesses Proves 'American Dream' Alive and Well," *Register-Pajaronian*, September 9, 1994, p. 6.

60. Mercedes Olivera, "Outside Tradition, Growing Numbers of Hispanas Are Entering the Work Force in Untypical Professions," *Register-Pajaronian*, October 5, 1991, p. 18.

61. Adair Lara, "If You're So Smart, Why Are You So Stupid?" *San Francisco Chronicle*, August 4, 1994, p. E 10.

62. Susanna Heckman, "ADA Burden Not All on Business," *Register-Pajaronian*, March 14, 1992, p. 11.

63. Burns W. Roper, "Race Relations in America," *The Christian Science Monitor*, July 13, 1990, p. 18.

64. Diane Ravitch, "Schools Aren't Guilty of Bias against Girls," *Register-Pajaronian*, December 27, 1993, p. 12.

65. Betty Friedan, *The Second Stage* (New York: Summit Books), 1981.

66. Mark Gerzon, *A Choice of Heroes: The Changing Faces of American Manhood* (Boston: Houghton Mifflin, 1983).

67. Bettijane Levine, "Women's Leadership Style More Inspiring, Study Shows," *Register-Pajaronian*, October 23, 1990, p. 18.

68. Ann Crittenden, "Temporary Solutions," *Working Women*, February 1994, p. 35.

69. Marilyn Ferguson, *Aquarian Conspiracy: Personal and Social Transformation in the 1980s* (Los Angeles: J. P. Tarcher, 1980).

70. Jean Houston, "The Church in Future Society," address to the Lutheran Brotherhood Colloquium, University of Texas, Austin, January 1979. See also Jean Houston, *The Possible Human* (Los Angeles: J. P. Tarcher, 1982).

71. Virginia Y. Trotter, "Women in Leadership and Decision Making: A Shift in Balance," *Vital Speeches*, April 1, 1975, pp. 373–375.

CHAPTER 5

The Job Market: Facts, Trends, Predictions

1. John Peers, Lecture at Mission College, Santa Clara, California, November 11, 1982.

2. Lester R. Brown, Christopher Flavin, and Sandra Postel, "A Planet in Jeopardy," *The Futurist*, May–June 1992, p. 10.

3. Jeremy Rifkin, "The Clocks That Make Us Run," *East West Journal*, September 1987, p. 44.

4. Elizabeth Schilling, "Raising Self-reliant Kids," *Register-Pajaronian*, February 12, 1994, p. 11.

5. "The Invisible Farmer," *The Christian Science Monitor*, October 20, 1993, p. 18.

6. *Statistical Abstracts of the United States* (Washington, DC: U.S. Bureau of the Census, 1990), p. 387, 395.

7. Priscilla Enriquez, "An Un-American Tragedy," *Food First Action Alert*, Summer 1992, p. 4.

8. Thomas J. Peters, "Competition and Change," *Santa Clara Magazine*, Summer 1989, p. 10.

9. Arthur S. Miller, "The Right to a Job," *San Jose Mercury News*, July 13, 1986, p. P-1.

10. "Matters of Scale," *World Watch*, September–October 1994, p. 39.

11. Chuck Matthei, "Why Do We Have a Housing Shortage?" *The Catholic Worker*, October–November 1987, p. 1.

12. Jonathan Rowe, "Just Words, But They Linger," *The Christian Science Monitor*, May 17, 1989, p. 12.

13. Barbara Marx Hubbard, "Critical Path to an All-Win World," *The Futurist*, June 1981, p. 31.

14. "Mitraniketan," *Community Service Newsletter*, March–April 1988, p. 1.

15. Alan London, personal conversation with author.

16. Lisa Genasci, "'Downsizing' May Not Be Worth the Savings," *Register Pajaronian*, July 7, 1994, p. 19; July 12, 1994, p. 14.

17. Jonathan Marshall, "'Downsizing' Trend Grinds On," *San Francisco Chronicle*, September 27, 1994, p. B1.

18. "U.S. Regains Its Edge in Technology After Lag," *Register-Pajaronian*, September 19, 1994, p. 12.

19. Frank Swoboda, "Labor Secretary Challenges National 'Competitiveness' Issue, *Register-Pajaronian*, September 24, 1994, p. 22.

20. Howell Hurst, "Focus," *INC.*, February 1991, p. 15.

21. Helena Norberg-Hodge, "Lessons from Traditional Cultures," *The Futurist,* May–June 1992, p. 60.

22. Paul Hawken, "Prophet of the Next Economy," *East West Journal,* April 1984, p. 34.

23. Robert Rodale, *Regeneration Project,* Rodale Press, (Emmaus, PA).

24. James Melton, "Can You Really Do Well by Doing Good?" *CO-OP America Quarterly,* Spring 1995, p. 13.

25. Susan Meeker-Lowry, *Catalyst,* Vol IX, No. 3 & 4, p. 7.

26. Stephen Phillips, "Small Bank Revives Urban Area," *New York Times,* January 30, 1986; see also *Targeted Investment,* May–June 1989 and other bank publications such as *The Bread Rapper.*

27. "Green Business," *CO-OP America Quarterly,* Winter 1994, p. 25.

28. Marj Halperin, "Women Helping Women Worldwide," *Building Economic Alternatives,* Spring 1987, p. 19.

29. Trickle Up Program, Inc., 54 Riverside Drive PHE, New York, NY 10024-6509.

30. Greg Ramm, "Community Investment Is Coming of Age," *Building Economic Alternatives,* Spring 1987, p. 9.

31. Christopher Flavin and Odil Tunali, "Getting Warmer," *World Watch,* March–April 1995, p. 10; also "Storm Warnings," *World Watch,* November–December, 1994.

32. Cynthia Pollock Shea, "Breaking Up Is Hard To Do," *World Watch,* July–August 1989, p. 10.

33. John Dillin, "Emerging Plans to Cut US Oil Imports," *The Christian Science Monitor,* February 7, 1991, p. 1; also Christopher Flavin, "Conquering U.S. Oil Dependence," *World Watch,* January–February 1991, p. 28.

34. Bill Cane, "Study Guide for Group Leaders, *Circles of Hope* (New York: Orbis Books, 1992, p. 6.

35. Christopher Flavin and Nicholas Lenssen, "Here Comes the Sun," *World Watch,* September–October 1991, p. 10.

36. "Vital Signs," *World Watch,* May–June 1990, p. 6.

37. Colin Norman, "The Staggering Challenge of Global Unemployment," *Futurist* (August 1978), p. 224.

38. Frances Moore Lappé and Joseph Collins, *Food First: Beyond the Myth of Scarcity* (New York: Ballantine, 1978), p. 1.

39. Michael N. Corbett, *A Better Place to Live, New Designs for Tomorrow's Communities* (Emmaus, PA: Rodale Press, 1981).

40. Sarah van Gelder, "Cities of Exuberance," *In Context,* 35, 1993, p. 46.

41. Laura Van Tuyl, "Her Design Is to Save the Earth," *The Christian Science Monitor,* January 28, 1991, p. 14.

42. Ed Ayres, "Breaking Away," *World Watch,* January–February 1993, p. 10.

43. "Eco-Actions," *CO-OP America Quarterly,* Winter 1992, p. 8.

44. Jessica Mathews, "The 'Missing Link' in Transportation Policy," *Register-Pajaronian,* August 27, 1994, p. 8.

45. Ayres, "Breaking Away," p. 10.

46. Christopher Flavin, "Conquering U.S. Oil Dependence," *World Watch,* January–February 1991, p. 28.

47. "Special Report," *Oxfam America News,* Winter 1983, p. 3.

48. "Citings," *World Watch,* May–June 1993, p. 8.

49. Charles B. Inlander and Ed Weiner, *Take This Book to the Hospital with You, A Consumer Guide to Surviving Your Hospital Stay* (Emmaus, PA: Rodale Press, 1985).

50. "Americans Spending Billions on Offbeat Medical Treatments," *Register-Pajaronian,* June 27, 1993, p. 1.

51. Center for Economic Conversion, 222 C. View St., Mountain View, CA 94041; (415) 968-8798.

52. George Hoffman, "Converting Swords into Environmental Plowshares: Laudable Transitions from Weaponry into Environmentally Benign Technology," *The Environmental Council,* Summer 1993, p. 9.

53. Michael Renner, "Monitoring Arms Trade," *World Watch,* May–June 1994, p. 21.

54. Hazel Henderson, "Will the Real Economy Please Stand Up," *Building Economic Alternatives,* Summer 1986, p. 3.

55. Odil Tunali, "Climate Models Growing More Accurate,: *World Watch,* May–June 1995, p. 6.

56. Robert Goodland, "Ecological Limit," *In Context* No 36, 1993, p. 12.

57. "Matters of Scale," *World Watch,* January–February, 1994, p. 39.

58. Howard Youth, "Flying into Trouble," *World Watch,* January–February 1994, p. 10.

59. Peer Weber, "Neighbors under the Gun," *World Watch,* July–August 1991, p. 35.

60. Lance Morrow, "The Weakness That Starts at Home," *Time,* June 4, 1979, p. 81.

61. Francois Dusquesne, "The Making of a Sacred Planet," *One Earth,* 2, p. 6.

62. Sandra Postel, *Last Oasis* (New York: W. W. Norton, 1992), p. 23.

63. John Todd, "Living Machines for Pure Water," *Mending the Earth, a World for Our Grandchildren* (Berkeley, CA: North Atlantic Books, 1991).

64. "New Ground," *Organic Gardening,* July–August 1989, p. 12.

65. David Clark Scott, "Retailers Move Early to Foil Yule Grinch," *The Christian Science Monitor,* November 18, 1985, p. 31.

66. "New Entries," *The Boycott Quarterly,* Spring 1994, p. 38.

67. Matthew Fox, "A Call for a Spiritual Renaissance," *Creation,* January–February 1989, p. 10.

68. Thomas Berry, *The Dream of the Earth* (San Francisco: Sierra Club Books, 1988), p. 73.

69. *Wild Earth, the Wildlands Project,* P.O. Box 492, Canton, NY 13617.

70. Thomas Gartside, "Planting 1,000 Trees," *The Christian Science Monitor,* March 6, 1990, p. 18.

71. "'Global Releaf' Project, *Greenhouse Gas-ette,* Spring 1989, p. 11.

72. Susan Meeker-Lowry, *Catalyst,* May–June 1987, p. 2.

73. Howard Youth, "Iguana Farms, Antelope Ranches," *World Watch,* January–February, 1991, p. 36.

74. Jo Roberts, "Rubber Tapper Chico Mendes Murdered," *The Catholic Worker,* March–April 1989, p. 1.

75. Beth W. McLeod, "Puppy Love,"*The Christian Science Monitor,* February 13, 1989, p. 14. Contact the Humane Society of the United States, 2100 L St. NW, Washington, DC 20037.

76. Joanna Poncavage, "Walnut Acres: The Farm That Gandhi Grew," *Organic Gardening,* February 1991, p. 58.

77. Phyllis Hanes, "Gardens Grow More Colorful," *The Christian Science Monitor,* June 21, 1989, p. 14.

78. John Ferrell, "Henry Ford's Vision of a Sustainable Future, *Earth Save,* Spring–Summer 1992, p. 15.

79. Elizabeth Schilling, "Natural Products Find Market Niche," *Register-Pajaronian,* January 14, 1991, p. 11.

80. "Earth Care," *Organic Gardening,* February 1991, p. 96.

81. *The Christian Science Monitor,* December 29, 1981, p. 11; July 7, 1986, p. 2.

82. Jodi L. Jacobson, "India's Misconceived Family Plan," *World Watch,* November–December 1991, p. 18.

83. Richard J. Barnet and John Cavanagh, "Think Global, Then Think Again," *CO-OP American Quarterly,* Fall, 1994, p. 15.

84. "In This Issue," *World Watch,* March–April 1990, p. 3.

85. Author visit and tour, September 30, 1994.

86. Beth Burrows, "Ethics and Other Irrational Considerations," *The Boycott Quarterly,* Spring 1994, p. 20.

87. "Finding His World," *Manas,* January 29, 1986, p. 2.

88. Chela Zabin, "Watsonville-based Business Had Its Start in the Kitchen," *Register-Pajaronian,* October 21, 1994, p. 1; phone conversation with author, October 29, 1994.

89. Quotes from Christopher Cerf and Victor Navask, *The Experts Speak* (NY: Pantheon Books, l984).

90. "Odds and Ends," *Ecology Action Newsletter,* October 1992, p. 4.

91. John Young, "The New Materialism," *World Watch,* September–October 1994, p. 37.

92. John Robbins, "Growing Impact," *Earth Save,* Winter 1991, p. 2.

93. "World's 'Vital Signs' Getting Better," *Register-Pajaronian,* October 19, 1992, p. 1.

94. Ed Ayres, "Environmental Intelligence," *World Watch,* July–August 1994, p. 6.

95. Christopher Flavin and John E. Young, "Will Clinton Give Industry a Green Edge?" *World Watch,* January–February 1993, p. 26.

96. Karl-Henrik Robért, "Planetary Pulse," *In Context,* 35, 1993, p. 6.

97. Robert Gilman interview with Bob Berkebile, "Restorative Design," *In Context,* 35, 1993, p.9.

98. *Tightwad Gazette,* RR1 Box 3570, Leeds, ME 04263.

99. Job Market Statistics synthesized from a variety of sources: "Ninth Annual Listing: Twenty-five Hottest Careers," *Working Women,* July 1994, p. 37; Knight-Ridder Survey, "Growth Occupations," *San Jose Mercury News,* September 4, 1994, p. D-1.

100. John Naisbett, *Reinventing the Corporation,* from Mission College *Work Experience Newsletter,* Fall l986.

101. David R. Francis, "Sizing up the Yuppies and the Oinks Gives Population Insights," *The Christian Science Monitor,* April 11, 1988, p. 14.

102. Hunter Lovins and Michael Kinsley, "Ingredients for Success," *Idea Bulletin,* Summer 1987, p. 3.

103. Adapted from Leonard Steinberg, Long Beach State University, Long Beach, California.

CHAPTER 6
Workplaces and Workstyles: Scanning the Subtleties

1. *Nation's Restaurant News,* December l984.

2. "MIT's Engineering Students Seek Better Ways to Coat M&Ms," *Register-Pajaronian,* January 2, 1991, p. 20.

3. Robert Levering and Milton Moskowitz, "The Workplace 100," *USA Weekend,* January 22–24, 1993, p. 4.

4. Adele Scheele, "Moving Over Instead of Up," *Working Women,* November 1993, p. 75.

5. Robert Vahl, Small Business Assistance Service, Clymer, NY, quoted in *In Business,* January–February 1986, p. 15.

6. James Kouzes and Barry Posner, "Credibility Makes a Difference," *Santa Clara Magazine,* Fall 1994, p. 12.

7. Jules Z. Willing, *the Reality of Retirement, the Inner Experience of Becoming a Retired Person* (New York: William Morrow and Company, Inc., 1981), p. 221.

8. Levering and Moskowitz, "The Workplace 100," p. 4.

9. Nancy K. Austin, "When Honesty Is the Best Management Policy," *Working Women,* May 1994, p. 25.

10. Erving Goffman, *Asylums* (New York: Doubleday, 1961).

11. Barbara Garson, "Women's Work," *Working Papers,* Fall 1973, p. 5.

12. U.S. Trust gets such information from a variety of sources, such as companies' annual reports, Securities and Exchange Commission reports, findings of the Investor Responsibility Research Center, the National Labor Relations Board, the Council on Economic Priorities, and the Interfaith Center on Corporate Responsibility.

13. Jeffrey W. Helms, "Green Investing," *Gardenia,* Winter 1994, p. 6; Anne Zorc, "Checking Up On Corporate Claims," *CO-OP America Quarterly,* Fall 1991, p. 16.

14. Loretta Graziano, "I'm Optimal, You're Optimal—An Economist's Way of Knowledge," *Propaganda Review,* Winter 1988, p. 36.
15. Graduation Pledge Alliance, Box 4439, Arcata, CA 95521.
16. Associated Press, "UAL Workers Sport 'Owner' Buttons," *Register-Pajaronian,* July 13, 1994, p. 16.
17. "Small Companies 'Rent-a-Staff,'" *Register-Pajaronian,* February 3, 1990, p. 16.
18. Ruth Walker, "The Expanding Work Week," *The Christian Science Monitor,* July 5, 1990, p. 19.
19. Hans Selye, 1936, 1950, cited in David Barlow and Mark Durand, *Abnormal Psychology* (Pacific Grove, CA: Brooks/Cole, 1995), p. 335.
20. "Pieces," *Good Money,* November–December 1984, p. 7.
21. John Kenneth Galbraith, "The Economics of an American Housewife," *Atlantic Monthly,* August 1973, pp. 78–83.
22. Studs Terkel, *Working* (New York: Avon, 1972), p. 4.
23. Bernard Lefkowitz, *BREAKTIME: Living without Work in a Nine to Five World* (New York, Penguin Books, 1979).
24. Charlotte-Anne Lucas, "Bechtel Employees Like Short Week," *Register-Pajaronian,* January 3, 1991, p. 16.
25. New Ways to Work, "Earthquake Fosters Flexibility," *Work Times,* September 1990, p. 1.
26. "Home Workers Not More Likely to Goof Off, Researcher Finds," *Register-Pajaronian,* June 8, 1993, p. 1.
27. Marilyn Gardner, "A Heroine—But Not Full-Time," *The Christian Science Monitor,* June 18, 1991, p. 13
28. Ann Crittenden, "Temporary Solutions," *Working Women,* February 1994, p. 32.
29. Al Bilk, "Troubling Trend in the Workplace," *Register-Pajaronian,* May 1, 1993, p. 11.
30. "Harried Americans Feel Starved for Time," *Register-Pajaronian.* March 9, 1992, p. 1.
31. Crittenden, "Temporary Solutions," p. 32.
32. Paula Ancona, "Temporary Workers in Demand," *Register-Pajaronian,* October 8, 1994, p. 24.
33. Stephen Barr, "Government Issues Rules On Temporary Employees, *Register-Pajaronian,* September 21, 1994, p. 14.
34. Susan Meeker-Lowry, *Economics as If the Earth Really Mattered* (Philadelphia, PA: New Society Publishers, 1988), p. 113.
35. Vivian Hutchinson, *Good Work, an Introduction to New Zealand's Worker Co-operatives,* Taranaki CELT, P.O. Box 4101, New Plymouth East, New Zealand.
36. *Building Economic Alternatives,* CO-OP America, 1612 K Street N.W., Suite 600, Washington, DC 20006.
37. Brochure, The Drucker Foundation, 666 Fifth Avenue, 10th Floor, New York, NY 10103.
38. Tom Richman, "The Hottest Entrepreneur in America," *Inc.,* February 1987, p. 50.
39. "Work and Workers for the 21st Century," *Workforce 2000, Work and Workers for the 21st Century* (Washington, DC: U.S. Department of Labor, Women's Bureau), December 1989, p. 60.
40. Richard Vega, "Fat Cats on Campus," *USA Weekend,* March 26–28, 1993, p. 8.
41. "Women's Business New Economic Force," *Register-Pajaronian,* April 1, 1992, p. 8; Virginia Littlejohn and Anita Alberts, "Healthy Entrepreneurism," *Working Women,* March 1994, p. 57.
42. "In the Short Term," *CO-OP America Quarterly,* Summer 1992, p. 12.
43. Tom Ehrenfeld, "The Demise of Mom and Pop?" *Inc,* January 1995, p. 46.
44. *Futurist,* February 1984, p. 82.
45. *Franchise Fact Sheet,* International Franchise Association, 1350 New York Avenue, NW, Suite 900, Washington, DC 20005, (202) 628-8000, Spring 1994; Echo Montgomery Garrett, "The 21st Century Franchise," *Inc.,* January 1995, p. 79.

46. Ylonda Gault, "Rising-Star Franchises," *Working Women,* November 1993, p. 85.

47. "Global Cooperation," *CO-OP America Quarterly,* Summer 1994, p. 22.

48. David E. Gumpert in cooperation with the Small Business Administration, "Building Your Business Foundation," *Working Women,* Special Advertisement Section, November 1993.

49. Luke Elliott, "$1,500 and a Kitchen Table," *Back Home,* Winter 1990–91, p. 20.

50. Jeremy Joan Hewes, *Worksteads* (Garden City, NY: Doubleday, 1981), pp. 5,7; see also Lefkowitz, *BREAKTIME.*

51. *Women and Office Automation: Issues for the Decade Ahead* (Washington, DC: U.S. Department of Labor, Women's Bureau, 1985), p. 24.

52. Marilyn Ferguson, *Aquarian Conspiracy: Personal and Social Transformation in the 1980s* (Los Angeles: J. P. Tarcher, 1982).

53. Alvin Toffler, *The Third Wave* (New York: Bantam Books, 1980), p. 387.

54. Richard Pitcairn and Susan Hubble Pitcairn, *Dr. Pitcairn's Complete Guide to Natural Health for Dogs and Cats* (Emmaus, PA: Rodale Press, 1982).

55. Bill Cane, *Through Crisis to Freedom* (Chicago: Acta Books, 1980), p. 8.

56. "Hotline Plugs Honest Mechanics," *Register-Pajaronian,* April 28, 1993, p. 5.

57. Robert Marquand, "Wendell Berry, Plowman-poet," *The Christian Science Monitor,* October 10, 1986, p. 1.

58. "Supporters and Buyers Beware," *CO-OP America Quarterly,* Winter 1994, p. 23.

59. *Occupational Outlook Quarterly,* Spring 1983, p. 11.

60. John Scherer and Bob Cosby, "Personal Productivity Audit," *JC Penny Forum,* May 1983, p. 26.

CHAPTER 7

The Job Hunt: Breaking and Entering

1. Martha Stoodley, "Choosing the Right Tool," *National Business Employment Weekly,* January 14, 1990, p. 9.

2. David Jacobson, "New Software 'Reads' Résumés in 5 Minutes," *Register-Pajaronian,* May 6, 1993, p. 18.

3. Hanna Rubin, "One Little Résumé and How It Grew," *Working Women,* April 1987, p. 100.

4. *Personnel Administrator,* May, 1981, pp. 71–78.

5. Toni St. James, Interview Workshop, California Employment Development Department, 1977.

6. St. James, Interview Workshop.

7. George S. Odiorne, "Bait and Switch, Corporate-Style," *Working Women,* May 1987, p. 50.

CHAPTER 8

Decisions, Decisions: What's Your Next Move?

1. David Keirsey and Marilyn Bates, *Please Understand Me: Character and Temperament Types* (Del Mar, CA: Prometheus Nemesis Books, 1978), p. 22.

2. Key Keyes, Jr., "Oneness Space," Living Love Recording (St. Mary's, KY: Cornucopia Center; Ken Keyes College, The Vision Foundation, 790 Commercial Avenue, Coos Bay, OR 97420).

3. Betts Richter and Alice Jacobsen, *Make It So!* (Sonoma, CA: Be All Books, 1979).

4. Olive Ann Burns, *Cold Sassy Tree* (New York: Dell Publishing, 1984), p. 379.

5. *OTA (Office of Technology Assessment) Report Brief,* September 1990.

6. Editorial, "Candidates Avoid the Hard Choices," *Register-Pajaronian,* September 8, 1994, p. 24.

7. "Shifting Patterns in Education and Training," *Women Workers: Trends & Issues* (U.S. Department of Labor, Women's Bureau), 1993, p. 91.

8. David R. Francis, "Business Leaders Say Dropout Problem Calls for Action," *The Christian Science Monitor,* March 8, 1991, p. 8.

9. "The More You Learn, the More You Earn," *Register-Pajaronian,* July 22, 1994, p. 17.

10. Susan Ager, "After Exiting the Executive Suite," *San Jose Mercury News,* October 25, 1981, p. 6E.

11. Ashleigh Brilliant, *I Have Abandoned My Search for Truth, and Am Now Looking for a Good Fantasy* (Santa Barbara, CA: Woodbridge Press, 1985), p. 118.

12. Walter Chandoha, *Book of Kittens and Cats* (New York: Bramhall House, 1973), p. 8.

13. Lyle Crist, "Twain's River Holds Depths for Exploring," *The Christian Science Monitor,* May 16, 1989, p. 17.

14. Alan Lakein, *How to Get Control of Your Time and Your Life* (New York: N.A. L. Dutton, 1989).

15. See Connie Stapleton and Phyllis Richman, *Barter: How to Get Almost Anything without Money* (New York: Scribner's, 1982).

16. Feature, *Catholic Women's Network,* September–October 1994, p. 10.

17. H. B. Gelatt, *Creative Decision Making* (Los Altos, CA: Crisp Publications, 1991), p. 11.

18. Joseph Campbell, *The Power of Myth* (New York: Doubleday, 1988), p. 91.

19. Ted Berkman, "Wanting It All," *The Christian Science Monitor,* January 27, 1983, p. 21.

INDEX